International Competitiveness and Environmental Policies

INTERNATIONAL STUDIES IN ENVIRONMENTAL POLICY MAKING

General Editor: Frank J. Convery, *Heritage Trust Professor of Environmental Studies and Director of the Environmental Institute at University College Dublin, Ireland*

This important new series will make a significant contribution to the development of policies to combat environmental problems. It is the result of a Europe-wide study of the use of market based instruments to formulate environmental policy and reduce degradation. International in scope, it will address issues of current and future concern across the globe, in both East and West and in developed and developing countries.

This series will provide a forum for the publication of a limited number of innovative, high quality volumes which will extend and challenge the current literature. It will demonstrate how economic analysis can make a contribution to understanding and resolving the environmental problems confronting the world in the late 20th century.

International Competitiveness and Environmental Policies

Edited by

Terry Barker and Jonathan Köhler

University of Cambridge

INTERNATIONAL STUDIES IN ENVIRONMENTAL POLICY MAKING

Edward Elgar

Cheltenham, UK• Northampton, MA, USA

Published by
Edward Elgar Publishing Limited
8 Lansdown Place
Cheltenham
Glos GL50 2HU
UK

Edward Elgar Publishing, Inc.
6 Market Street
Northampton
Massachusetts 01060
USA

A catalogue record for this book
is available from the British Library

Library of Congress Cataloguing in Publication Data

International competitiveness and environmental policies / edited by
    Terry Barker, Jonathan Köhler.
        (International studies in environmental policy making series)
    Includes bibliographical references.
        1. Environmental policy—Economic aspects. 2. Competition,
International. I. Barker, Terry. II. Köhler, Jonathan, 1960– .
III. Series.
HC79.E5I5315   1998
333.7—dc21   97–39248
                                                           CIP

ISBN 1 85898 778 4

Printed and bound in Great Britain by Bookcraft (Bath) Ltd

Contents

v

List of figures

List of tables

List of contributors and discussants

Terry Barker	DAE, University of Cambridge.
Frans Berkhout	SPRU, University of Sussex.
Paul Ekins	Environmental Policy Unit, Department of Economics, University of Keele.
Norman Glass	HM Treasury.
Rolf Iten	INFRAS, Switzerland.
Nick Johnstone	International Institute for Environment and Development, London.
Jonathan Köhler	DAE, University of Cambridge.
Carl C. Koopmans	CPB Netherlands Bureau for Economic Policy Analysis.
Stephen Potter	Design Innovation Group, The Open University.
Najma Rajah	Department of the Environment.
Eirik Romstad	Department of Economics and Social Sciences, Agricultural University of Norway, Oslo.
Robin Roy	Design Innovation Group, The Open University.
Sue Scott	ESRI, Dublin.
Clare Smith	School of the Environment, University of Sunderland.
Mark Smith	Design Innovation Group, The Open University.
Stefan Speck	Environmental Policy Unit, Department of Economics, University of Keele.
Rolf-Ulrich Sprenger	IFO, Munich.
Grahame Thompson	Faculty of Social Sciences, The Open University.

Preface

This book has been developed from the proceedings of a workshop 'Environmental Policies and International Competitiveness' held at Madingley Hall, University of Cambridge in October 1996. The workshop was organised by the Department of Applied Economics, University of Cambridge as part of a Concerted Action on 'Market-based Instruments for Sustainable Development' funded under the Programme 'Human Dimensions of Environmental Change' and coordinated by Professor Frank Convery of University College, Dublin. The chapters in the book have been revised, some extensively, and considered comments have been added to give the reader different perspectives on the issues.

The Cambridge workshop followed a previous workshop on 'Environmental Taxes and Charges, National Experiences and Plans' organised in Dublin in February 1996 by the European Foundation for the Improvement of Living and Working Conditions, where the issue was considered by government officials, business leaders and trade unions (from the Workshop Proceedings obtainable form the Foundation). Various governments in Europe are considering or have introduced environmental taxes usually accompanied by compensating measures such as reductions in taxes on employment.

The Dublin workshop also heard the industry view which emphasised that one of the main reasons why business leaders opposed such taxes was their effect on competitiveness. The Cambridge workshop addressed this concern directly and this book does the same. Competitiveness is a legitimate concern both for environmental taxes and regulations, but it is clear from the evidence that the introduction of new taxes and regulations is an opportunity to improve competitiveness as well as a threat to established price and cost structures. The 1996 OECD Report on 'Implementation Strategies for Environmental Taxes', reviewing the evidence so far, found that 'The trade and investment impacts which have been measured empirically are almost negligible' (p.18). The limitation of this finding is that there is relatively little experience of environmental policy and model predictions for competitiveness effects of possible future policies vary considerably. 'Probably all that can be said with confidence is that the effect of a carbon tax policy on competitiveness could be substantial' (p.18). So there is a need for further research.

The Cambridge workshop set the scene for future work by bringing together researchers currently working in this area and the book contains revised and extended versions of the papers presented. The aim is to cover the issues associated with competitiveness in a comprehensive manner, so there is a double emphasis – survey chapters combined with a wide range of theoretical and empirical approaches.

Chapter 4 of this book is a revised version of the authors' report *Competitiveness and the Carbon Tax* which was produced for the Department of the Environment. © Crown copyright 1996. Reproduced with the permission of the Controller of Her Majesty's Stationery Office. The Department does not take responsibility for the views expressed in the chapter or for the accuracy of the review. The authors acknowledge with gratitude the comments given by the Department of the Environment and members of its Academic Panel, when the original report was presented.

The review in Chapter 4 has been sent to lead authors of the main studies discussed, both for comment and to ensure that their findings are not misrepresented. Replies were received from Alan Manne, Joaquim Oliveira–Martins, Jack Pezzey, Thomas Rutherford and Heinz Welsch and these have been incorporated into the chapter. We are grateful to them for taking the trouble to comment; in particular we wish to thank Joaquim Oliveira–Martins and Jack Pezzey for giving us extensive suggestions which have allowed us to improve the presentation. Finally the authors wish to thank Clare Bryden, formerly with Cambridge Econometrics, for help in producing the original carbon tax report and various comments on the text and tables.

Cambridge
July 1997

Foreword

It is the responsibility of the research community to seek after truth. And this is not easy, in a world where, as Camus says, we are all special cases.

The European Commission (Directorate XII) provides financial support for a network of research institutions coördinated by the Environmental Institute, University College, Dublin, devoted to the study of the design and use of market based instruments for sustainable development. The network operates as follows: a number of themes have been identified, and a workshop has been, or will be, organised on each of these. Scholars, policy practitioners and others come together, a number of keynote papers on the theme are presented, these are discussed at some length, and then in most cases, the organisers of the theme in question bring together the (revised) papers into an edited volume. Themes which have been, or will be, thus addressed in regard to market based instruments include: non–market valuation, voluntary agreements, international trade, environmental effectiveness, institutional aspects, tradable permits, green tax commissions, and competitiveness.

This volume is the product of the workshop on competitiveness organised and hosted by the Department of Applied Economics, University of Cambridge.

The impetus towards the Single Market has been driven in part by a concern that Europe is 'falling behind' the US and Japan. There is a perceived need to capture economies of scale, to break down barriers to competition, to energise the firms and sectors of the economy across Member States by exposing them to competitive forces. The rhetoric of competitiveness has been in the air now for over a decade. And it has become more fevered as the evidence seemed to show that the European economies are not performing as well their global competitors, in particular in regard to product innovation and growth in real output and employment.

Into this context came the proposal from the Commission to impose a European Union–wide tax on carbon and energy, with the objective of stimulating energy conservation and a switch to less carbon–intensive fuels, in the context of stabilising emissions of greenhouse gases. There was a parallel proposal to recycle the revenues, all or part in the form of tax reductions on labour. But, as the Irish politician and orator Edmund observed 'To tax and to please, no more than to love and be wise, is not given to men' (in: On American Taxation).

Not surprisingly, widespread opposition emerged amongst the energy intensive sectors to this proposal, with much of the argument based on the alleged negative effects which such a proposal would have, if implemented, on competitiveness.

It is timely therefore to step back from the debate and review the evidence, to look at the theory and the practise, ranging from the global economy and that of the nation state to the situation of the individual firm.

And this is the contribution which this book makes: it provides an important context for those in the policy process to assess the competitiveness issue, to evaluate the various arguments which are proposed. It provides scholars with a benchmark from which to undertake more work in this rapidly emerging field.

This is the first of a series of books on transnational environmental policy issues: the Series on International Studies in Environmental Policy Making which will be produced by Edward Elgar Publishing Ltd.

Frank J. Convery
Series Editor

1. Introduction

Terry Barker and Jonathan Köhler

1 ENVIRONMENTAL POLICIES AND COMPETITIVENESS

Government policies to reduce environmental pollution and global warming are often criticised as damaging the economy, particularly by reducing international competitiveness. This book addresses this issue directly by examining some of the policies concerned and their effects on competitiveness. The general position can be summarised as follows.

First, it is important to distinguish between 'command and control' environmental regulation and 'market–based incentives' such as fiscal policy to increase the price of a product in order to achieve an environmental objective. Regulation has been the traditional way of managing environmental problems; fiscal policy is seen as a newer, less costly alternative, especially in reducing greenhouse gas emissions; but both types of instrument can be useful depending on the nature of the environmental problem and the non–environmental benefits associated with the instrument. The competitive effects of regulation take place as a result of compliance costs and any stimulation of new technology (see Adams, 1997); the effects of fiscal policy take place through higher prices, higher fossil fuel prices in the case of carbon taxation, offset by lower labour costs if revenues are recycled, with again a possible stimulation of new technologies.

Second, regulation may well be more costly than the fiscal policy and the nature of the costs is different. However, in both cases the costs tend to be identifiable, localised and immediate, whereas the benefits tend to be diffused over many people and firms, over areas nowhere near the original source of the pollution and over long periods of time. Correspondingly the competitive losses may be more apparent and immediate and the competitive advantages more hidden and distant. Those who might lose from environmental policies are likely to be more vociferous than those who might gain. This point is well illustrated in the controversy which surrounded the proposed introduction of an EU-wide carbon/energy tax and in the nature of the discussions at several UN conferences on climate change, for example the 1995 conference in Berlin. In the discussion of the European proposal, the arguments were particularly fierce. The threat of effective policies to reduce fossil fuel use challenged the energy–producing and using industries, two of the more powerful, well–organised and influential of industrial sectors. One of the main arguments in opposing the move towards environmental policies, was that such policies will increase firms' costs relative to their competitors, making them less profitable and reducing employment and investment (Ikwue and Skea, 1994).

Third, there has been a substantial debate in the US on the costs and benefits of environmental regulation on competitiveness, that is 'command and control' policies, a debate which is addressed in Chapter 3 below. Porter and Van der Linde (1995) argue that studies of the effect of compliance costs on competitiveness have ignored long term productivity gains from innovation. Regulation, and environmental fiscal policy, may stimulate new technologies in reducing pollution and waste and in saving energy, by creating a climate of resource–saving technological progress. However, evidence is hard to find. Jaffe and Stavins (1994) conclude that there is little to document the view that regulations have adversely affected international competitiveness, but that there is also no support for the revisionist hypothesis that regulations stimulate innovation.

Fourth, the effects of environmental taxation policies as proposed and implemented by national governments and the European Commission are judged in most studies, including those presented below, to have very small effects on prices and costs (OECD, 1996 and 1997); indeed, the effects are so small that it is difficult to measure them and distinguish them from the background of continual changes in costs and prices due to wage changes, exchange rate changes and technical change. Fiscal policies are in many cases just beginning to tackle the problem and the effects may be small because the policies do not go far enough, but it is reassuring that there is no evidence that overall economic performance has been harmed to any significant extent by such policies. Indeed if such policies are well designed and introduced gradually, they can increase economic well–being as well as improve the environment.

Fifth, since environmental policies may improve the quality of life, they may also improve competitiveness by making a locality or a country more attractive as a place to live and work. This is a rather nebulous improvement, but may be very important in the long term particularly in economic sectors such as research and development where the well–being of the workforce is important to economic success.

Sixth, environmental policies, if they are part of a general drive to raise standards, reduce waste, and modernise a national industry, may well lead to net increases in costs (although there are instances of spectacular savings being made through use of new technologies), but the reduction in price competitiveness, assuming that the national exchange rate remains unchanged, may be more than offset by an increase in quality. This can take the form of better service, shorter waiting time, better design, less waste in the use and disposal of the product, as well as in new product attributes attractive to the purchaser.

This introduction sets the chapters which follow in the context of the general debate on international competitiveness.

2 WHAT IS COMPETITIVENESS?

'Competitiveness' continues to be a word that excites economists, industrialists, and politicians. It represents a notion that is at the core of neoclassical economic thinking – that the way to generate the greatest possible (economic) wealth is through the operation of 'agents' bidding against each other in price competition to buy or sell a limited quantity of goods and services in a 'market'. It also represents a notion at the core of new thinking in economics, such as that in Porter's *The Competitive Advantage of Nations* (Porter, 1990), in which cost and price competitiveness are set alongside and compared with non–price factors such as quality, variety and availability in a dynamic context.

Because the idea is fundamental in understanding the working of the economic system and in devising policies for firms and governments, it is applied in many different contexts. There is the perception that nation states and groups such as the European Union and the North American Free Trade Association, NAFTA, compete with each other, which broadens the idea to encompass politics as well as economics.

In recent years there has been a surge in the academic study of competitiveness, with a survey of the debate given in the **Oxford Review of Economic Policy** (1996). In her assessment, Boltho (1996) takes the definition of international competitiveness in the short term as 'equated with the real value of the exchange rate' and in the long term as 'virtually synonymous with trend productivity growth' (p.3). There are difficulties with this definition, as she acknowledges, namely the distinction between short and long terms, what is meant by the real exchange rate in practice, and whether labour productivity is sufficient to measure long-term competitiveness.

The alternative OECD definition is 'the degree to which (a country) can, under free and fair market conditions, produce goods and services which meet the test of international markets, while simultaneously maintaining and expanding the real incomes of its people over the longer term' (OECD, 1992, p.237). This places less emphasis on the exchange rate and the current account of the balance of payments. This definition is more general and conveys what most commentators mean by competitiveness. It is explored in more detail by Thompson in Chapter 2 and by Ekins and Speck in Chapter 3 below.

3 COMPETITIVENESS AND CURRENCY EXCHANGE RATES

The promotion of national competitiveness is sometimes based on the idea that economies should be run on the basis of firms competing to sell their products. However firms are not countries and it can be misleading to propose policies for countries based on the analogy with firms. Different aspects of this issue are explored in the Chapters which follow, but since the analogy is so persuasive in common usage, it is also worth setting out the problems with it here.

There is a crucial difference between firms competing against other firms for shares in a particular market and countries competing against other countries in many markets: in the case of countries, the exchange rates of their currencies can vary to offset any long-term competitive advantages either may have over the other. Both firms and countries can transform themselves in the competitive process, with firms changing their pricing strategies, developing new products and even relocating to other countries; but only countries adjust their external relations with other countries through variations in exchange rates and firms must accept the consequences. For example, if the firms in one country are successful competitors on the world market, they may find that the currency of their country appreciates, reducing their price competitiveness.

The underlying issue is the ability of firms to sell their products in competition with firms from other countries (leaving aside a discussion of multinationals). It is this which worries politicians and is used by industrialists to lobby a government exploring new environmental policies. However, it is not enough to argue that if such policies lead to a reduction in competitiveness, then the exchange rate will adjust to maintain long-run competitiveness. The weakness of the argument can be shown by considering the important differences for national policy and analysis in the two cases of nations with currencies in chronic appreciation or depreciation.

If a country finds that large current account surpluses continue to escalate in the form of holding of foreign currency or transfer on capital account, for example increasing ownership of foreign assets, the exchange rate may appreciate or if the national government holds it fixed, it may be periodically revalued. The appreciation will result in a fall in price competitiveness, but it will not necessarily weaken non–price competitiveness. Indeed it may strengthen it by forcing firms which rely on price competitiveness to switch to an emphasis on non–price attributes or to go out of business. Over the long term increasing non–price competitiveness will be offset by decreasing price competitiveness. A good example of the process is to be found in the Japanese economy since 1985. Yoshitomi (1996, p.68–9) provides convincing evidence that during a period when the yen appreciated substantially in relation to costs and foreign prices from 1990 to 1995, Japanese exports have moved substantially upmarket.

The opposite case is a country with low or falling non–price competitiveness which sees its currency depreciate unless it can borrow more and more from abroad. There are asymmetries in the inflation process such that it is easier to generate more inflation than less. This is partly a result of the downward rigidity of money wage rates as workers are reluctant to accept wage cuts and employers are reluctant to impose them. If this is so, then a depreciating currency will lead to more domestic inflation. In addition, reliance on price and costs competitiveness will drive a nation's trade down market, away from higher quality goods and services. Lower quality products also tend to be those with lower income elasticities, so that the nations with depreciating currencies find that their markets grow more slowly than those of their competitors, even when real prices remain unchanged. Firms and products become more price competitive as a result of the depreciation, but the poor performance in terms of non–price competition is not addressed.

Therefore countries are in a different position from firms in that they may, if they are free to do so, depreciate their currency to bring about a short-term improvement in national competitiveness. However depreciation may be unattractive as an act of policy because of the risk that it will set off a domestic wage–price spiral, that it will become ineffective through the competitive depreciation of other currencies, or, as we have argued, that it has the long-term effect of encouraging price competition at the expense of quality competition.

4 COMPETITIVENESS AND TECHNOLOGY

The debate on competitiveness and trade has brought to the fore discussion of the role of technology in affecting trade and prices. It has become clear that the identification of international competitiveness with relative unit costs or prices is much too restrictive. Fagerberg (1996, p.40–41) shows that there is no simple correlation between decline in price competitiveness as measured by unit labour costs and growth in market share of exports for 12 industrial countries 1978–94; in fact there is more correlation between the change in the share of R&D in GDP and the change in export shares. In the econometric explanations for exports and imports, many investigators have introduced measures of technical change and innovation, as surveyed by Fagerberg (1996), with the general conclusion that such measures should be considered at least as important as those of price and cost factors for explaining changes in export and import market shares. These findings support several of the conclusions in the papers which follow which compare any effects on prices and costs of environmental policies with effects on technology.

5 DOES CARBON TAXATION DAMAGE COMPETITIVENESS?

Global warming is an international environmental problem and as such requires international negotiations and solutions. Carbon taxation to reduce greenhouse gas emissions is particularly important in the discussion of international competitiveness and environmental policy. The issue of competitiveness is important for two groups of reasons. Firstly, the estimation of such effects is vital to the design of appropriate policies at the national and regional level (for example which industries to exempt) and to the outcome of negotiations at the international level. Secondly, it is used by interest groups in a political context to oppose environmental policies.

The international **economic** significance of the unilateral adoption of carbon taxation is related to the effects on particular sectors. Such taxation will increase the costs of production for those sectors which use carbon intensively, but if the revenues from such taxes are used to reduce employment taxes, the costs of other sectors will decline. Carbon–intensive producers in other regions which do not impose the tax will gain a cost advantage, allowing them to increase market share at the expense of firms in the country which has adopted the tax. Again this loss will be offset by gains in price competitiveness and market share of employment–intensive sectors, if tax revenues are recycled so as to reduce labour costs. The international **environmental** significance of the such taxation is to some extent merely a reflection of this process, since other countries will increase their production in carbon-intensive sectors. It is also, however, related to the depressing effect that the tax may have on the price of fossil fuels in world markets, encouraging producers to adopt more carbon–intensive processes in all sectors.

The Chapters in this book show that the widely held view of adverse economic and environmental consequences of a national or EU-wide unilateral greenhouse gas abatement policy should be qualified if not even, in some circumstances, reversed. The effects on income and GDP, not including the environmental benefits, are generally insignificant if the revenues are recycled as reductions in taxes on employment, and are in some cases positive. Many studies of trade, as quoted above, have shown that relative cost effects, such as those arising from a carbon tax, are not the sole or even the most important determinants of trade. Since the implementation of a tax achieving substantial abatement, for example 50 per cent reductions in CO_2 emissions, will certainly lead to a fundamental transformation of the economy, the analyses in the literature which are limited to cost effects, with no beneficial effects from improvements in non-price competitiveness or from revenue recycling, will be misleading. The pace of technological innovation may change, the entire tax structure may adjust, and the whole direction of economic development may shift.

Similarly, the apparent negative environmental effects through leakages which are found in many studies can also be examined critically. If OECD incomes are reduced as a result of abatement policies, then the rest of the world will export less to the OECD and incomes, and therefore emissions, are also likely to be lower, offsetting any price effects in world markets from reduced OECD demand for fossil fuels. Similarly if gas and coal markets are restricted to particular regions through high transport costs, then there may be instances when emissions actually fall in the face of falling world oil prices. One example of this is in the prospective use of fossil fuels in China: at present the use of coal in China is expected to grow strongly, but if oil prices fell in relation to coal prices in China, there may be substitution from coal to oil, reducing overall emissions and supporting the world oil price.

6 COVERAGE OF THE BOOK

The book is divided into three parts: (1) broad coverage of the field in the surveys of Chapters 2, 3 and 4, (2) macroeconomic studies and (3) microeconomic studies.

Chapter 2 by Grahame Thompson discusses why competitiveness has become so important in international discourse and as an objective for national governments. He compares different ways of looking at the issue and settles for the geo-economic approach, looking at trade and foreign direct investment (FDI) flows between the three blocs NAFTA, the EU and Japan. He discusses different measures of international competitiveness: changes in unit labour costs; changes in the shares of world exports of goods and services; and FDI performance. Thompson points out that FDI flows are more footloose and less integrated than trade flows. He explores some of the anomalies in the use of unit labour costs to measure competitiveness and argues that both inward and outward FDI should be considered in assessing competitiveness. His conclusion is to council against international competitiveness as a near universal criterion to measure the effects of policies.

Chapter 3 by Paul Ekins and Stefan Speck is a general survey of the literature concerned with the effects of environmental policies on competitiveness. They find that at the firm and sector level and given intelligent policy design over all sectors, there will not be a significant loss of competitiveness. The same is true at the national level. There could be severe transition effects, but these can be ameliorated by the gradual and predictable introduction of environmental policies.

Chapter 4 by Terry Barker and Nick Johnstone is a more specific survey of modelling work that has been undertaken on the competitiveness effects of carbon taxation and the carbon leakage problem. The reported effects on international price competitiveness were very small, but those on leakage rates differed widely. The models considered fall into two broad groups: general equilibrium models and macroeconometric models. None of them were originally designed to deal with the competitiveness issue and in some cases very little work has gone into making them appropriate. The review concludes that in most of the models the representation of global energy–environment–economy interactions as a dynamic system leaves much to be desired and that many models do not capture important features of responses to energy price and carbon tax changes, for example the effects on CO_2 emissions of changes in world real income arising from the unilateral introduction of an OECD carbon tax.

Two macroeconomic studies report evidence from studies of international environmental policies. In Chapter 5, Clare Smith reports the results of a study using a global econometric model to investigate carbon leakage. For a relatively modest tax that would reduce emissions by 14 per cent from the base case, she finds a 6 per cent leakage by 2030 in the case of an OECD–wide carbon tax, or a 12 per cent leakage by 2030 for an EU–wide tax. However, competitiveness effects would probably be reduced by structural readjustment. Oil–exporting countries face a loss in revenues. Carl Koopmans in Chapter 6 reports studies for a world–wide energy tax of 50 per cent which show that there would be a 0.25 per cent per year decrease in world income. A national tax for the Netherlands at this level would require exemptions for the energy–intensive sectors to be acceptable, in which case Dutch employment would rise slightly with a negligible loss in growth. Energy use in the Netherlands would then decrease by 3.5 per cent. The way to avoid undesirable leakage effects is to cooperate with other countries to solve the Prisoner's Dilemma associated with who introduces a tax first. Both the EU and the OECD could provide a suitable forum for international agreements on the introduction of carbon taxes.

The final part contains four studies of firms' behaviour in the context of environmental policy. Chapter 7 is a theoretical study by Eirik Romstad of trans–boundary pollution and alternative policies to control it. Tradeable permits and taxes are shown to be equivalent only if a system of lump sum payments removes the increased loss of competitiveness with taxes. A game theoretic treatment of trans–boundary pollution shows that choosing the instrument with lower costs increases the possibility of a cooperative solution for emission reductions. He then examines the Porter hypothesis, that environmental policies promote innovation, giving production efficiency gains that may lead to an absolute advantage over firms that are not regulated. There is little empirical support for this.

A national case study for Germany by Rolf–Ulrich Sprenger is included as Chapter 8. Germany is a particularly interesting case – it is a very large exporter and has a relatively long history of environmental awareness and policy action. Once again, the evidence shows that for most sectors, competitiveness effects are negligible, although firms that face severe international competition may suffer even from a slight increase in costs due to compliance with environmental regulations.

Turning to business management, Frans Berkhout examines life cycle approaches to the management of the environmental impact of products in Chapter 9. The main effect of demands for increased environmental stringency will be on the producers of final goods and services, who will find themselves competing over this aspect of their products. Increased producer responsibility for products in the short term and changing patterns of product ownership that create new markets in the longer term would provide firms with incentives to take a positive role in product policy. The final Chapter is an empirical study of green product development by Robin Roy, Mark Smith and Stephen Potter. Firms did not set out to produce a 'greener' product, rather environmental factors were considered in pursuit of commercial aims. Environmental regulation would be needed to encourage the adoption of a more comprehensive 'ecodesign' approach and more green products.

The general opinion of the contributors is that carefully designed environmental policies will have a small or insignificant effect on the ability of firms to compete in international markets. Taking into account the characteristics of the macroeconomic models, high estimates of carbon leakage in the literature do not appear to be well founded, with many estimates small or even negative. The firm studies demonstrate that there is considerable potential for firms to compete and make profits by developing green products and adopting a comprehensive approach to the management of the environmental impacts of products. However, the conclusions are necessarily based on evidence which is open to interpretation and often inconclusive. The models suffer from significant problems, especially in the use of data; and green product development and management is still in its infancy, especially in the UK. So these findings should be taken as a basis for further work, rather than as a consensus achieved.

REFERENCES

Adams, J. (1997) 'Environmental policy and competitiveness in a globalised economy: conceptual issues and a review of the empirical evidence', Chapter 4 in *Globalisation and Environment: Preliminary Perspectives*, OECD, Paris, forthcoming.

Boltho A. (1996), 'The assessment: international competitiveness', *Oxford Review of Economic Policy*, **12**(3), 1–16.

Fagerberg, J. (1996) 'Technology and Competitiveness', *Oxford Review of Economic Policy*, **12**(3), Autumn, 39–51.

Ikwue T. and J. Skea (1994), 'Business and the genesis of the European Community carbon tax proposal', *Business Strategy and the Environment*, **3**(2), Summer, 1–10.

Jaffe A.B. and R.N. Stavins (1994), 'Environmental Regulation and Technology Diffusion: The Effects of alternative policy Instruments', Harvard University John F. Kennedy school of Government Faculty Research Working Paper Series: R94-20.

OECD (1992), *Technology and the Economy: The Key Relationships*, OECD, Paris.

OECD (1996), 'Pollution abatement and control expenditure in OECD countries', OECD Environment Monograph, OECD/GD(96)50, OECD, Paris.

OECD (1997), *Environmental Taxes and Green Tax Reform*, OECD, Paris.

Oxford Review of Economic Policy (1996), Issue on International Competitiveness, **12**(3), Autumn.

Porter, M. (1990), *The Competitive Advantage of Nations*, The Free Press, New York.

Porter, M. and C. van der Linde (1995), 'Toward a New Conception of the Environment–Competitiveness Relationship', *Journal of Economic Perspectives*, **9**(4), Fall, 97–118.

Yoshitomi, M. (1996), 'On the changing international competitiveness of Japanese manufacturing since 1985', *Oxford Review of Economic Policy*, **12**(3), Autumn, 61–73.

PART ONE

Reviews of the Literature

2. International competitiveness and globalization: frameworks for analysis, connections and critiques

Grahame Thompson[*]

1 INTRODUCTION

A key point raised in this chapter is why we have all become so preoccupied with being 'competitive'. The emphasis on 'competitiveness' now threatens to pervade all aspects of our economic and social lives. This is obviously so for companies and nations; whether their activity is in the traded goods sectors or not, whether it is privately produced or collectively provided. All these are now equally subject to the criteria of competitiveness. But it is increasingly so for individuals. We are also required to become 'competitive' in the way we conduct our lives, which goes under the headings of being 'flexible', 'innovative', 'imaginative', 'entrepreneurial', and the like. Thus the discourse of competitiveness has become pervasive. In part this has to do with a perceived growth in uncertainties and risks in the late–capitalist world. This is itself driven by the end of the long boom and the coincidental emergence of stagflation and a difficulty in generating a new sustained upswing for the world's economies. As a result we are required to be competitive so as to generate or maintain our own 'security' in an as yet to be

* This chapter is based upon two papers: 'Some Observations on the "International Competitiveness Debate" and International Economic Relations' given at the ESF-EMOT Workshop: *Globalization and Industrial Transformation in Europe*. Malaga, Spain, January 9-12, 1997 and 'International Competitiveness and Globalization: Connections and Critiques' given at the conference: *Globalization: Critical Perspectives,* The University of Birmingham, March 14-16, 1997. I am grateful to the participants at these conferences for helpful comments after the presentation of the papers.

fully reinvigorated and still potentially hostile world. But security here has less to do with politico–military matters, and more to do with becoming or remaining **economically competitive**. Geoeconomics is replacing geopolitics as the driving force for international security. So it is the performative outcomes in terms of our economic status that will establish and maintain our personal securities as well.

In the international economic domain there are probably five relatively separate trends that can account for this growth in the discourse of competitiveness.

The first, and most obvious, has to do with the collapse of the Cold War. Whilst the Cold War was in place competitiveness remained couched in fundamentally geopolitical terms – the struggle between the two main politico–ideological formations locked all remaining world issues into a single geomilitary dimension. Once this was over the **differences** between countries came newly to the fore, and particularly the differences between them in terms of their economic performance as measured by their competitiveness.

A second important development was the perceived unsuccessful nature of large scale and grandiose 'industrial policy' initiatives. Twenty-five years ago critical economic discourse was much more concerned about different industrial policies and restructuring initiatives by governments. As it is these are now seen to have been a failure (though this is not to suggest that there were all actually failures). In the wake of this, it is the emphasis on 'competitiveness' that has taken hold of both the private and public consciousness in terms of economic matters.

A third trend is the move towards policies of liberalization and privatization in terms of domestic institutional changes. Although these are often argued to be the results of internationalization and even the globalization of economic activity, it is suggested that they are fundamentally driven by domestic decisions and policy changes (see Thompson, 1997c). Whatever the reason, however, the result has been a reinvigorated emphasis on competition and market driven solutions to economic problems.

A fourth issue involves the relative 'success' of those mainly inter–governmental organizations of international economic regulation and management that have governed the world economy in the post–Second War period, like the OECD, the GATT/WTO, the IMF and World Bank. The activity of these organizations resulted in a general opening–up of the world economies as protectionist barriers to economic activity were eliminated or drastically reduced. In the absence of tariff barriers or capital controls the underlying economic competitiveness of different countries were exposed, hence the growth in a concern with this aspect of their economies.

Finally, and something that brings all these different aspects together, there has been an undoubted growth of interdependences and integration amongst the world economies since the end of the Second World War. This process, sometimes known as 'globalization', when combined with the end of the semi–fixed exchange rate regime in the early 1970s and other developments mentioned so far, served to announce afresh the importance of the relative competitiveness of different countries.

So there is a very clear and close relationship between the growth of the discourse of international competitiveness and that of 'globalization', something returned to in a moment. First the chapter outlines in more detail the main ways in which 'international competitiveness' is discussed in the international political economy literature, since this can act as a frameworking device for the chapter as a whole. It then moves on to look specifically at the economics literature, where different conceptions and emphasis of international competitiveness are considered. The discussion is undertaken with the UK position to the forefront, since it is a very interesting example, but one that needs to be placed in a comparative international context.

2 EXPLANATORY FRAMEWORKS FOR INTERNATIONAL COMPETITIVENESS AND GLOBAL SECURITY

In this section I delineate three contrasting approaches to the analysis of international competitiveness from broadly within the international political economy literature. Each of these approaches is indicative of a larger number of specific studies.

The first is termed the 'domestic interests approach'. Essentially, this looks for the **sources** of international competitiveness, and seeks them in the configuration of **domestic** relations between the 'interest groups' or 'social partners'. It is illustrated in Figure 2.1 using Jeffrey Hart's analysis of post–War advanced industrial economies (Hart, 1992), where, in this case, the interests groups are business, labour and the state. (This is part of a much larger body of literature in

Structure of interest	Interest Group		
	State	Business	Labour
More than one group dominates	Japan (State and Business)	Germany (Business and Labour)	
A single group dominates	France	USA	UK

Figure 2.1 Domestic interests approach

the IPE tradition that stresses similar patterns and processes for understanding relative national economic performative outcomes.) In Hart's particular analysis those countries whose economic organization is dominated by an exclusive attachment to a single nodal interest group have suffered relative to those whose organization is more broadly balanced. The strategic choices he offers the USA and Britain, for instance, to improve their competitive performance is to move towards a position similar to the one already occupied by Japan and Germany respectively, where no one group is predominant.

A number of critical comments can be made about this approach. Whilst not wishing to totally deny its continued pertinence, the overall result looks dated. Britain, for instance, could hardly any longer be placed in the position as illustrated – as totally beholden to labour – yet its performative outcome has not greatly improved and continues a relative decline. Germany and Japan are also in flux in respect to the 'balanced' position as their economies falter. In addition there is a question as to the accuracy of the original positioning anyway. Was the state quite so unimportant to the economic success of post–war Germany as might be suggested from this figure? Similar comments could be made about the USA. And perhaps the key role supposedly played by the state in Japan has been exaggerated? Broadly speaking, this analysis relies upon a particular configuration of post–war 'social settlements' in each country, one that is now being eroded by neo–liberal policy changes and international integrative developments. Whilst the full consequences of these for comparative international competitiveness remain unclear, it reduces the confidence in the model as indicated.

The second approach stresses the interactions between key actors in the conduct of **international** economic relations rather than domestic ones. Here the actors are more narrowly drawn than in respect to Figure 2.1. Just two key types of agents are identified – governments and companies – and the issue is the relationships between them. Stopford and Strange (1991) suggest that it is government–company relationships (and to a lesser extent company–company relationships) that provide the arenas in which decisions for international competitiveness will be decided or fought over. They see international competitiveness as being conditioned by both comparative and competitive advantage (although the differences between these, and the relative importance attributed to each of them, are not sufficiently distinguished in their analysis – see below). In addition, they pay particularly close attention to the business tactics and strategies of multinational corporations, though without neglecting the role of purely domestic companies. An added feature of the Stopford and Strange approach is to downplay government–government interactions as the strategic site for struggles for international competitiveness.

The actor interactions approach has some obvious virtues. It focuses upon significant and important issues. But the analysis also suffers from a number of weaknesses. First, its analysis of government–company interactions is directed at the relationships between the less developed economies and the multinational corporations in the main, so the role of the more developed countries as continued strategic players in their own right is somewhat neglected. Secondly, the complexity of the strategies, tactics, locational decisions, governmental reactions, and the like, explored in the analysis does not lend itself easily to any generalization (this may be one of the reasons why this useful book has been relatively neglected in the debate). The book ends rather 'in the air', however, without being able to suggest much about the general nature of the internationalized economy being analysed. The sources of competitiveness are thus multiple and unlikely to be systematised (it is all ' complex process' with no simple model as to where that process might lead – either intellectually or practically).

The final approach discussed in this section is the geoeconomic approach. This stresses the strategic interrelationship between the three main player countries/groups within the international system – the Triad (Japan/East Asia, USA/NAFTA and Germany/EU). The analysis by Sandholtz et al. (1992) (collectively known as the Berkeley Roundtable on the International Economy – BRIE) is overwhelmingly concerned with redefining the nature of international security, in which it sees the issue of international competitiveness as being critical.

Two features animate their analysis; the collapse of the Cold War and the decline of US hegemony. The first is seen as heralding the potential end of geopolitics as a new geoeconomics based upon international competitiveness replaces it. The emphasis shifts from a predominantly militarily driven system of inter–state/bloc rivalry, based upon deep ideological and systemic socio–economic organizational differences, to a system based around 'peaceful' economic competition between states and blocs with military matters subsidiary to this (at least in the first instance). The second implicates the US's ability to 'manage' the newly evolving system and fix its own security. The decline of hegemony is put down to a decline in economic power and the loss of international competitiveness, so the remedy is obvious – to restimulate the American economy. But how? This question, of course, has preoccupied many American analysts since the 1970s.

The geoeconomics approach has the advantage of setting the problem of competitiveness squarely within an international system, and one where state or bloc rivalry between the advanced industrial states continues to figure prominently. The thrust of the approach is to look for the possible **consequences** of a differential or similar competitiveness record amongst the Triad (in terms of its security implications), rather than to concentrate upon the **causes** of any differential competitiveness (though this element is by no means neglected). Although the nodal points are represented by single countries (Japan, USA and

Germany) a feature of the analysis is to link these to the formation of definite economic blocs (East–Asia, NAFTA and the EU). An obvious potential problem here is whether such an East–Asian bloc, formed around Japan, is actually emerging. The EU looks the most coherent bloc, with NAFTA a long way behind in terms of institution building. Such that there is an East–Asian bloc based upon Japan, it is driven by commercial activity rather than by any institution building. Explicit and complex institution building is eschewed by the 'Asian way' and rejected within the APEC process, for instance (Yamazawa, 1998).

3 EXPLORING THE GEOECONOMIC APPROACH

The geoeconomic approach probably represents the most fruitful way of thinking about the question of international competitiveness and its implications. As is argued in Hirst and Thompson (1996), the Triad alone was responsible for 75 per cent of FDI flows during the 1980s, some 70 per cent of trade in 1992, and a similar percentage of GDP. Since the mid–1980s the growth of FDI has eclipsed that of trade growth and now figures as the central driving force in the international economy. Although the growth of FDI flows declined somewhat in the early 1990s, and their direction of flow moved more in favour of the non–Triad countries, the older pattern began to reestablish itself again after 1992 (Hirst and Thompson, 1996, Figure 4.1 p.79). In addition, the intra–Triad dominance was reinforced by important subsidiary flows of investment between that group of countries and a geographically discrete group of smaller 'client' states (Hirst and Thompson, 1996, chapter 3 and Figure 3.6). Relatively isolated clusters of main actor and client states are emerging, which are geographically discrete and stabilizing. The essential character of this process is illustrated in Figure 2.2, which shows which member of the Triad dominates the inward FDI in particular countries. Thus whilst **intra**-Triad investment relationships are particularly strong, a pattern of further discrete but robust **inter**-linkages between each of the Triad members and more marginalized country clusters is also evident. These country groupings tend to be regionally specific and geographically 'adjacent' to one or other of the Triad members. Further, this testifies to the **lack of multilateral integration** in FDI flows and stocks since the clusters indicate a geographical and regional discreteness in the relationships between countries. The direction of FDI relationships is first amongst the Triad countries themselves and then secondly between one or other of the Triad powers and its cluster of client states, rather than between the smaller states themselves.

There are two sets of points to be drawn from this analysis. The first is to emphasize the enormous geographical concentration of FDI in the Triad and a

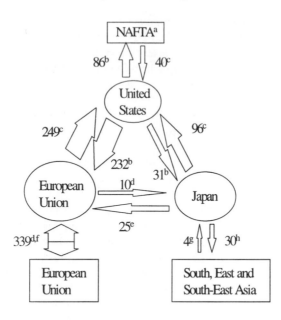

World inward FDI stock: $2,080 bn

Source: UNCTAD, Division on Transnational Corporations and Investment, FDI database

Notes:

a Canada and Mexico
b United States outward FDI stock
c United States inward FDI stock
d Outward FDI stock of Austria, Finland, France, Germany, Italy, Netherlands, Sweden and the UK. Data for Austria are for 1991 and data for France and the Netherlands are for 1992.
e Inward FDI stock of Austria, Finland, France, Germany, Italy, Netherlands, Sweden and the UK. Data for Austria are for 1991 and data for France and the Netherlands are for 1992.
f For Sweden, the data reflect FDI to and from all European countries. Intra-European Union FDI, based on inward stocks, is $225 bn.
g Data are based on approvals/notifications and represent those from countries other than those in North America and Europe.
h Estimated by multiplying the values of the cumulative flows to the region according to FDI approvals by the ratio of disbursed to approved/notified FDI in developing countries.

Figure 2.2   FDI stock among Triad members and their clusters, 1993 (Billions of dollars)

few other states. The second point concerns the comparison of the multilateral integration of FDI and that of trade: FDI between members of the Triad and their respective clusters of client states is less integrated than trade (UN, 1993, Chapter VII; UN, 1996, Chapter 1), whereas between the Triad members themselves, FDI is more integrated than trade, although as we have seen, links remain extremely geographically discrete.

The greater integration of FDI between Triad members as compared to that of trade means that FDI relationships are more 'open' to cross-integration between the core countries and the different sets of cluster states than they are in the case of trade relationships, perhaps because they are more dependent on physical links and hence more closed to these cross fertilizations between regionalized blocs and clusters.

This has two possible further implications. First it means that 'protectionist' sentiment on the part of the different trading blocs and major states is likely to be lower in the field of investment than it may have been in the case of trade. Secondly, it makes investment potentially as liable to genuine multilateral regulation as is trade, if not more so (and trade has shown itself highly amenable to this form of management in the past). Both of these features could act to undermine any inward looking development of regionalized trading blocs. Given that investment is tending to displace trade as the driving force of international integration the likelihood of competitive and antagonistically poised trade or investment blocs emerging is made less likely if this analysis is correct. Thus the potential for security of the system needs to be considered in this context. There are more incentives for continued minimal cooperation between the Triad blocs than for outright dissent amongst them.

Why are investment relationships less sticky and intense than ones involving trade? The 1993 UN report suggests there are two possible reasons; a) geographical distance is less of an inhibitor to FDI than it is to trade because transactions costs are lower with respect to the former; b) national endowment advantages in respect to FDI are less specific than they are with respect to trade. The factors important for successful FDI are more widely distributed geographically than they are for trade, hence, while FDI remains highly concentrated it is less concentrated than is trade.

The second major point to draw from this analysis is to reemphasize the still enormous geographical concentration of FDI in the big three and a few other states. And similarly it is to reemphasize this concentration even more so in respect to trade flows than investment flows, as just pointed out above.

4 MEASURES AND TRENDS IN INTERNATIONAL ECONOMIC COMPETITIVENESS

This section moves away from the analysis of the overall framework in which international competitiveness can be considered to look more closely at the idea of international **economic** competitiveness. We might begin to develop the importance of international competitiveness for the UK economy, for instance, by first reminding ourselves of the two main ways it is discussed in the literature. These are in terms of 'ability to sell' and 'locational attractiveness' (Dluhosch, Freytag and Kruger, 1996). Accepting for a moment the usefulness of the notion of 'national competitiveness', a country's ability to sell internationally will depend on its relative cost structure, its productivity and its exchange rate, so the policy areas more or less identify themselves automatically here (though not necessarily the policy options). The ability to sell approach is the traditional one. It focuses on the current account of the balance of payments, particularly the trade account. A premier measure of competitiveness in this case is the relative unit labour cost (RULC), usually in manufacturing (Thompson, 1997a; Auerbach, 1996). This is usually associated with shares in world exports.

The locational attractiveness approach arises in the context of the internationalization and efficiency of financial markets, increased capital mobility, and the way that intertemporal investment decisions are thought to follow a logic of utility maximization in an interdependent world economy. This approach would stress how balance of payments adjustments are secured via capital flows, and would look more to the decisions of private agents in terms of their investment choices, and thus focus on the capital account of the balance of payments. A premier measure of competitiveness with this approach are FDI and other investment flows. The policy areas here have to do with making a country attractive for investors, so they embrace a wider set of options than just the traditional ones associated with the ability to sell.

Although these two approaches are often presented as though it is a matter of choice between them (one is correct and the other is not), it is probably best to think of them as complementary and interdependent rather than as competitors. It will now be useful to examine how the UK has fared in relationship to both these main measures over the post–Second World War period (Thompson, 1997a).

In the case of the RULC and 'ability to sell', the long–term trend until the late 1970s was for the UK economy to show an **improving** competitiveness position. There was a dramatic loss of international competitiveness between 1979 and 1981 and subsequently the longer–term trend of improving competitiveness, measured by RULC, tended to reestablish itself. The story for the US economy is much the same as this, though the loss of competitiveness for the US lasted longer in the 1980s (to 1985) before the reemergence of the older trend. The sources of improvements in the UK were mainly through exchange rate adjustments (devaluations), while for the US they were mainly through domestic labour cost adjustments. Comparing these experiences with those of Japan and Germany is instructive since there the trends were more or less the exact opposite. Japan and Germany had been **losing** competitiveness in RULC terms over almost the entire period since the 1960s (Thompson, 1987 and 1997a).

Thus the counter–intuitive paradox here, noted first by Kaldor in the 1970s (Kaldor, 1978), was that as the US and the UK were improving their international competitiveness, they were losing on their trade accounts, and while Japan and Germany were losing their international competitiveness, they were improving or maintaining their trade account surpluses. In fact, this seeming paradox is one shared for a larger range of advanced economies as shown in Fagerberg (1996). The relationship between the growth in market share of exports and the growth in relative unit labour cost is **positive** and **greater than one** (slope 1.17) for the twelve countries[1] examined (Fagerberg, 1996). In particular, there is a close relationship between the growth in market share for exports and the change in R&D as a share of GDP. The very strong correlation and high value of the slope indicates the way market share seems to be driven by technological innovation rather than by relative labour costs.

This is probably a well known result amongst economists, but it is important rhetorically and polemically. In as much that governments insist on driving down their relative labour costs in the name of some expected beneficial effects to their current account, if historical experience is anything to go by there may be no such benefits. To a large extent it is this kind of a result that led to a disillusionment with the RULC measure of international competitiveness, and the rise in popularity of the locational advantage approach. Let us now examine this in the UK context.

A great deal is made of the record of the UK as a destination for FDI, demonstrating the success of liberalization, deregulation and policies for flexibility adopted in the UK over the past fifteen years or so. However, this success should not be exaggerated. The UK has been a consistent **net exporter** of FDI in every year since the growth of FDI took off in the early 1980s, except for small surpluses in 1982 and 1990 (HMSO, 1996). In addition, the UK has been a net exporter of portfolio investment (HM Treasury, 1996). During the 1980s it became the largest single outward FDI investor in the world. Moreover, even before the 1980s the UK was also a large external investor. The result was that in 1995 whilst the stock of inward investments was £160bn, the stock of outward investments was much larger at £219bn. This would seem to indicate to the 'locational non–attractiveness' of the UK economy in this regard. The only large industrial economy that displays a long term locational advantage on this measure is the USA, which during the 1980s became a consistent net importer of capital (this position changed in the early 1990s, however). The other major European economies and Japan, for instance, have also been net exporters, mainly to the USA and the southern EU members. This might be the expected and unexceptional result – the rich countries with 'excess' capital exporting it to the poorer ones with high demands – **except** for the highly anomalous position until recently occupied by the USA. The US proves the rule in undermining the commonly accepted approach.

The argument about the UK's unique attractiveness as a destination for foreign investment in Europe is also undermined by the fact that France had larger FDI inflows than the UK did between 1991 and 1995, despite all the talk about the supposed detrimental effects of the Social Chapter (Barrell and Pain, 1997, Table 2, p.65). UK companies were the largest single investor in France over this period. The benefits of inward investment to the UK also tend to be exaggerated given that a growing percentage of these are accounted for by service industry investments, which have not shown significant increases in productivity, and are the results of takeover and acquisition activity.

An important (policy) issue arises here concerning the quality of official analysis in this area It is claimed that inward investment has served to preserve 770,000 British jobs (HMSO, 1996, p.139), but given the net FDI exporting position, wouldn't we expect there to be an overall **net loss** of jobs for the UK? British industry is being 'hollowed out' by this process. As far as can be judged there are no official UK calculations of this potential impact. By contrast, other advanced countries do make these kinds of calculations. MITI, for instance, estimates that Japanese multinationals operating abroad employed just under 2m workers in 1993 (MITI, 1996a, p.25) while multinationals from overseas operating in Japan only employed 169,000 workers (MITI, 1996b, p.24).

Secondly, it is claimed that outward FDI added positive flows to the balance of payments in terms of interest, profit and dividend receipts at £24bn in 1995. But the net position was much less, at only £6bn. Also, what are the possible loss of **export receipts** to the UK economy as a result of the net export of its investment capital? The MITI studies mentioned above follow up the basic statement of the net employment loss position with a discussion of the possible 'second round' impacts of the export of FDI. Their argument is that Japanese overseas FDI has had an overall positive impact on the Japanese economy, and even on Japanese employment (MITI, 1996a, pp.38–42). This is because the investment has stimulated the purchase of Japanese capital goods. Such an 'export inducement effect' has outweighed the 'export substitution effect'. But this is not quantified in the report. It is only asserted, with the proviso that this net positive impact could soon wear off as the overseas investment 'matures'. One important thing the government could do for the UK, therefore, is to establish a serious and ongoing 'social audit' on the full consequences of FDI flows into and out of the economy, so as to provide proper information on which to base public discussion and official decision making. In this respect the emphasis placed upon FDI as a measure of success might also be challenged. FDI measures changes on the liability side of companies balance sheets, not the asset side. This is one reason why FDI can fluctuate so much; as a response to companies manipulation of their liabilities. More emphasis needs to be directed to the productive asset side of company activities before a true picture of the extent and effects of inward investment can be properly calculated (see Thompson, 1997b).

Clearly, both the approaches indicated above suffer analytical and policy problems, so perhaps we should not expect too much from either of them. The RULC approach continues to emphasize international cost and price competition. A possible resolution of the 'Kaldor paradox' mentioned above, then, is to highlight 'quality' rather than 'quantity' as the growing determinant of international success (which is itself linked to the technological inventiveness aspect, as indicated above). In principle, this would seem extremely important and potentially fruitful. Whilst it would be impossible to ignore prices and costs altogether, the emphasis is shifting to quality indicators. Here the UK has a mixed record to say the least. The disastrous consequences of ignoring quality can be judged by the recent beef crisis. Studying the ways continental Europe, and elsewhere, go about establishing and monitoring agricultural quality norms and standards, for instance, would be useful. Do we need a new 'economy of conventions' in this regard? (Wilkinson, 1997). The Anglo–American tradition tends to leave these important matters to either self–regulation, or to the concerns of the consumption end of economic activity (retail chains and consumer choice), or to universalized information and dissemination packages. In Europe, and elsewhere, it is managed much more at the production level, or in respect to **local** producer/municipal organizations (who do the monitoring themselves), and/or has a stronger institutionalized base. The advantage of establishing, monitoring and regulating quality is that it is not so affected by 'globalization' as are other more overt policy initiatives. It need not implicate treaty commitments already entered into with international organizations governing trade and commerce.

The way this has taken hold (perhaps only half–heartedly, however) in the UK is via 'benchmarking' (CBI, 1993). The trouble with this is that it may just encourage a simple 'copying' of already existing products, techniques and processes, which mirrors current best practice. Competitive advantage is gained by an innovative capacity to jump to a new performance plateau, so benchmarking leaves all this work still to be done. But this may be a too cynical view. Enhancing and developing the benchmarking process at least provides a means by which best practice technique could be diffused. By and large British companies are unused to this and are often openly hostile to the levels of cooperation it requires. If they refuse to cooperate, however, there is little that can be done at present. In general terms the UK has a smaller stock of 'world class companies' than the size of its economy would warrant, something that a programme of international benchmarking might serve to alter.

5 THE COMPETITIVENES OF COUNTRIES AND THE COMPETITIVENESS OF COMPANIES

The introduction of the nature of British companies serves to raise a number of other issues associated with international competitiveness. The RLUC and FDI measures pertain to economies rather than to companies, and it may be worthwhile trying to keep these two apart at a number of levels. To start with there is a dispute about comparative advantage and competitive advantage; the one pertaining to the economy, the other to its companies. In terms of conventional trade theory an economy always has a **comparative advantage** in some line of production, so there are always mutual gains from trade. This rather attractive result may, however, not be the case if we take seriously the notion of **competitive advantage**. It is not clear that an economy will always have a competitive advantage in some line of production if such a competitive advantage is dependent upon the success of its companies. Some companies may be unsuccessful in all lines of production, whilst others are successful. This is doubly so if we take the dynamic increasing returns modelling literature seriously (Authur, 1996). Bandwagon effects, positive feedbacks, learning by doing, and so on can all lead to successful cumulative growth trajectories for companies or products, that completely out–compete others (but which do not necessarily lead to the most efficient or optimal outcomes overall) (see also Kaldor, 1981). On the other hand, those companies that are out–performed will suffer from a cumulative decline and eventually go out of business. If one country has a critical mass of internationally competitively successful companies located on its territory that country will demonstrate a **revealed absolute competitive advantage**, characterized by an increasing share of world trade and/or sustained appreciation of its currency. On the other hand, if a country is unlucky enough to have a set of companies located on its territory who lose out in the competitive struggle then a cumulative downwards spiral might result. Thus revealed **absolute** competitive conceptions may be taking over from **comparative** advantage ones. Here we must register a crucial distinction, however. Absolute competitive conceptions would apply to those sectors, usually manufacturing and services, where competitive advantage can be deliberately created and fostered (by either public policy or the policies pursued by firms). This includes the developments associated with intra–industry trade in particular. Comparative advantage would still seem to apply to those sectors whose success remains dependent upon natural comparative factor endowments, like primary production (agriculture and mineral extraction).

Even such a perceptive commentator of these matters as John Kay (1994) fails to fully register these key conceptual distinctions about trade theory (as does the farther of the competitive advantage approach, Porter, 1990). Kay has argued, for instance, that the UK maintains a national **comparative** advantage in areas where the English language is important – publishing and audio–visual media, and tertiary education; in areas like chemicals and pharmaceuticals; in aviation electronics and engines; in insurance and some other financial services; and in retailing. These have been British success stories, based upon the competitiveness of British firms. Clearly, in our terminology, the key to a revealed **competitive** advantage for the UK economy is the competitive advantage of the companies in these fields. It is important, therefore, for both companies and governments to recognize and foster those factors that account for the present configuration of company performative success, and to nurture those that might present opportunities to construct new competitive advantages in the future. From the Kay perspective, however, there is little point in trying to enhance the existing domestic competitive configuration of sectors or branches where other countries and their firms already demonstrate current comparative advantage. Trying to emulate the current comparative success of elsewhere is unlikely to enhance the long–run strengths of the home economy, he argues. However, this can be successful at times, as is shown by the decision to foster the European aircraft industry against the predominant strength of that in the USA. Thus contrary to the fine grain of Kay's strictures a country should not totally write off the potential of a coordinated attempt to emulate or outperform already highly successful international competitor companies.

A further important consequence of stressing the differences between companies and countries is that we can draw a sharper distinction between what might be good for a company and what might be good for an economy. These two do not always coincide. For instance, what firms do to improve their international efficiency and competitiveness may have detrimental effects upon the economy as a whole, as in the case of the way the labour market operates to displace problems of employment and training away from firms and on to the economy as a whole. The decisions by UK companies over FDI mentioned above is another potential example of this mismatch. Thus there may well be very efficient and internationally competitive firms operating in an economy while that economy overall is becoming less internationally competitive or declining relatively. Indeed, this could be a pattern settling in around the UK economy. Small 'pockets' of economic efficiency, wealth and competitiveness, coalescing around successful firms or branches of industry, coexisting within a generalized poor performance of the aggregate economy characterized by stagnation, growing poverty, inequality and inefficiency. The future, therefore, could be for the emergence of a form of 'leopard spot' economy – islands of success set within a sea of increasing social disintegration and poverty.

The case just described is one where the companies on a territory are internationally successful while the economy overall is not. Is the reverse a possibility, or are there asymmetries here? Though more difficult to envisage, there seems no reason that a country might be successful while its companies are not. In particular, a country might be very successful in attracting FDI – which is deployed to meet home demand – though the companies on the territory may be less successful in meeting international standards or demand.

An important corollary of this is the question as to whether it is sensible to think of countries competing economically at all. Whilst companies clearly compete – they can either grow and expand or go out of business – countries cannot go bankrupt and disappear in the same way if they are not economically successful. Almost the only way a country can disappear is if it is conquered by another after a war. Thus the type of competition that countries are involved in *qua* countries is arrayed along quite a different dimension to that given by economics. Clearly, there is some truth in this argument, and in an ultimate sense countries do not compete amongst themselves in quite the same way as companies do, or with the same consequences. But at another level countries clearly do compete in economic terms, even if just to attract FDI. But their competition is also wider than this, expressed in terms of such diverse characteristics as comparative living standards or military power.

Finally there is one further big difference between firms and nations in regard to their economic activity. Firms tend to 'export' the vast bulk of their produce – well up to 99 per cent one suspects. They sell it on the market 'outside' of their own institutional boundaries and they do not consume much of it themselves or allow their own workers to do so. Indeed, they do not sell much on the open market to their own workers either. However, this is not the case with nations. The bulk of their product (measured by GDP) is consumed 'internally' to the nation, and by its own citizens, so that only a small percentage is exported. This varies between nations, of course. While the US exported just under 10 per cent of its GDP in 1993, the UK exported much more at nearly 25 per cent and Germany a higher proportion at 32 per cent. But, as has been pointed out by Krugman (1994), the three largest economic blocs as a whole in the global economy (the US, Japan and the EU) exported about the same amount – 10 per cent to 11 per cent in 1993. (The reason for the differences between individual EU countries and the EU as a whole is accounted for by intra–EU country trade.)

The point made by Krugman is that perhaps the emphasis given to trade and international competitiveness in popular economic and political discussion is misplaced if it only involves about 10 per cent of GDP. For the purposes of economic growth and living standards the real issue then becomes one of changes in national productivity *per se* without worrying too much about the international dimension or comparisons of this. This means that considerations of international competitiveness should only pertain to a much smaller section of the economy –

the internationally traded sector – and we should resist the 'expansion' of the
concern about being 'competitive' to all other aspects of economic life. There
remains a large 'sheltered sector', particularly involving welfare expenditures and
a large section of the privately traded service economy, that is not, and need not

*Table 2.1   Developments in the openness of economies: sum of exports and
imports as a percentage of GDP*

	1972	1982	1992
USA	12	19	22
Japan	19	28	17
EU12	16	23	19
OECD average[a]	40	52	48
Asian NIEs			
Hong Kong	122	146	252
Singapore	192	321	279
Taiwan	70	87	74
Korea	39	62	51
Thailand	31	42	66
Indonesia	29	41	48
Malaysia	63	91	139
Phillipines	30	36	48
India	7	13	16
China	–	15	36
Eastern Europe			
Hungary	67	77	61
Poland	–	33	35
Czechoslovakia	–	66	82

Note: a   Unweighted mean (excluding Turkey).
Sources: Complied from: *BEQB*, February, 1996, Table B, p.72; *European Economy* 42, 1989;
           European Economy 58, 1994; *Statistical Yearbook of the Republic of China.*

be, subject to all the vagrancies and pressures associated with being 'internationally competitive'.

Clearly, this argument is all very well and has its place. But it could be accused of leading to complacency and a disarming attitude. Engaging in international trade has important 'demonstration effects' for domestic economic activity overall and potential 'learning effects' for new exporters. Without it the general level of domestic productivity for those sectors not engaged in international trade could easily fall behind best practice and its activity levels stagnate.

We can also take these arguments one step further by considering the comparative data given in Table 2.1. There may be dangers when **too great** a proportion of economic activity is devoted to the international market. Table 2.1 gives data on the general openness of economies (exports plus imports as a percentage of GDP) over the period between 1972 and 1992.

Perhaps countries like Thailand, Malaysia, Hong Kong, Singapore, Taiwan, Korea and the Philippines are the vulnerable ones in the international economy. Their whole prosperity is built on exporting, without a large 'sheltered' domestic sector to fall back on. The less vulnerable economies are those like the Triad which have about 80 per cent of their GDP as purely domestic economic activity which could act as a cushion if times became difficult. These economies could more easily ride out any downturn in global economic activity that might be caused by trade policy or other economic changes. Most of the East Asian NIEs are in effect trade policy captives of either the USA or Japan with one of which they have large trade surpluses. Changes in domestic policy sentiment in these later countries could have serious impacts on the East Asian NIEs. The East Asian NIEs are clearly highly dependent upon the continuation of a liberal and open international trading system, something that still largely rests in the hands of the Triad. Of course as these NIEs mature they may well follow the characteristics of the older advanced economies and become less dependent upon trade for their prosperity. But these points should warn us against loosing sight of the continued structural vulnerability of the East Asian NIEs, particularly as their GDP growth rates and exports growth rates slump (*Financial Times,* 11 April, 1987). They may not be as competitive as they seem, or as we are led to fear.

6 SOME FINAL CONSIDERATIONS

A great deal is made in policy circles of the need to improve the overall supply side of the UK and older European economies, by promoting specific education and training programmes, improving R&D expenditures, creating the 'climate for enterprise', and so on, (for example HMSO, 1994). But we might wish to be modest in any expectations that can be generated from policies designed to promote international competitiveness organized around the concerns expressed so far in this chapter. Historical reflection demonstrates that there is no systematic or robust evidence to causally link economic innovativeness, educational levels, R&D expenditures, training competencies, or any of the other worthy supply–side initiatives that are often spoken about, with international economic performance and success (Edgerton, 1996). Much more important than these specific measures are the general institutionalized operation of the labour market (for example, centralized *vs* decentralized bargaining), the forms of the 'social settlement' between the social partners or organized interest groups, the form of the financial system, the constitutional nature of company governance systems, and so on. The question is, how far are these institutionalized structural features of the British and other systems open to reform or policy initiatives?

And as a final footnote it should be emphasized that all these approaches concentrate exclusively on **economic** measures of international competitiveness. In fact this emphasis typifies all debate in this field. But it is worth making the point that this narrowly defined way the international competitiveness debate has been set up leads to a neglect of other important elements that go to make a nation 'competitive', many of which are non–economic. For instance, the idea that a country can be successful in the modern world without it having a lively, innovative, pluralistic and open political and aesthetic culture is hardly credible. Yet these are precisely the issues neglected and dismissed by the headlong rush to redefine everything in terms of economic competence and managerial perogative. A country that refuses to actively foster a critical 'culture of ideas' will quickly become marginalized and isolated. This will eventually impact on its international competitiveness in an adverse way.

7 CONCLUSIONS

Just as in the case of the discussion of 'globalization', the discussion of 'international competitiveness' must be treated with great caution. The strong globalization thesis serves to disarm policy makers and undermine strategic thinking about national economic management. It leads to diminished expectations about what can be achieved in the face of market forces and the decisions of private transnational economic actors (Hirst and Thompson, 1996). Similar comments could quite easily be made about the connected discourse of 'international competitiveness'. This chapter has served introduce the way the term 'international competitiveness' has entered our everyday discourse about economic matters, and to raise issues about the limited usefulness of the concept and some of the ambiguities in the trends it is supposed to embody. There is no need for all economic activity to be subject to the dictates of being 'internationally competitive', and we should be careful to distinguish the operation of companies and of economies in the discussion of the concept.

NOTES

1. USA, Japan, Germany, France, Italy, UK, Canada, Belgium-Luxembourg, Netherlands, Korea, Taiwan, Hong Kong.

REFERENCES

Arthur, W.B. (1996), 'Increasing returns and the new world of business', *Harvard Business Review*, July–August, 100–109.

Auerbach, P. (1996), 'Firms, competitiveness and the global economy', Chapter 12 of Mackintosh, M., Brown, V., Costello, N., Dawson, G., Thompson, G. and Trigg, A. (eds), *Economics and Changing Economies*, International Thompson Business Press, London.

Barrell, R. and N. Pain, (1997), 'The growth of foreign direct investment in Europe', *National Institute Economic Review*,160, April, 63–75.

CBI (1993), *Survey of Benchmarking in the UK: Executive Summary 1993*, CBI and National Manufacturing Council, London.

Dluhosch, B., A. Freytag, and M. Kruger, (1996), *International Competitiveness and the Balance of Payments: Do Current Account Deficits and Surpluses Matter?*,Edward Elgar, Cheltenham.

Edgerton, D. (1996), *Science, Technology and the British Industrial 'Decline', 1870–1970.* Cambridge University Press, Cambridge.

Fagerberg, J. (1996) 'Technology and Competitiveness', *Oxford Review of Economic Policy*, **12**(3), Autumn, 39–51.

Hart, J. A. (1992), *Rival Capitalists: International Competitiveness in the United States, Japan, and Western Europe*, Ithaca, Cornell University Press.

Hirst, P.Q. and G.F. Thompson (1996), *Globalization in Question*, Polity Press, Cambridge.

HMSO (1994), 'Competitiveness of UK Manufacturing Industry', *Trade and Industry Committee, 2nd Report*, 20 April, HCP 41-I, HMSO, London.

HMSO (1996), *Competitiveness. Creating the Enterprise Centre of Europe*, Cm 3300, HMSO, London.

HM Treasury (1996), 'Overseas investment and the UK', *HM Treasury Occasional Paper 8*, June, HM Treasury, London.

Kaldor, N. (1978), 'The effect of devaluations on trade in manufactures', in N. Kaldor, *Further Essays in Applied Economics*, Duckworth, London.

Kaldor, N. (1981), 'The role of increasing returns, technical progress and cumulative causation in the theory of international trade and economic growth', *Economie Appliquee*, **34**(4), 593–617.

Kay, J. (1994), *The Foundations of National Competitive Advantage*, The Economic and Social Research Council, Swindon.

Krugman, P. (1994), 'Competitiveness: A Dangerous Obsession', *Foreign Affairs*, **74**(2), March/April, 28–44.

MITI (1996a,) 'Summary of "The Survey of Trends in Overseas Business Activities of Japanese Companies"', International Business Affairs Division, January (N–96–2), MITI, Tokyo.

MITI (1996b), 'The 28th Survey of Trends in Business Activities of Foreign Affiliates', International Business Affairs Division, (N–96–3), MITI, Tokyo.

Porter, M. (1990), *The Competitive Advantage of Nations,* The Free Press, NY.

Sandholtz, W., M. Borrus and J. Zysman et al. (1992), *The Highest Stakes: The Economic Foundations of the Next Security System*, Oxford University Press, New York.

Stopford, J. and S. Strange (with John S. Henley) (1991), *Rival States, Rival Firms: Competition for World Market Shares,* CUP, Cambridge.

Thompson, G.F. (1987), 'The Supply Side and Industrial Policy', in Thompson, G., Brown, V. and Levacic, R. (eds), *Managing the UK Economy,*Polity Press, Cambridge.

Thompson, G.F. (1997a), 'Some Observations on the "International Competitiveness Debate" and International Economic Relations', Paper given at the ESF–EMOT Workshop: *Globalization and Industrial Transformation in Europe*. Malaga, Spain, 9–12 January, 1997.

Thompson, G.F. (1997b,) 'Where do Transnational Corporations Conduct their Business Operations and What are the Consequences?', Paper prepared for the ESF–EMOT Workshop: *The Role of National Institutions and Forms of Economic Organisation*, Berlin, Germany, 30 January – 1 February, 1997.

Thompson, G.F. (1997c), '"Globalization" and the possibilities for domestic economic policy' *Internationale Politik und Gesellschaft* , 2, 161–71.

United Nations (1993), *World Investment Report 1993. Transnational Corporations and Integrated International Production*, United Nations, NY.

United Nations (1996), *World Investment Report 1995. Transnational Corporations and Competitive*ness, United Nations, New York.

Yamazawa, I. (1998), 'Economic integration in the Asia–Pacific region' in Thompson, G.F. (ed), *Economic Dynamism in the Asia–Pacific: The Growth of Integration and Competitiveness*, London, Routledge.

Wilkinson, J. (1997) 'A New Paradigm for Economic Analysis?', *Economy and Society*, **26**(3), August.

3. The impacts of environmental policy on competitiveness: theory and evidence

Paul Ekins and Stefan Speck[*]

1 INTRODUCTION

Considerations of competitiveness are of importance to environmental policy for both economic and environmental reasons:

1. **Economic** – if environmental policy produces negative impacts on competitiveness it will be associated with corporate, sectoral or national economic decline, which will make its introduction politically difficult or impossible.
2. **Environmental** – if domestic 'dirty' (environmentally–intensive) industry declines, to be replaced by a growth in foreign 'dirty' industry, overall environmental impacts may not change. If the environmental effect were local, then a cleaner domestic environment will have been bought at the cost of a loss of competitiveness (and gain in foreign competitiveness will entail a worse environment there). If the environmental effect were global (for example greenhouse gas emissions), then loss of national competitiveness will have brought no environmental gain at all.

Whether environmental policy has had, or is likely to have, effects on

[*] This chapter is an extension of work commissioned by the Climate Change Working Group of the UK Government's Advisory Committee on Business and the Environment, whose support is gratefully acknowledged.

competitiveness, is a hotly contested issue, with views ranging across a wide spectrum, from the perception that past environmental regulation has been costly and damaging to competitiveness and could well be so in the future, to the view that well–formulated environmental policy could actually have positive impacts on competitiveness.

One reason for this divergence of opinion is the complexity of the concept of competitiveness itself, with no consensus as to how it should be defined or measured, and a clear need to distinguish between the different levels – the firm, business sector and national economy – being considered. Another reason is the many influences on competitiveness and the consequent difficulty in identifying the particular influence of environmental policy. As will be seen, a number of analytical techniques have been used to address this difficulty and, given the complexities involved, it is perhaps not surprising that their results differ. To gain insights into the future impacts of environmental policy, modelling is often used. The models and assumptions employed vary widely, again introducing the likelihood of different outcomes.

This paper seeks to analyse and explore these differences with a view to arriving at some general conclusions about the impact of environmental policy on competitiveness, in a way that complements the more detailed analysis and empirical evidence that is presented in other papers in this book. Section 2 considers various definitions of competitiveness and the different levels of economic activity to which the concept is applied. Section 3 examines the impact of environmental policy at the firm level. Section 4 reviews the evidence on the effects of past environmental policy on the macroeconomy. Section 5 looks in detail at the possible effects on competitiveness of environmental taxes and of 'eco–tax reform'. Section 6 explores the various modelling projections of the possible effects of environmental taxes on competitiveness in the future. Section 7 concludes.

2   DEFINITIONS AND LEVELS

Competitiveness basically denotes the ability of a national economy, or a productive sector, to sell its goods and services in domestic and world markets. There are many possible indicators of competitiveness, some of which become policy targets in their own right and even become taken for competitiveness itself. Underlying these indicators is the insight that being competitive is important because it enables goods and services to be produced and sold, which contributes to or increases national or sectoral output and incomes. These indicators include: income per head; balance of trade; exchange rate movements; unit labour costs; generation of employment; labour productivity; market share; profitability; firm growth; share of world exports. Exports are relevant because they indicate competitive success in markets outside national borders. Opportunities to trade are advantageous to competitive firms because they give them access to larger markets, enabling them to increase output and, perhaps, realise economies of scale.

At the firm level environmental policy may have implications for competitiveness if it imposes on some firms costs which are not imposed on their competitors. However, it may not always be the case that environmental policy imposes costs on firms; even where it does the costs may not be substantial enough to affect competitiveness; or the policy may generate benefits for the firm to set against the costs. These are some of the issues which are discussed in Sections 3 and 4. In principle, however, it is clear that environmental policy, especially when stringent and effectively enforced, and whether implemented through environmental taxes and charges, regulations or voluntary agreements, could affect competitiveness.

From the aggregate performance of a country's firms, national statistics of output, exports, employment and so on may be derived. If a country's firms are generally competitive, then the country will have a constant or rising share of world exports, a strong exchange rate with a consequent ability to increase imports, and an above–average income growth. If a country's firms are not generally competitive, then its share of world exports will decline, a weak exchange rate will limit the possibility to import and income growth will be below average. Reductions in the competitiveness of certain economic sectors will be marked by bankruptcies and job losses. If the affected sectors were major export earners, and imports stay constant, then exchange rate depreciation may occur, introducing import–inflation into the economy, with further negative macroeconomic knock–on effects. Under such circumstances it is sometimes said that national economic competitiveness is in decline.

However, there is a limit to the implied analogy between countries and firms. Countries do not go bankrupt, as firms do. If some economic sectors become uncompetitive because of environmental policy, the economy will restructure so that others take their place. This may involve costs. The new activities may not be as productive as those they replace. Loss of competitiveness by economically important sectors could lead to substantial transition costs and, perhaps, a higher equilibrium rate of unemployment. Economic restructuring could be very painful. Such considerations lead to a conclusion that, although national competitiveness is a different concept from competitiveness at the firm level, it is no less important.

It should be clear that effects on competitiveness will only arise if environmental policy in different countries imposes different levels of costs on competing firms. Thus, although the economic effects of environmental policy may be measured in terms of reduced labour productivity, or reduced rates of economic growth, these are only effects on competitiveness if they differentially affect some firms and not their competitors. However, because in practice environmental policy and the regulations to which it gives rise are not greatly harmonised between countries (although such harmonisation is more apparent in groups of countries like the European Union), such measures are often interpreted as implying effects on competitiveness.

3   THE EFFECT OF ENVIRONMENTAL POLICY ON THE COMPETITIVENESS OF FIRMS

Companies have adopted, or been required to adopt, a range of practices in response to present, or the prospect of future, environmental policy. Such practices include environmental monitoring, accounting and reporting, and the adoption of a corporate environmental policy, of an environmental strategy and action plan to give it effect, and appropriate communication of environmental outcomes, both internally and externally. Increasingly these practices are being integrated into a formal environmental management system.

The conventional economic view is that the realisation of environmental benefits through environmental policy is likely to entail economic costs. In their review of studies in this area, Christainsen and Tietenberg (1985, pp.372-3) identify five reasons which have been put forward why environmental policy may constrain the growth of productivity, income and, where this policy is not applied to all competitors, competitiveness:

- Investments in more pollution control may crowd out other investment.
- More stringent abatement requirements for new plant may prolong the life of older, less productive, plant.
- Pollution control equipment requires labour to operate and maintain with no contribution to saleable output.
- Compliance with environmental regulations absorbs managerial and administrative resources with no contribution to saleable output.
- Uncertainty about present and possible future regulations may inhibit investment.

One result of these possible cost increases resulting from environmental policy is that affected industries will move to countries which have less stringent or no environmental policies, an issue studied by Lucas et al. (1992). They found that the growth rate of the toxic intensity of manufacturing was both higher in the poorest countries and increased through the 1970s and 1980s. The authors consider that this is consistent with the hypothesis that 'stricter regulation of pollution–intensive production in the OECD countries has led to significant locational displacement, with consequent acceleration of industrial pollution intensity in developing countries' (Lucas et al., 1992, p.80). This result showing the absolute and relative growth of pollution–intensive industry in poor countries is confirmed by Low and Yeats (1992) through quite different non–econometric analysis of trade statistics. However, while Low and Yeats agree that the result is consistent with the Lucas displacement hypothesis, they stress that there are a number of other possible explanations, including that the strong growth of 'dirty' industries is a normal occurrence at an early stage of development.

It must be emphasised that the Lucas et al. result is only concerned with compositional, and not technical, effects. Its 'toxic intensity' was calculated using constant technologies, so that the increase in such intensity refers only to a proportional increase in the output of the toxically intensive sectors. The environmental impact of this compositional change would be reduced, and could be completely counteracted, if improvements in technique rendered the environmentally intensive sectors less toxic. Moreover, a different conclusion from the Low and Yeats analysis is provided by an input–output study of CO_2 emissions from the UK and West Germany by Proops et al. (1993). Their results indicate that the CO_2 embodied in the net imports of these two countries increased only marginally from 1970–1990, and that at the end of the period both countries still exported more embodied CO_2 than they imported (Proops et al., 1993, p.177). This does not suggest the displacement of energy intensive industries from those countries.

Other studies, surveyed by Dean (1992, pp.16–20), give conflicting results, but overall do not suggest that the forces for displacement are very great. One study since Dean's survey, however, examined the effect of pollution abatement expenditures on the productivity of factories in the paper, oil and steel industries, finding that: 'Plants with high compliance costs have significantly lower productivity levels and slower productivity growth rates than less regulated plants. The impact of compliance costs is stronger for total factor productivity than for labour productivity, and stronger for productivity growth rates than for levels. The magnitude of the TFP impacts indicates that the compliance costs have a larger than expected effect' (Gray and Shadbegian, 1993, p.2). Jaffe et al. (1995, p.152) say that subsequent work by Gray and Shadbegian has shown these effects on productivity to be 'largely an artefact of measurement error in output'.

Against their reasons for possible increases in cost from environmental policy, Christainsen and Tietenberg only cite one possible positive influence of environmental regulation on output, the protection and improvement of the health of workers, but this is extremely difficult to assess and is routinely excluded from models of this issue. They ignore possible cost reduction, first–mover advantages and stimulation to innovation, which have become important elements in the debate on this issue, as will be seen.

The natural resources that are used in economic processes normally have to be purchased. The discharge of wastes during or at the end of a process represents a failure to use productively all the purchased inputs. The waste resource is also wasted money. Moreover, disposal of the waste will often have to be paid for. Waste management costs, while vital once wastes have been generated, are also a waste of money in that they add nothing to the service delivered by a product. Finally, where the processes or products involved are potentially toxic or otherwise hazardous, they will be subject to regulations and controls, compliance with which may also be costly. Therefore environmental management systems can actually result in net savings and improve competitiveness, if they lead to changes in company practices which save money in excess of the cost of implementing the management systems.

Smart 1992 (p.3) gives five reasons why it can benefit corporations to move 'beyond compliance' with regulations in their environmental performance:

–   Preventing pollution at source can save money in materials and in end–of–pipe remediation.
–   Voluntary action in the present can minimise future risks and liabilities and make costly retrofits unnecessary.
–   Companies staying ahead of regulations can have a competitive edge over those struggling to keep up.
–   New 'green' products and processes can increase consumer appeal and open up new business opportunities.
–   An environmentally progressive reputation can improve recruitment, employee morale, investor support, acceptance by the host community and management's self–respect.

Smart gives many examples of firms which have benefitted financially for these reasons from voluntary environmental management initiatives:

–   Between 1975 and 1992 the 3M Corporation saved more than $530 million from all the projects in its 3P (Pollution Prevention Pays) programme (Smart 1992, p.13).
–   Feeling exposed because of its status as highest reporter of listed substances in the Toxic Release Inventory of the US Environmental Protection Agency, Dupont's CEO reports that the company embarked on an ambitious emissions reduction programme. 'The result is a total air emission reduction of **80 per cent** within one year. Our investment of just over $250,000 results in annual savings of $400,000 – instead of a $2 million investment for an incinerator that would have cost an additional $1 million annually to maintain and operate' (Smart, 1992, p.191; emphasis in original).
–   Under its Tank Integrity Program, Chevron replaced all its old underground petrol tanks with double–walled fibreglass tanks although this was not strictly required. However, a Chevron Vice–President notes: Making right

contamination from a leaking tank could cost the company $250,000 or more. If such a liability could be prevented with an expenditure of $25,000 to $50,000, then it's well worth it' (Smart, 1992, p.103).

– Pacific Gas and Electric adopted a programme on Customer Energy Efficiency, which involved it investing in the more efficient use of energy by its customers, and sharing in the resulting financial savings. Its 1991 measures under this programme reduced emissions of nitrogen oxides by 445 tons, of sulphur oxides by 120 tons and of carbon dioxide by 340,000 tons, and earned the company $45.1 million before taxes.

A similar view of the possibly beneficial effects of corporate environmental action came from the Business Council for Sustainable Development (BCSD), which stated: 'Many of the waste reduction and environmentally positive programs in business are economically viable and are providing positive rates of return in relatively short time periods' (Schmidheiny, 1992, p.96).

Examples given by the BCSD include Northern Telecom, which, in phasing out its use of ozone–depleting CFC–113 between 1988 and 1991, spent $1 million putting a substitute in place, but saved $4 million on purchasing the CFC, associated taxes and waste–disposal (Schmidheiny 1992, p.230). In India Harihar Polyfibres implemented 200 projects at its pulp mill between 1983 and 1989, aimed at resource efficiency. Although its production increased by 20 per cent in this period, energy consumption fell by 60 per cent, chemical consumption by 55 per cent and the effluent load by 55 per cent. $69.5 million was invested in the projects, but the payback period was under two years (ibid., pp.272–3).

Other examples come from California, where several companies have found that investment in industrial water conservation can result in substantial savings of water with a payback period of a year or less. For example, the California Paper–Board Corporation cut its water consumption by 72 per cent from 2.5 to 0.7 million cubic metres per year with a payback period on investment of only 2.4 months (Brown et al., 1993, p.34). In another example, Ayres and Walter (1991, p.251) report that the average return on investment for 167 energy–savings projects undertaken by the Louisiana Division of Dow Chemical Co. over the years 1982–88, as part of an 'energy–contest' initiative, was 198 per cent.

Three other examples of reduced effluents, reduced water usage and cost–saving are given in CEST, 1991, p.40. A subsequent project of CEST in the UK's Aire and Calder valley resulted in 11 participating companies identifying 542 options for cost saving waste reduction that saved over £2 million almost immediately with the prospect of similar savings in future, with over 70 per cent of the measures having a payback of less than a year (CEST, 1994, pp.6–7).

In all these cases investment is required to achieve environmental benefits, but it yields net financial as well as environmental gains, and so can be justified in terms of financial return irrespective of environmental considerations. In a competitive market it is surprising that there are so many opportunities for profitable investment that appear to have been overlooked. It appears that business managers have been widely unaware of the **economic**, let alone the environmental, costs of resource use and waste disposal, and needed the pressure of public opinion drawing attention to the latter before they gave serious consideration to the former.

One reason for this lack of managers' awareness may be a flawed accounting system which fails to register all the financial benefits of environmental investments, because of incorrect accounting of firms' actual environmental expenditure, whether this is for abatement, source reduction, monitoring or regulatory compliance. Obviously, unless firms know how much they are paying to prevent or monitor environmental damage, they will not feel the correct incentive to move towards products and processes that are inherently less environmentally damaging – and which could save them money. Ditz et al. (1995) report on nine case studies which were carried out on five large and four medium–sized firms, to see whether their environmental expenditures were correctly reported in their management accounts. In each case they found they that were not, but that, because environmental expenditures were sometimes subsumed under non–environmental headings, real environmental expenditures were substantially larger than they appeared in the accounts, financially justifying environmental improvement measures which before had not appeared economic.

Revised accounting procedures which would remedy this failing have been called Total Cost Assessment (TCA) (Jackson, 1993, pp.200ff.). Table 3.1 shows one application of TCA to an investment that converted a solvent/heavy metal to an aqueous/heavy metal-free coating at a paper coating company. The company analysis column shows how the company's conventional accounting system assessed the project's costs and benefits. The TCA column includes costs and benefits that were accounted in the company analysis under headings which obscured their relation to the project. These hidden, or indirect, costs and benefits included costs of waste management, utilities (energy, water, sewerage), pollution control/solvent recovery and regulatory compliance. It can be seen that the project under TCA was substantially more profitable than with the conventional company analysis.

The Smart (1992) 'beyond compliance' studies were of US corporations, but very similar results were reported in a recent study of UK business: 'The main benefits reported from investment in cleaner production systems were cost savings through improved waste management, improved public image for the company and staff motivation, cost savings through better energy management, improved process efficiency, and increased profitability. Substantial savings could be made through energy management systems and relatively simple "housekeeping" modifications to production processes. Longer term gains in competitiveness were expected by many firms, mainly large corporations with sophisticated strategies for environmental management' (Christie et al., 1995, p.xi).

Table 3.1   *Financial data for a project comparing conventional company analysis with a Total Cost Assessment (TCA)*

	Company analysis	TCA	Difference %
Total capital costs	$623,809	$653,809	6
Annual savings (bit)[1]	$118,112	$216,874	84
Net present value, years 1–10	($98,829)	$232,817	336
Net present value, years 1–15	$13,932	$428,040	2972
IRR, years 1–10	12%	24%	12
IRR, years 1–15	16%	27%	11
Simple payback (years)	5.3	3	–43

Note: 1) before interest and taxes.

Source: Jackson 1993, p.203

In addition to cost reduction, pressures on companies from environmental policy can achieve economic benefits by stimulating creativity and innovation which results in new products or new business opportunities. Thus the Costa Rican firm RICALIT developed a fibre cement in 1981–2 to replace its asbestos cement which was subject to increasing concern over safety. The substitute proved both less expensive and more manageable than asbestos cement, and was highly profitable, with sales more than doubling to over $6 million in 1991 (Schmidheiny, 1992, pp.215–6). An example of a new business opportunity is that presented by energy conservation to traditional energy supply companies. The New England Electric (NEE) company realised as long ago as 1979 that energy conservation made more economic sense than providing new supply, but it was not until 1989 that the utilities' regulatory system permitted the company to make a financial return on investments in conservation. In 1990 NEE spent $71 million on energy conservation projects, saving 194,300 MW–hours of electricity and $161 million. NEE retained $8.4 million (9 per cent) of this $91 million net saving, the rest being passed on to customers. NEE projects that it could spend $100 million a year to the year 2000 on economically viable conservation projects in its service area (ibid., pp.187–8).

Such experiences have caused De Andraca and McCready (1994, p.70) of the Business Council for Sustainable Development to dismiss fears that environmental policy is likely to damage an economy: 'Concerns about pollution havens, free riders or an exodus of capital and jobs from countries with tough standards are unsubstantiated.' They emphasise in contrast the competitive benefits to be gained by innovation and eco–efficiency induced by stringent regulations and high prices of environmental resources. Considerations of this sort have led Porter (1990, pp.647–8) to hypothesise that environmental regulations may be good for economic competitiveness:

> Stringent standards for product performance, product safety, and environmental impact contribute to creating and upgrading competitive advantage. They pressure firms to upgrade quality, upgrade technology and provide features in areas of important customer (and social) concern. ... Particularly beneficial are stringent regulations that anticipate standards that will spread internationally. These give a nation's firms a head start in developing products and services that will be valued elsewhere.

In a later publication Porter and Van Der Linde (1995, p.111) emphasise market–based instruments, instead of or as well as regulation, as very often the most effective way to give firms the incentive to overcome the various obstacles to corporate innovation and technological change, including lack of information and organisational inertia.

The Porter 'win–win' hypothesis of the economic, as well as environmental, benefits of environmental regulation runs clearly counter to economists' normal assumptions of efficient, competitive markets. It has been attacked as being at best a marginal phenomenon with regard to the costs of environmental regulation as whole. Palmer et al. (1995, pp.127–8) estimate that Porter's 'innovation offsets' amount to only a few percent of the total costs of conforming to environmental regulations, which in the US have been estimated by the EPA at $135 billion in 1992. They contend that the vast majority of these costs conform to the standard economic trade–off model, whereby environmental benefits are gained at the sacrifice of economic growth.

However, it is indisputable that the environmental protection industry that has sprung up at least partly as a result of environmental regulation is now a major industrial sector in its own right, which OECD (1991, p.198) and Business International (1990, p.157) value at $70–100 billion in OECD countries and probably half as much again world–wide. It is not implausible that there should be a first mover advantage to environmental regulation, in that those countries which early develop new technologies in response to stringent domestic regulations will be well placed in world markets if those regulations are imposed in other countries. Porter (1990, pp.648–9) gives examples where Japan, Germany, the US and Switzerland have, in different instances, all benefitted from first–mover advantages and thereby improved their national economic performance.

Several conditions must be fulfilled for a first–mover advantage to be realised in practice: first–mover regulations must correctly anticipate the regulations to be imposed elsewhere; first–mover firms must be able to compete with firms in other countries once regulations have been imposed there; and the benefits from being a first mover must give a reasonable rate of return on capital invested, which must also be at least as good as the opportunity cost of not investing it elsewhere, and must outweigh the costs of complying with the first–mover regulations elsewhere in the economy. These are non–trivial conditions. Even in a situation where they may be met, it is likely that several countries may seek a first–mover advantage for themselves. While such advantage may be a welcome side–effect from environmental policy that is desired for its environmental gains, the risks of not achieving it mean that it is unlikely to be an appropriate motivator for environmental policy in itself.

The other element of the Porter hypothesis, that environmental policy can stimulate innovation that more than offsets the costs of complying with the policy, is more difficult to analyse in general terms, not least because of the inherent unpredictability of innovation.

Innovation is the very stuff of markets and gives to capitalism its uniquely dynamic quality among economic systems. Producers are always looking for opportunities to innovate, in order to cut costs and to develop new products which will cause consumers to innovate (i.e. change their consumption patterns). In itself, innovation need not be of particular benefit to the environment. There are plenty of new products and technologies which cause environmental damage, while the economic growth to which innovation gives rise can also pull more energy and materials through the economic system to the detriment of the environment.

However, markets' restless search for innovation can be harnessed by environmental policy to environmental ends. The most important component of such policy is probably use of the price mechanism, the basic means of coordination of markets, the implications of which will be discussed further in Section 5. There is little doubt that firms are uniquely attentive to prices in both absolute and relative terms, and they give important signals too to consumers. However, price changes need to be both gradual and anticipated if they are to avoid economic disruption, such as the premature scrapping of capital, and encourage innovation rather than retrenchment. Innovation takes time and cannot be produced to order. Firms must be given the time, and perhaps financial support, to develop a new generation of low environmental impact products and technologies.

There are numerous other policy instruments which can and should be used to reinforce the unremitting signals from the price mechanism. The differing nature and advantages of different policy instruments mean that environmental policy needs to be carefully designed to maximise the chances that firms will respond to it innovatively rather than defensively. Porter and van der Linde (1995, p.110) give three conditions for the design of environmental policy to encourage innovation: the adoption of clear goals, with a flexibility which allows firms to attain them in their most cost–effective way; the encouragement of continuous improvement through the use in policy of economic incentives, voluntary agreements and the dissemination of information; and better co–ordination of environmental regulation, between industry and regulators and between regulators themselves at different levels (local, national, supranational). Wallace (1995, pp.250, 266), on the basis of his case study of six European countries, regards the last condition as the most important of all:

> The choice of instrument will frequently have less of an influence on the prospects for harnessing innovation than the political climate of industry–regulator relationships and the nature of day-to-day industry–regulator interactions. ... Stable long-term policies and effective dialogue can create a culture which rewards proactive, responsible firms and reduces the risk of investing in innovative solutions.

However, such considerations do not imply that environmental policy is a certain stimulator of innovation, and it may not be either efficient or effective in this role. In this case, as with the possible gain of first–mover benefits, it seems that environmental policy should be justified on environmental grounds, rather than on the grounds of possible competitive advantage. However, in the implementation of environmental policy, care should be taken not to discriminate against innovation and, if possible, to encourage it. This is most likely to be done through an approach that derives from a stable policy that allows time for measures of compliance to be put in place; that focuses on outcomes, rather than the means of achieving them; and that fosters continuous improvement by permitting targets to be met in a flexible and cost–efficient way.

4   THE EFFECTS OF ENVIRONMENTAL POLICY ON THE COMPETITIVENESS OF THE MACROECONOMY

Just as there is no consensus about the competitiveness effects of environmental policy on firms, so there are conflicting views about the aggregate effect of such policy on the macroeconomy. Christainsen and Tietenberg (1985, p.378) note in their review of this issue: 'The extent to which past increases in regulation caused productivity to decelerate – and price increases to accelerate – remains controversial.' However, the studies they survey permit the conclusion, with regard to the US in the 1970s, that 'environmental regulations cannot escape some of the blame for the slowdown in the rate of productivity growth. ... A reasonable estimate would attribute, say, 8–12 percent of the slowdown in productivity growth to environmental regulations. This amounts to a reduction in the growth rate of labour productivity of 0.2–0.3 percentage points.'

A later study by Jorgenson and Wilcoxen (1990, p.315) found that environmental regulation reduced the US GDP growth rate by an average of 0.19 per cent p.a.

between 1973 and 1985. The authors say that 'This is several times the reduction in growth estimated in previous studies', but it actually appears very close to the range identified by Christainsen and Tietenberg as above. Jorgenson and Wilcoxen's interpretation of the significance of their numbers is also very different to the earlier study's, for they consider their results 'show that pollution abatement has emerged as a major claimant on the resources of the US economy' (Jorgenson and Wilcoxen 1990, p.315), while Christainsen and Tietenberg (1985, p.380) say that the adverse effect on economic performance in the United States 'has not been large in magnitude'. An even more recent estimate, by Nordhaus (1993a), estimates the 'drag on economic growth' that depletion, pollution and defensive environmental expenditures may exert in the years up to 2050, concluding that the growth rate may be reduced by 0.3 per cent per annum, or nearly 20 per cent of the per capita 1.6 per cent per capita per annum growth that he projects (Nordhaus 1993a, p.38). Of this 0.3 per cent per annum, about 23 per cent was due to the effects of environmental policy, including mitigation of the greenhouse effect.

Another review of the macroeconomic effects of environmental policy covers the same literature as Christainsen and Tietenberg, and notes their overall conclusion, but considers: 'There are numerous methodological and practical criticisms that throw doubt on the accuracy and validity of the aggregate productivity measures showing the negative impact.' (OECD, 1985, p.88). It also draws attention to the facts that 'For a number of other OECD countries, less comprehensive studies indicate that the negative effects are much smaller' (ibid., p.87); and that some disaggregated industry studies suggest that some results from or changes in pollution control, such as cost saving, the development of cheaper pollution control technologies and the accelerated development of new production processes, 'have either added to productivity growth or helped to reverse the earlier falling trend' (ibid., p.87). Thus, unlike Christainsen and Tietenberg, the OECD acknowledges some of the cost saving effects of environmental improvement that have been reported in the previous section.

Reviewing the reported effects of environmental policy on economic growth and employment, the OECD study identifies several conflicting forces at work on the macroeconomy as a result of environmental programmes. First the extra investment and operating expenditure creates extra demand, boosting output and employment, which is further reinforced by the multiplier effect. However, in due course the costs of the programme feed through into higher prices which constrain GDP growth. Overall, the study concludes that the effect on growth is indeterminate, being positive in some studies and negative in others, while the effect on employment is positive. But overall: 'The main conclusion which emerges from [these results] is that the macroeconomic effect of environmental policies is relatively small. Most of the figures reported ... are in the range of a few tenths of a percentage point per year. Furthermore, it is important to recall that these small effects were registered during a period (the 1970s) of peak pollution control activity, when efforts were directed not only at limiting ongoing pollution, but also at cleaning up the backlog caused by the neglect of the environment during the 1950s and 1960s' (OECD, 1985, p.10).

The passage of time seems to have confirmed the OECD view of low costs from environmental regulation rather than the reverse. Thus Pearce (1992, p.27) claims that 'there is no evidence that industrial competitiveness has been affected by environmental regulation'. Grossman and Krueger (1994, p.20) concur: 'The available evidence does not support the hypothesis that cross–country differences in environmental standards are an important determinant of the global patterns of international trade.' Jaffe et al.'s (1995, p.157) recent review concludes that 'studies attempting to measure the effect of environmental regulation on net exports, overall trade flows, and plant location decisions have produced estimates that are either small, statistically insignificant or not robust to tests of model specification'. This view was broadly endorsed by the OECD in 1996: 'The trade and investment impacts which have been measured empirically are almost negligible' (OECD 1996, p.45). Rather than market failure, Jaffe et al. (ibid., p.158) cite data limitations, the low proportion of environmental expenditures in firms' overall costs, the small difference between US regulations and those of its major competitors, and the preference of many countries to standardise their pollution controls to those of the most stringent countries, as the probable reasons for the lack of any significant effects of environmental regulation on competitiveness. However, it is not clear that these reasons are incompatible with the Porter hypothesis, which Jaffe et al. reject largely on theoretical grounds.

However slight the past effect of environmental regulations on competitiveness, four observations are pertinent. The first is that this may not hold true for the future. Past environmental policies have not resulted in a diminution of environmental concern and the new goal of sustainable development seems to be requiring more stringent policy, with more potential effects on competitiveness, than in the past.

Second, the past legacy of environmental damage has by no means been completely addressed. Brown et al. (1993) identify the US as facing clean–up costs of $750 billion for hazardous waste sites and $200 billion for nuclear weapons manufacturing facilities (Brown et al. 1993, p.10) Such clean–up problems face all industrial countries to some extent and it is not clear that such clean up is likely to yield 'win–win' gains of the kind hypothesised by Porter.

Third, there is widespread agreement that in today's global economy 'ever fiercer competition prevails' (HMSO, 1993, p.1). The assessment of the US Office of Technology Assessment seeks to take these points into account. It agrees that 'environmental regulations generally have a small effect on US manufacturing competitiveness' but cautions that 'they can have a larger effect in particular sectors with high environmental compliance costs' and that current 'more intense' international competition and stricter environmental regulations 'leave open the possibility that environmental regulations could be more of a competitive disadvantage than before' (OTA, 1992, p.8).

Finally, it seems likely that environmental policy in the future will make more use of environmental taxes than in the past. Such taxes have distinctive implications for competitiveness, which need to be examined separately from an assessment of the impacts of an environmental policy which has so far relied largely on regulation.

5 THE EFFECTS ON COMPETITIVENESS OF ENVIRONMENTAL TAXES

Even though environmental regulations do not seem to have had a significant impact on competitiveness, there is widespread agreement among economists and policy analysts that they are a less efficient way of achieving many environmental goals than the use of economic instruments, such as environmental taxes and charges, tradable permits and other means of direct financial incentives for environmental improvement. There are several reasons for the greater efficiency of these market–based instruments:

–   They equalise the marginal cost of abatement across polluters, so that all the cheapest options for abatement are implemented first.
–   They can be as effective for diffuse sources of pollution, which are difficult to regulate, as for point sources.
–   By becoming incorporated into the prices of products, environmental taxes in particular give incentives to consumers as well as producers to shift away from environmentally intensive consumption.
–   Because environmental taxes are payable on all a particular use of the environment (unlike regulations which permit its free use once the regulatory requirements have been met), they give an incentive for continual environmental improvement at all levels of use.
–   By raising revenue, environmental taxes provide the means to give earmarked subsidies, where appropriate, to achieve environmental improvements beyond those arising from the price effect, or to reduce distortionary taxes elsewhere. Where these are labour taxes, greater employment may result. Such a shift in the burden of taxation from labour to the use of environmental resources is sometime called ecological (or simply eco) tax reform.

A variety of environmental taxes and charges have been implemented, especially in North European countries, in recent years (see OECD, 1995 for a survey). Although they allow society as a whole to achieve environmental goals more cost effectively than total reliance on regulation, in one way environmental taxes and charges raise more serious competitiveness issues than regulations for firms that are in particularly environmentally intensive sectors. This is because, after compliance with regulations firms may use the environment without further payment; with environmental taxes firms pay for **all** use of the environment, even that which is within the limits specified by society. Of course, it is this continuing payment which gives the incentive for continual improvement which is a feature of environmental taxes.

Because of fear of their potential competitiveness effects, most countries that have introduced environmental taxes have given vulnerable firms or sectors tax exemptions or concessions. These reduce the economic efficiency of the environmental tax and reduce the economic advantage to be gained from clean production systems. They also slow down the process of structural change in the economy such that energy– and environment–intensive economic sectors both become less intensive and less important economically relative to less environment–intensive sectors. It is therefore important to note that the overall effects on business competitiveness from the tax will depend on how the tax revenues are recycled through the economy: while environmentally–intensive sectors may end up worse off, clean businesses are likely actually to benefit from it. The mechanism at work is clearly shown in Pezzey (1991), who simulated the introduction of a carbon tax in the UK.

The effect on competitiveness of a carbon tax will be determined by a number of influences, including:

–   the size of the carbon tax and the nature and extent of the offsets (how the revenues are recycled through the economy).
–   the carbon intensity of the product.
–   the trade intensity of the product (ratio of exports plus imports to production).

Because the second two of these influences differ between countries, even the imposition of an identical tax–offset arrangement in all countries would differentially affect their competitiveness. Table 3.2 presents some relevant data for the UK to gain some insights into the carbon tax's competitiveness effects.

In Table 3.2, Row 1 is the relative production of the different sectors of UK industry compared to the total production of all those sectors in seven industrial countries. It can be seen that, in terms of absolute value, the UK's most important industrial sectors are machinery and food, followed by chemicals, transport equipment, paper and iron and steel. Row 2 shows the relative contribution of each UK sector relative to the seven countries' total output in that sector. Overall the UK produces 7.2 per cent of the seven countries' output in these sectors, but a greater share than this of their iron and steel (11.3 per cent), chemicals (9.4 per cent), non–metallic minerals and food (8.8 per cent), paper (8.6 per cent) and cloth and

Table 3.2   Sectoral competitiveness effects for a carbon and energy tax

Key: AI – All industry; IS – Iron and steel; CH – Chemicals; NFM – Non–ferrous metals; NMM – Non–metallic minerals; TE – Transportation equipment; M – Machinery; F – Food and so on; P– Paper; W – Wood; CL – Cloth and so on.

UK	AI	IS	CH	NFM	NMM	TE	M	F	P	W	CL
1 RP	72	06	09	01	03	07	19	14	07	02	05
2 SP	72	113	94	45	88	49	64	88	86	67	76
3 TI	59	25	62	124	28	108	77	30	29	43	83
4 Icc	1.6	4.0	3.8	4.5	4.4	0.8	0.6	0.7	0.8	0.1	0.8
5 Icco	0.0	2.4	2.1	2.9	2.8	-0.7	-1.0	-0.8	-0.7	-1.4	-0.7
6 SCco	0.0	-0.6	-1.3	-3.5	-0.8	0.8	0.7	0.2	0.2	0.6	0.6
7 SCeo	0.0	-0.5	-1.7	-4.2	-0.9	0.9	0.8	0.3	0.2	0.7	0.7

Notes:
1. Value of UK production by sector relative to value of total output of tradable manufactures in 7 countries (US, Japan, Germany, France, UK, Italy, Spain) in 1985 (* 1000)
2. Value of sectoral production of UK relative to value to total output in that sector of seven countries (*1000)
3. Trade intensity: percentages of exports plus imports to domestic production
4. Impact cost of a tax of $100 per ton of carbon with no offset: percentage of sectoral value of production
5. Impact cost of a tax of $100 per ton of carbon with offset (uniform subsidies per unit value of production): percentage of sectoral value of production`
6. Sectoral competitiveness (trade intensity * [–]impact cost) under carbon tax with offset: relative impact on output, arbitrary scale
7. Sectoral competitiveness (trade intensity * [–]impact cost) under energy tax ($100/toe) with offset: relative impact on output, arbitrary scale

Source:	Pezzey (1991) Tables	6.3	6.5	6.8	6.9	6.11	6.16
	pp.	106	107	110	111	113	115.

so on (7.6 per cent). Row 3 gives the UK's trade intensity in these sectors, defined as the percentage ratio of exports plus imports to production in that sector. It can be seen that the highest trade–intensities are in non–ferrous metals, transport equipment, cloth and machinery. Row 4 indicates the cost impacts on the different sectors of a carbon tax of $100 per ton of carbon levied on fuel inputs, with no tax offsets. It therefore indicates relative sectoral carbon intensities. It is clear that iron and steel, chemicals, non–ferrous metals and non–metallic minerals are the most carbon–intensive sectors. Row 5 shows the sectoral impact cost of the carbon tax when revenues are rebated as uniform subsidies per unit value of industrial production. All entries with a negative sign indicate that these sectors have experienced a cost–improvement due to the carbon tax plus offset. These are the sectors of below average carbon intensity. Row 6 translates these cost (and therefore price) effects into relative effects on output by using the trade intensity as a proxy for price elasticity (based on the intuition that the higher the ratio of traded products in a sector, the more domestic price changes will affect that trade). This is clearly a crude approximation and can only be used to give indicative effects. Row 7 is as Row 6, except for an energy tax plus offset. Differences are due to differential consumption by sector of non–carbon energy (for example nuclear electricity).

There are many reasons why these results should be treated as rough approximations, not least in that they only take account of immediate, first–round effects of the relative price changes, rather than eventual adjustments to equilibrium. But the main mechanisms through which imposing environmental taxes influences sectoral competitiveness are clear.

First, as in Row 4, the imposition of a broad–based environmental tax, such as a carbon or energy tax, will increase the costs of all sectors, with a greater impact on those sectors that make the greatest use of the environmental good in question (in this case the carbon–intensive sectors IS, CH, NFM, NMM). Row 5 then shows that these costs can be completely offset in all but these four sectors by recycling the revenues from the tax back to the sectors that paid them. In this example this is done on the basis of sectoral output, so that any sector that is less than averagely carbon intensive will end up better off. The recycling could just as easily be done by reducing employers' labour taxes (for example employers' National Insurance contributions in the UK), in which case the sectors that end up better off will be those whose labour intensity is more above average than their carbon intensity. The point is that as long as the revenues are returned to industry, losses of price competitiveness in the carbon–intensive sectors will be counter–balanced by gains in the non–carbon intensive sectors. Moreover, the carbon–intensive sectors will only lose competitiveness to the extent that they do not reduce their carbon intensity at a rate equal to the tax being applied. This point is discussed further below.

International competitiveness depends not only on cost increases but also on the trade intensity of the affected products. Relative price rises of untraded goods may affect demand for those goods in domestic markets, but they will not affect international trade. Row 6 shows that the low trade intensity of IS and NMM (both sectors comprising heavy, bulky goods including iron and cement) substantially reduces the trade impacts that these sectors will suffer from the carbon tax. Indeed, the trade impacts on CH are also reduced by the medium trade intensity of this sector, leaving NFM as the only sector in which a high trade intensity and high cost increase from the tax may cause significant trade effects from the tax. Against this it may be noted that 57 per cent of UK exports in 1995 were to EU countries, so that if the carbon tax was imposed on an EU–wide basis (as was the proposal from the European Commission in 1991), all the trade effects for these sectors would be much attenuated.

Table 3.2 clearly shows the difference between the impacts from environmental taxes on sectoral and national competitiveness. The cost increases in the four most affected sectors will impair their position in domestic markets with respect to the products of other sectors. The six sectors whose costs are decreased by the revenue recycling will be particular beneficiaries from the shift in relative prices. For the country as a whole, however, there is no reason for thinking that its competitiveness will be affected at all by the shift.

Table 3.3 shows the export share of the sectors identified in Table 3.2, plus some others, aggregating the sectors in the UK Input–Output Tables of 1989 to get as close as possible to Pezzey's classification. The four sectors relatively disadvantaged by the tax–plus–rebate account for 16 per cent of UK exports. On the other hand, 30.4 per cent of UK exports are in the six relatively advantaged sectors. In addition, three other sectors have been identified (FS, AE, OM, see Table 3.3 for the code) which have a similar energy intensity to some of the relatively advantaged sectors, and so might also be expected to benefit from the tax–plus–rebate. Adding in their export share takes the proportion that might be expected to benefit to around 55 per cent of UK exports. On these figures it may well be that the UK's international trading position would be improved by the tax–plus–rebate arrangement.

Table 3.3   Export share of various UK sectors as a percentage of total UK exports in 1989

IS	CH	NFM	NMM	TE	M	F	P	W	CL	FS	AE	OM
2.2	11	2.1	0.5	13	8	4.7	2	0.4	2.2	13	6.8	4.9

Sectors as in Table 3.2 plus:
FS – Financial and other non–transport services; AE – Aerospace equipment manufacturing and repairing; OM – Office machinery and computer equipment.

This conclusion would appear to be borne out by the experience of Denmark, which has a small, open economy, and which has been a pioneer in the area of environmental taxation. According to its Ministry of Economic Affairs: 'Danish experience through many years is that we have not damaged our competitiveness because of green taxes. In addition, we have developed new exports in the

environmental area' (Kristensen, 1996, p.126). The study of the Norwegian Green
Tax Commission (1996, p.90) has also endorsed this essential conclusion:

> Reduced competitiveness of an individual industry is not necessarily a problem for
> the economy as a whole. ... It is hardly possible to avoid loss of competitiveness
> and trade effects in individual sectors as a result of policy measures if a country has
> a more ambitious environmental policy than other countries or wishes to be an
> instigator in environmental policy. On the other hand, competitiveness and
> profitability will improve in other industries as a result of a revenue neutral tax
> reform.

Investment, Efficiency and Technical Change

Implementing a carbon tax will increase the relative price of fossil energy compared
to other inputs, an effect which may be enhanced by reducing taxes on these other
inputs (for example labour, capital). As has been seen, this need not affect overall
business competitiveness. But the change in relative prices could affect economic
development in a number of other ways.

Increased scrapping

A change in relative prices caused by the imposition of a carbon tax might affect
economic development by making existing capital equipment uneconomic, thereby
bringing forward its scrapping date. This could be a major potential source of
adjustment costs related to the tax.

One would expect that the least disruptive imposition of a carbon tax would be one
introduced initially at a low level, with modest annual increases over a substantial,
pre–announced period of time. This would allow responses to the tax to be
synchronised with normal investment schedules. If a carbon tax were introduced in
this gradual, expected way, it is unlikely that experience gained in response to the
energy price shocks of the 1970s would provide a reliable guide to the economy's
response. Elasticities derived from these responses should, therefore, be treated
with caution when applied to this different situation.

Ingham and Ulph (1991a) have developed a vintage model of the UK
manufacturing sector, which allows firms to change their machines' energy/output
ratio, according to relative factor prices, both between different machine vintages
and with existing machines. Technical change is thus at least partly endogenised.
The model clearly confirms the above intuition. There is a significant increase in the
tax rate required to meet, and the associated cost of meeting, a given target if the
target date is brought closer or if action is delayed, or if the target entails cutting
existing emissions rather than preventing future growth. As Ingham and Ulph
(1991a, p.143) say: 'It is much more expensive to undo the effects of
emissions–generating plant already installed, than it is to offset the effects of
emissions–generating plant yet to be installed.'

Moreover, the Ingham and Ulph model suggests that the increased scrapping may lead to higher long term growth that outweighs the short term adjustment costs. The authors find that 'in the short run output falls, and this induces considerable scrapping of equipment which leads to lower costs and prices, and output being higher in the longer term than in the case where demand is determined exogenously. In the extreme case, output growth rises from 2 to 4.4 per cent' (Ingham and Ulph 1991b, pp.198–9).

Improvements in energy efficiency

In another application of the model mentioned in the previous section, Ingham et al. (1992, pp.128–9) identify, for UK manufacturing, the separate contribution to the decline in the energy/output ratio of relative factor prices, output and an exogenous component of technical progress. They conclude that in the period 1971–80 'changes in energy prices have explained all the improvements in energy efficiency' (p.129), as expressed in the UK manufacturing sector's energy/output ratio (this is clearly different from reductions in energy intensity due to changes in the structure of production of industry as a whole, which was not considered in the model). Although Ingham et al. stress the tentative nature of their result, at the least it suggests what might have been expected from theory, namely that technical change in the achievement of energy efficiency would increase with the price of fossil energy.

Whether or not investment and improvements in energy efficiency will accelerate with a carbon tax, many analysts have argued that market failures are preventing the implementation of some cost–efficient energy conservation measures now (for example Lovins and Lovins, 1991; Jackson and Jacobs, 1991; Jackson, 1995). It is possible that complementary government initiatives to encourage energy conservation and efficiency, and investment in clean energy technologies, would cost relatively little and significantly increase the energy elasticities on the basis of which the costs of a carbon tax are calculated, thereby reducing the cost of achieving any given CO_2 reduction target. Jackson (1991) provides evidence that the energy market is far from perfect. He finds that out of 17 technological possibilities for the reduction of CO_2 emissions, eight could be implemented at negative cost on the basis of current prices, saving a total of 165 million tonnes of CO_2 per year by 2005, or 24 per cent of UK 1991 emissions. On this analysis the UK could exceed the Toronto target for CO_2 emissions (20 per cent reduction from 1988 levels by 2005) **and** save money. This is not an unrepresentative result. After reviewing this issue, Cline (1992, p.227) decides that a reasonable estimate is that the first 22 per cent of carbon emissions from base can be cut back at zero cost. The IPCC survey of this literature (Bruce et al. 1995, pp.310–8) finds that zero cost emission reductions by 2025/2030 estimated by various studies ranged from >61–82 per cent (for the US) and from >45–60 per cent for other OECD countries. Clearly a rising energy price would increase the number of cost–effective efficiency measures and the probability that they would be implemented.

Changed investment opportunities
The changing relative price of energy would change patterns of investment and demand. There are opposite tendencies at work here. One tendency is the possible complementarity between energy and capital, a still unresolved issue (Solow, 1987). If energy and capital are complements, then increasing the price of energy will reduce the demand in production for both energy and capital, thereby reducing both investment and growth. A related tendency working in the same direction is the possible energy–using bias of technical change, already mentioned in the context of energy efficiency (Hogan and Jorgenson 1991). The results of Jorgenson's empirical work in this area have showed that productivity growth had an energy–using bias in 32 out of 35 sectors studied, (Jorgenson 1990, p.83), which would mean that, in these sectors, increasing the price of energy would reduce productivity growth.

A third negative effect on investment of an energy price increase is the obvious one that certain investments involving energy intensive capital goods or processes would become uneconomic and would not, therefore, be made. However, working in the opposite direction to all these growth–reducing tendencies is the stimulus that the relative price change would give to energy–saving investment. If it is true that many presently economic opportunities for energy saving remain unimplemented because of market failures, then it might be expected that a continuously increasing energy price, by providing a continuously increasing incentive to correct such failures, would result in substantial investments in energy efficiency and further innovation in this area. If energy efficiency could be increased at the same rate as the price of energy, then the negative effect of the rising price on investment plans would be cancelled out. There would also be a positive stimulus with regard to the development of non–fossil energy technologies. Such technical change would be what Grubb (1995, p.305) calls 'induced technology development', which he speculates may be a cause of asymmetrical elasticities of energy demand, for which there is now substantial evidence (in general falls in energy prices have not increased energy demand by as much as the preceding energy price increases reduced it). Grubb concludes: 'If price rises stimulate technical development and in addition governments take further associated action to encourage energy saving, long–term solutions may emerge at relatively lower cost as a result of the accumulation of technical change in the direction of lower CO_2–emitting technologies, infrastructure and behaviour' (ibid., p.309).

As for the issues of energy/capital complementarity and technical bias, it is possible that all the empirical results showing energy/capital complementarity or the loss of productivity induced by energy price rises owe more to the inflationary and recessionary effects of the 1970s and the **kind** of energy price rises then experienced, than to the fact of the price rise itself (see Barker et al., 1995, pp.11–12).

Technologies do not emerge from on high. They evolve in response to pressures, which may be the competitive forces of the market, or the demands of public policy. Grubb et al. (1995, p.420) point out that the no regrets potential for increased energy efficiency in the UK in 1980 was identified as about 20 per cent. In 1990 it was again identified as about 20 per cent, despite the fact that the earlier 20 per cent had largely been realised. They comment: 'It seems a curious feature of energy efficiency studies that they seem regularly to identify cost effective potentials of around 20–30 per cent of current demand, almost irrespective of the potential already exploited. ... The persistence of such results suggests that investing in greater energy efficiency helps itself to stimulate and identify options previously overlooked.'

This analysis of the possible impacts on sectoral and national competitiveness from the imposition of environmental taxes leads to several important conclusions:

1. Where the revenues from the tax are recycled back to the affected industries, there are no grounds for thinking that there will be any long term effects on national competitiveness whatever. For the UK, sectors which would benefit have a higher share of exports than those which might be negatively affected, so that UK trade performance might even be improved by such a measure.
2. Even those sectors which might be negatively affected could offset the effects of the tax if they were able to increase the rate at which they improved environmental efficiency in those areas affected by the tax. There are good theoretical and empirical grounds for believing that the tax itself, and the rise in relative price of environmental inputs that it would induce, would help to bring about such improvements.
3. In order to avoid the costly premature scrapping of capital, to give time for industrial adjustment, and to influence future investment plans, environmental taxes should be introduced at low levels and gradually escalated according to a pre-announced schedule.

6 THE FUTURE EFFECTS OF ENVIRONMENTAL POLICY ON COMPETITIVENESS: MODELLING ENVIRONMENTAL TAXES

The conclusions from the previous section about the effects of environmental taxes on competitiveness largely derive from simple simulation and analysis. However, there is now a substantial literature which has sought to estimate competitiveness effects through detailed modelling of the environmental taxes. Most of this modelling relates to the possible introduction of carbon/energy taxes.

The models used for this purpose vary in terms of theoretical underpinning, structure, basic assumptions and the treatment of different parameters. The implications of these differences for their results are dealt with in detail elsewhere in this book (Chapter 4), and will only be discussed here insofar as they add insights to the earlier analysis. In fact there are only a few studies which tackle competitiveness and energy taxation questions directly and even these do not deal with the issue of competitiveness separately. It is mainly regarded as an issue synonymous with other questions such as changes in economic growth and employment and in the rate of inflation. In what follows, first the studies of the macroeconomic effects of an energy tax will be analysed and then those of the sectoral effects.

Model Results of Macroeconomic Competitiveness Effects

Chapter 4 in this book deals with this issue in great detail, so that only one issue will be highlighted here: the importance of the means of recycling the tax revenues.

Many of the studies that model carbon/energy taxes have found the imposition of the tax to result in reductions in GDP, or costs, which have tended to predominate in discussion of this issue. For example, the Stanford Energy Modelling Forum exercise found: 'The costs of achieving a 20 percent reduction in CO_2 emissions (in the U.S.) relative to today's level range from 0.9 percent to 1.7 percent of U.S. GDP in 2010' (Gaskins and Weyant 1993, p.320).

However, these results, and others showing costs, were generated by returning the carbon tax revenues to households on a lump sum basis, rather than by reducing distortionary taxes. It is clear that such a procedure is suboptimal. For example, Jorgenson and Wilcoxen argue: '(Lump–sum recycling) is probably not the most likely use of the revenue. ... Using the revenue to reduce a distortionary tax would lower the net cost of a carbon tax by removing inefficiency elsewhere in the economy' (Jorgenson and Wilcoxen 1993, p.20). This is precisely the effect that is obtained in all models that do in fact reduce distortionary taxes to offset a carbon tax. Jorgenson and Wilcoxen (1993, Table 5 p.22) themselves find that a 1.7 percent GDP loss under lump–sum redistribution is converted to a 0.69 percent loss and a 1.1 percent gain by reducing labour and capital taxes respectively.

This effect has also been shown in the work of Nordhaus. Nordhaus (1991a), on the basis of an abatement–cost curve derived from his survey of extant models in Nordhaus (1991b), and his own calculation of a global warming damage function, arrived at an efficient level of a carbon tax of $7.33 per ton CO_2 equivalent (Nordhaus, 1991a, p.934). By 1993, using his own DICE model, the optimum carbon tax had fallen to $5.24 per ton CO_2 equivalent. Using a carbon tax of $56 per ton to cut emissions in 1995 by 20 percent from 1990 levels caused an annualised global GDP loss of $762 billion (Nordhaus, 1993b, p.315). However, these DICE results came from recycling the carbon tax revenues through lump sum rebates. When instead carbon taxes are used to reduce other, burdensome taxes, assumed to have a deadweight loss of $0.30 per $ of revenue raised, then the optimal tax rate becomes $59 per ton, emissions go below the 20 percent cut, and annualised GDP **rises** by $206 billion. Nordhaus notes: 'The importance of revenue recycling is surprising and striking. These findings emphasize the critical nature of designing the instruments and use of revenues in a careful manner.' (Nordhaus, 1993b, p.317) Gaskins and Weyant confirm the importance of revenue recycling: 'Simulation with four models of the US economy indicate that from 35 percent to more than 100 percent of the GDP losses could ultimately be offset by recycling revenues through cuts in existing taxes' (Gaskins and Weyant 1993, p.320).

A similar result was found in the modelling work of the Norwegian Green Tax Commission, the brief of which was explicitly to examine the possibilities of using a tax shift to achieve both environmental and economic goals, as part of a long term process of structural reform towards sustainable development. The Commission made a number of recommendations for implementing an ecological tax reform in Norway, which are detailed in Moe (1996). Its modelling of this issue indicated that an increase in green taxes amounting to about 1 per cent of GDP, permitting a 2–3 per cent reduction in payroll taxes, would generate a 0.2 per cent increase in real disposable income, and a 0.7 per cent increase in employment, by 2010.

In addition to the GDP level, another macroeconomic indicator which is highly sensitive to the tax offsets to a carbon tax is inflation. Clearly, a carbon tax, by raising the prices of fossil fuels, will raise the general price level; but offsetting it with reductions in VAT or other taxes will tend to reduce the price level. Different offsetting arrangements can vary the overall price effects from being inflationary to being largely inflation neutral. Reducing VAT tends to offset the carbon tax's inflation more than reducing other taxes. In fact, using VAT the tax 'package' can be designed to be inflation neutral, to eliminate the effect of inflation on other variables in the model (for example wages).

Although the carbon tax in a tax reform package might be regarded as an extra economic constraint, it would be offset by loosening, or even removing, the constraints represented by other taxes. The effect on macroeconomic variables such as output cannot be deduced a priori but will depend on the relative elasticities of demand and substitution of the goods and services affected by the package.

However, the preservation of broad neutrality with regard to inflation would appear to be an important consideration if negative macroeconomic impacts from a carbon tax are to be avoided. For, example, the study by Yamaji et al. (1993, p.27) shows output losses in the Japanese economy of 5 per cent in 2005 following the imposition of a carbon tax, even when the tax is offset by reductions in income tax. This is because inflation induced by the increased demand due to higher disposable incomes largely erodes the nominal output gains due to recycling the revenues. It would have been interesting to see results from this model from offsetting the carbon taxation by reducing indirect taxes, which might have been expected to have resulted in lower inflation as well as maintaining demand.

A number of modelling exercises have sought to incorporate other environmental taxes as well as carbon/energy taxes. Thus Barker and Lewney (1991) have combined a carbon tax designed to reduce UK CO_2 emissions back to 1990 levels by 2005, a fourfold rise in industrial pollution abatement expenditures by 2000, and an intensified water clean–up policy. This reduces GDP in 2010 by less than 1 per cent (Barker and Lewney, 1991, Table 7, p.35). Similarly the Netherlands National Environmental Policy Plan (NEPP) projected the decrease of a number of emissions and waste discharges by between 70 per cent and 100 per cent, and a doubling of environmental expenditures: by 2010 GDP had grown to 95 per cent above its 1985 level, in contrast to a 99 per cent growth with a base case of unchanged policy (MOHPPE 1988, Table 5.2.3, p.110; when other countries implement the same measures as the Netherlands, Dutch GDP actually grows by 0.5 per cent).

Finally, Table 3.4 gives some macroeconomic results from the wide–ranging report from DRI and other consultancies, commissioned by the European Commission (DRI, 1994). DRI modelled three scenarios for six of the larger European Union economies (EU–6): a Reference scenario (REF) containing 'all policy measures and actions agreed by the end of 1992' (DRI 1994, p.27); a Policy–in–the–Pipeline scenario (PIP), incorporating policies or proposals that had been the subject of a directive, mainly comprising 'command and control' measures, except for the European Commission's carbon–energy tax; and an Integrated scenario (INT), mainly using market instruments, including environmental taxation, to internalise environmental costs. DRI also modelled a variant of the INT scenario, called INT+, in which all the revenues from INT's environmental taxes were used to reduce employers' non–wage labour costs such as social security payments or, in the UK, employers' National Insurance Contributions.

All the scenarios yielded environmental improvement compared to the base (REF), but PIP resulted in not inconsiderable costs as well. In contrast, as Table 3.4 shows, INT, and especially INT+, had broadly neutral macroeconomic results, with both scenarios showing an increase in employment. These results are in line with the theoretical conclusions that market–based instruments are less costly than direct environmental regulation, and that environmental policy need not incur macroeconomic costs. These macroeconomic effects seem small, and, where they are negative, certainly seem less than the environmental benefits achieved. Both Christainsen and Tietenberg and the 1985 OECD study stress that the macroeconomic costs are only one side of the environmental policy picture. According to the former: 'One basic and overriding point should be made with respect to environmental regulations. The contributions to economic welfare which they are intended to make are, by and large, not reflected in marketed or measured

Table 3.4   *Percent change in key economic variables in 2010 INT and INT+ vs. REF in the EU-6*

	INT vs. REF	INT+ vs. REF
Real GDP at market prices	0.91	1.06
Final consumption	0.90	1.04
Fixed investment	1.44	1.68
Consumer price index	3.39	2.51
Wholesale price index	3.35	2.49
Employment	1.28	2.74
Unemployment rate[1]	–0.58	–1.17
Trade balance, US$ million[2]	57.39	46.97
Current account balance, US$ million[2]	86.82	74.63
Government borrowing, per cent GDP	3.60	3.77
Change compared to REF	-0.51	-0.34

Notes:
1. Difference in unemployment rate in 2010 between scenarios.
2. Change in levels in 2010 between scenarios.

Source: DRI 1994, Table 4.7, p.58

output. ... Although they are difficult to quantify, let alone value, numerous studies have indicated marked increases in these outputs from environmental policy. ... If this is in fact the case, the effect of these regulations on 'true' productivity would be positive and not negative, and the inclusion of the outputs of these regulations in the numerator of the standard productivity measures would both offset the negative effects of other factors on productivity growth and change the **sign** of the effect attributable to environmental regulations' (Christainsen and Tietenberg, 1985, p.388).

Model Results of Sectoral Competitiveness Effects

Analysing the impacts of an environmental tax on the sectoral level requires a disaggregated modelling framework. The estimation of the price effects induced by the imposition of an environmental tax is often carried out using a cost driven input–output price model. The impacts on competitiveness are then analysed by the development of the sectoral prices following the introduction of an environmental tax and the respective recycling measures of the generated revenues. The price increase induced by, for example, an energy tax affects not only the economic sectors producing energy products. The prices of all economic sectors are increasing depending on how much energy is required, directly and indirectly via intermediate goods, in the production of the goods.

Using such an approach Barker (1995) has examined the issue of competitiveness using the MDM–E3 model for the UK economy analysing the implications for industrial costs of a $10 per barrel carbon/energy tax in the UK, with compensating cuts in employers' National Insurance Contributions (NIC). By taking into account indirect and feedback effects from the carbon tax, this goes further than the Pezzey analysis discussed earlier, which only analysed the carbon tax's direct effects. Barker's result shows again the importance of how the generated revenues are redistributed: 'If the taxes are not compensated, most industries' prices rise as they face higher energy and labour unit costs. However if NIC contributions are reduced to keep the PSBR ratios at base levels then all industries' costs fall depending on their use of labour – and the most labour–intensive industries will have the largest reduction in costs' (Barker 1995, p.19). Table 3.5 shows that for most sectors the effects from the reduction in labour costs more than offsets the effects from the increase in energy costs. The macroeconomic differences from the base case scenario are negligible: growth and inflation are slightly higher while the balance of payments experiences a small fall.

The German Institute for Economic Research (DIW, 1994) analysed the effects of an ecological tax reform imposing an energy tax, which rises annually by 7 per cent in real terms, and recycling the generated revenue to firms by cutting the employers' social insurance contributions and also to private households via a per capita allowance (lump–sum or 'eco bonus'). The modelling framework was based on an input–output model linked to an aggregated, macroeconomic, business cycle model of Germany before unification. This approach permitted sectoral as well as macroeconomic analysis. The research team concludes:

> The study shows that a tax reform along these lines ... would have positive economic effects, even if it were implemented in a single country. The reform induces a process of ecological and economic structural change which would be conducive to employment. There are no grounds for the fear that such an

ecological tax reform would endanger German competitiveness. (Bach et al., 1994, p.3).

Table 3.6 presents some of the sectoral results in detail. The price increase following the imposition of the energy tax is highest in energy–intensive sectors such as iron and steel, chemical products, non–ferrous metals, quarrying, cellulose, pulp and paper and transport services (the energy producing sectors are

Table 3.5   Some sectoral price effects for the UK from an ecological tax reform

Sector	change in fuel costs	change in labour costs	% difference from base net changes in costs
Other Mining	+1.9	–0.4	+1.6
Food	+0.4	–0.3	+0.1
Clothing and Leather	+0.1	–0.6	–0.5
Wood and Wood Products	+0.2	–0.8	–0.6
Paper, Printing and Publication	+0.4	–0.6	–0.2
Chemicals nes	+1.9	–0.3	+1.6
Non–met. Min. Prod	+2.3	–0.5	+1.8
Basic Metals	+3.0	–0.4	+2.6
Elect. Engineering	+0.5	–0.8	–0.3
Motor Vehicles	+0.2	–0.3	–0.1
Retailing	+0.4	–0.9	–0.5
Communications	+0.7	–0.9	–0.2
Banking and Finance	+0.2	–0.3	–0.1
Public Administration	+0.3	–0.9	–0.6
Education	+0.3	–1.1	–0.7
Health/Social	+0.3	–1.0	–0.7
Waste Treatment	+0.4	–3.4	–3.1

Source: Barker 1995, p.18

Table 3.6   Sectoral price effects of an ecological tax reform for Germany

(price changes in per cent after 5 years)

Sector	Energy Tax	Compen -sation	Net effects
Iron and Steel	+9.3	–1.3	+8.0
Cellulose, Pulp, Paper	+4.9	–0.9	+4.0
Water	+4.9	–1.0	+3.9
Chemical Products	+3.8	–0.9	+2.7
NF–metals	+3.1	–0.9	+2.2
Quarrying	+3.4	–1.2	+2.2
Glass	+3.3	–1.1	+2.2
Extraction of Minerals	+3.6	–1.5	+2.1
Sea Transport	+2.2	–0.8	+1.4
Ceramic Goods	+2.9	–1.5	+1.4
Agriculture	+2.5	–1.3	+1.2
Products of rolling mills/metal casting	+2.6	–1.4	+1.2
Railways	+4.7	–3.6	+1.1
Construction	+1.4	–1.5	–0.1
Market–related services provided by the health and veterinary system	+0.5	–0.7	–0.2
Development services	+0.9	–1.1	–0.6
Electrotechnical products	+0.9	–1.2	–0.3
Engineering products	+1.0	–1.4	–0.4
Wholesale services, recycling	+0.7	–1.2	–0.5
Social insurance services	+0.9	–1.4	–0.5
Insurance services	+0.5	–1.1	–0.6
Services provided by private organizations	+0.7	–1.9	–1.2
Postal services and communications	+0.4	–1.7	–1.3
Government services	+0.9	–2.3	–1.4

Source: DIW, 1994, Tables 6.3–3 p.138; 6.4–2 p. 148; 6.5–1 p.154.

not considered). The recycling measure leads to price reductions highest in the sectors having the highest wage costs. The net effects of the higher tax burden induced of the energy tax and the compensation shows that the costs of energy–intensive sectors, that is iron and steel, cellulose, paper and pulp, chemical products, non–ferrous metals, quarrying, water supply are rising and that sectors, such as mechanical engineering, electrical engineering, service sectors and construction, are facing a decline in their burden. It is worth mentioning a particular consideration with respect to the chemical industry. The DIW researchers note: 'In the chemical industry, the rise in costs varies significantly between the various areas of production. Energy costs amount to 5 to 6 per cent of total costs in the production of basic goods and chemical fibres, whereas energy represents just 1 per cent of total costs in the production of soaps, and body–care products, pharmaceutical products and photo–chemical products' (Bach et al., 1994, p.4). As with the Pezzey analysis of an earlier section, it is also true that some of the sectors, such as parts of the quarrying sector and water supply, which experience a significant increase in costs from the tax, are not much traded internationally, so that international competitiveness effects in these sectors will not be great.

The implications of the analysed ecological tax reform on the economy as a whole were also analysed incorporating alternative assumptions concerning monetary and fiscal policy. The outcome of the sensitivity analysis was that '(I)n none of the variants studied did the ecological tax reform have a significant effect on economic growth and competitiveness' (Bach et al. 1994, p.6).

Most countries that have already introduced carbon/energy taxes, such as Denmark, Sweden and Norway, grant energy–intensive industries a lower tax rate than, for example, households. Thus Swedish manufacturing industries are completely exempt from the energy tax on mineral fuels and are eligible for a 50 per cent reduction of the carbon tax on mineral fuels. A study by Oliveira–Martins, Burniaux and Martin (1993) showed that, for a given emission–reduction target, the tax exemption of energy–intensive industries in the EU does not affect the output level of these industries. This outcome arises because the exemptions result in higher tax rates for the rest of the economy, so that the costs of the other sectors are higher and total output falls. A similar result has been reported by Böhringer and Rutherford (1997) in their analysis of the consequences of exempting energy–intensive sectors from a carbon tax. They find that wage subsidies to export– and energy–intensive sectors, rather than tax exemptions, retain more jobs and are less costly. The study's general conclusions are: 'Welfare losses associated with exemptions can be substantial even when the share of exempted sectors in overall economic activity and carbon emissions is small. Holding emissions constant, exemptions for some sectors imply increased tax rates for others and higher costs for the economy as a whole' (Böhringer and Rutherford, 1997, p.301).

Two further studies of the effect of carbon/energy taxes on economic performance have been carried out for the Austrian economy (WIFO 1995, Koeppl et al., 1996) and the Swiss economy (INFRAS 1996). Their results are of very much the same pattern as has already been reported: the taxes can have significant negative impacts for particular sectors, but the overall impact on the economy is either slightly positive (Austria) or negligible (Switzerland).

7 CONCLUSIONS

Despite the many influences on competitiveness and the complexities involved in separating out those due to environmental policy from the rest, some fairly clear conclusions emerge from the many studies of this subject that have been carried out:

1. Paying attention to environmental management can lead to cost savings and innovation which yield commercial benefit. Clearly for any particular company it is not possible to say for certain in advance whether and to what extent such benefits will be forthcoming, but there is now substantial case study evidence that many companies of different sizes in different sectors have been able to achieve environmental gains at zero or negative net cost.
2. The evidence for either first mover competitive advantage or regulation induced innovation is not strong enough to justify environmental policy on its own. Such policy should remain clearly motivated by its prospective environmental benefits. However, the facts that the environmental business sector is a source of fast growing business opportunity, and that innovation offsets to the costs of regulation are by no means uncommon, greatly reduces the likelihood that the costs of well formulated environmental policy will have a significant negative impact on competitiveness.
3. Studies confirm this insight. Although two decades of environmental policy have required substantial costs for environmental protection to be incurred at the company level, there is little evidence of this having had negative effects on the competitiveness of even the most affected sectors.
4. National competitiveness is a fundamentally different concept to the competitiveness of firms. In particular, if revenues from environmental taxes on industry are recycled to industry, then the negative effects on some sectors will be balanced by positive effects on others. However, if important economic sectors go into sudden decline, there will be costs of transition, in terms of bankruptcies and unemployment, possible exchange rate adjustments and a reduction in economic activity that are likely to be painful and politically unpopular. This reinforces the case for well formulated, cost–effective environmental policy.

5. Such policy is likely to contain an appropriate mix of instruments, including market–based instruments, regulations and negotiated agreements. Environmental taxes and other policy instruments should be imposed gradually and predictably, to minimise adjustment costs and ensure that they are taken into account in investment plans. Environmental policy should seek to encourage innovation and continuous improvement by being stable and focused on outcomes, rather than the means of achieving them, and by being informed by effective dialogue between government, business and environmental stakeholders.

6. Negative effects of environmental policy on the competitiveness of even the most affected sectors will be offset if firms in the sector respond by improving the efficiency of their use of the relevant environmental resources.

7. Exemptions of environmentally intensive sectors from environmental taxes reduce the efficiency of the taxes and increase the overall costs of attaining a given environmental improvement.

8. The modelling of even stringent future environmental policy does not suggest that this need have negative effects on the competitiveness of the macroeconomy.

There is substantial variance between these conclusions and the common perception, especially in business circles, that environmental policy, and in particular environmental taxes, represent a major threat to competitiveness. While this perception has some validity for a small number of sectors that are intensive users of energy and other environmental resources, other sectors stand to benefit from a policy of ecological tax reform, and the affected sectors can reduce the negative impacts as per point 6 above. The superficially attractive policy of exempting potentially negatively affected sectors from environmental taxes actually increases the costs of environmental improvement to society at large.

REFERENCES

Ayres, R. and J. Walter (1991), 'The greenhouse effect: damages, costs and abatement', *Environmental and Resource Economics*, **1**, 237–70.

Bach, S., M. Kohlhaas and B. Praetorius (1994), 'Ecological tax reform even if Germany has to go it alone' in *Economic Bulletin*, DIW German Institute for Economic Research, **31**(7), 3–10.

Barker, T. (1995), 'Taxing pollution instead of employment: greenhouse gas abatement through fiscal policy in the UK', *Energy and Environment*, **6**(1), 1–28.

Barker, T., P. Ekins and N. Johnstone (eds) (1995) *Global Warming and Energy Demand*, Routledge, London/New York.

Barker, T. and R. Lewney (1991), 'A Green scenario for the UK economy' in Barker, T. (ed), *Green Futures for Economic Growth: Britain in 2010*, Cambridge Econometrics, Cambridge, 11–38.

Böhringer, C. and T.F. Rutherford(1997), 'Carbon taxes with exemptions in an open economy: a general equilibrium analysis of the german tax initiative', *Journal of Environmental Economics and Management*, **32**, 189–203.

Brown, L.R. et al. (1993), *State of the World*, Earthscan, London.

Bruce, J., H. Lee and E. Haites (eds) (1995), *Climate Change 1995: Economic and Social Dimensions of Climate Change*, contribution of Working Group III to the Second Assessment Report of the Intergovernmental Panel on Climate Change (IPCC), Cambridge University Press, Cambridge.

Business International (1990), *Managing the Environment: the Greening of European Business*, Business International, London.

CEST (Centre for the Exploitation of Science and Technology) (1991), *Industry and the Environment: A Strategic Overview,* CEST, London.

CEST (Centre for the Exploitation of Science and Technology) (1994), *Waste Minimisation: a Route to Profit and Cleaner Production*, CEST, London.

Christainsen, G. and T. Tietenberg (1985), 'Distributional and Macroeconomic Aspects of Environmental Policy' in A. Kneese and J. Sweeney (eds) *Handbook of Natural Resource and Energy Economics*, **1**, Elsevier Science Publishers, Amsterdam, 345–93.

Christie. I., H. Rolfe and R. Legard (1995), *Cleaner Production in Industry: Integrating Business Goals and Environmental Management*, Policy Studies Institute, London.

Cline, W.R. (1992), *The Economics of Global Warming*, Institute for International Economics, Washington DC.

Dean, J. (1992), 'Trade and the environment: a survey of the literature' in P. Low (ed), *International Trade and the Environment*, World Bank Discussion Paper 159, World Bank, Washington D.C., 15–28.

De Andraca, R. and K. McCready (1994), *Internalizing Environmental Costs to Promote Eco–Efficiency*, Business Council for Sustainable Development, Geneva.

Ditz, D., J. Ranganathan and R.D. Banks(1995), *Green Ledgers: Case Studies in Corporate Environmental Accounting*, World Resources Institute, Washington D.C.

DIW (Deutsches Institut für Wirtschaftsforschung; German Institute for Economic Research) (1994), *Wirtschaftliche Auswirkungen einer ökologischen Steuerreform*, Berlin.

DRI (1994), *Potential Benefits of Integration of Environmental and Economic Policies: an Incentive–Based Approach to Policy Integration*, report prepared for the European Commission, Graham and Trotman, Kluwer, New York/ London .

Gaskins, D.W. and J.P. Weyant (1993), 'Model Comparisons of the Costs of Reducing CO_2 Emissions', *American Economic Review (AEA Papers and Proceedings)*, **83**(2), May, 318–23.

Gray, W. and R. Shadbegian (1993), 'Environmental Regulation and Manufacturing Productivity at the Plant Level', National Bureau of Economic Research (NBER) Working Paper 4321, NBER, Cambridge MA.

Grossman, G. and A. Krueger (1994), 'Economic Growth and the Environment', NBER Working Paper 4634, February, Cambridge MA: National Bureau of Economic Research.

Grubb, M. (1995), 'Asymmetrical price elasticities of energy demand' in Barker, T., Ekins, P. and Johnstone, N. (eds) (1995), *Global Warming and Energy Demand*, Routledge,London/New York, 305–310.

Grubb, M., T. Chapuis and M. Ha Duong (1995), 'The economics of changing course: implications of adaptability and inertia for optimal climate policy', *Energy Policy*, **23**(4/5), 417–32.

HMSO (Her Majesty's Stationery Office) (1993), *Realising Our Potential: A strategy for science, engineering and technology*, Cm.2250, HMSO, London.

Hogan, W.W. and D.W. Jorgenson (1991), 'Productivity Trends and the cost of reducing CO_2 emissions, *Energy Journal*, **12**(1), 67–86.

INFRAS (1996), *Economic Impact Analysis of Ecotax Proposals*, Zürich, Switzerland.

Ingham, A. and A. Ulph (1991a), 'Market–based instruments for reducing CO_2 emissions: the case of UK manufacturing', *Energy Policy*, **19**(3) (March), 138–48.

Ingham, A. and A. Ulph, (1991b), 'Carbon Taxes and the UK Manufacturing Sector' in Dietz, F., Van der Ploeg, F. and Van der Straaten, J. (eds) (1991), *Environmental Policy and the Economy*, Amsterdam: Elsevier, 197–239.

Ingham, A., J. Maw and A. Ulph (1992), 'Energy conservation in UK manufacturing: a vintage model approach' in Hawdon, D. (ed) *Energy Demand: Evidence and Expectations*, Surrey University Press, Guildford, 115–41.

Jackson, T. (1991), 'Least–Cost Greenhouse Planning', *Energy Policy*, January/February, 35–46.

Jackson, T. (ed) (1993), *Clean Production Strategies: Developing Preventive Environmental Management in the Industrial Economy*, Lewis Publishers, Boca Raton (FL)/London.

Jackson, T. (1995), 'Price elasticity and market – overcoming obstacles to ensure energy efficiency' in T. Barker, P. Ekins and N. Johnstone (eds) *Global Warming and Energy Elasticities*, Routledge, London, 254–66.

Jackson, T. and M. Jacobs (1991), ' Carbon Taxes and the Assumptions of Environmental Economics' in T. Barker (ed) *Green Futures for Economic Growth*, Cambridge: Cambridge Econometrics, 49–67.

Jaffe, A., S. Peterson, P. Portney and R. Stavins (1995), 'Environmental regulation and the competitiveness of us manufacturing: what does the evidence tell us?', *Journal of Economic Literature*, **XXXIII** (March), 132–63.

Jorgenson, D. (1990), 'Productivity and Economic Growth' in E.R. Berndt and J.E. Triplett (eds) (1990) *Fifty Years of Measurement: the Jubilee of the Conference on Research in Income and Wealth*, University of Chicago Press, Chicago 19–118.

Jorgenson, D. and P. Wilcoxen (1990), 'Environmental Regulation and US Economic growth', *RAND Journal of Economics*, **21**(2), Summer, 314–40.

Jorgenson, D. and Wilcoxen, P. (1993), 'Reducing US Carbon Emissions: an Econometric General Equilibrium Assessment', *Resource and Energy Economics*, **15**(1) (March), 7–25.

Koeppl, A., K. Kratena, C. Pichl, F. Schebeck, S. Schleicher and M. Wueger (1996), 'Macroeconomic and sectoral effects of energy taxation in Austria', *Environmental and Resource Economics*, **8**, 417–30.

Kristensen, J.P. (1996), 'Environmental Taxes, Tax Reform and the Internal Market – some Danish Experiences and Possible Community Initiatives' in *Environmental Taxes and Charges: NATIONAL Experiences and Plans*, European Foundation for the Improvement of Living and Working Conditions, Dublin, and Office for Official Publications of the European Communities, Luxembourg.

Lovins, A.B. and H.L. Lovins (1991), 'Least cost climatic stabilization', *Annual Review of Energy and Environment*, **16**, 433–531.

Low, P. and A. Yeats (1992), 'Do "Dirty" Industries Migrate?' in Low, P. (ed.) *International Trade and the Environment*, World Bank Discussion Paper 159, World Bank, Washington DC, 89–103.

Lucas, R., D. Wheeler and H. Hettige (1992), 'Economic Development, Environmental Regulation and the International Migration of Toxic Industrial Pollution: 1960–88' in Low. P. (ed) (1992), *International Trade and the Environment*, World Bank Discussion Paper 159, World Bank, Washington DC 67–86.

Moe, T. (1996), 'Ongoing work in the Norwegian Green Tax Commission' in *Environmental Taxes and Charges: National Experiences and Plans*, European Foundation for the Improvement of Living and Working Conditions, Dublin, and Office for Official Publications of the European Communities, Luxembourg.

MOHPPE (Ministry of Housing, Physical Planning and Environment) (1988), *To Choose or to Lose: National Environmental Policy Plan*, MOHPPE, The Hague.

Nordhaus, W.D. (1991a), 'To slow or not to slow: the economics of the greenhouse effect', *Economic Journal*, **101** (July 1991), 920–37.

Nordhaus, W.D. (1991b), 'The cost of slowing climate change: a survey', *The Energy Journal*, **12**(1), 37–65.

Nordhaus, W.D. (1993a), 'Lethal Model 2:the Limits to Growth Revisited', Cowles

Foundation Paper No. 831, Yale University, New Haven.

Nordhaus, W.D. (1993b), 'Optimal Greenhouse Gas reductions and tax policy in the "DICE" model', *American Economic Review* (Papers and Proceedings), **83**(2) (May), 313–7.

Norwegian Green Tax Commission (1996), *Policies For A Better Environment and High Employment*, 1996, Oslo.

OECD (Organisation for Economic Cooperation and Development) (1985), *The Macroeconomic Impact of Environmental Expenditure*, OECD, Paris.

OECD (Organisation for Economic Cooperation and Development) (1991), *The State of the Environment*, OECD, Paris.

OECD (Organisation for Economic Cooperation and Development) (1995), *Environmental Taxes in OECD Countries*, OECD, Paris.

OECD (Organisation for Economic Cooperation and Development) (1996), *Implementation Strategies for Environmental Taxes*, OECD, Paris.

Oliveira–Martins, J., J.-M. Burniaux and J.P. Martin (1992), 'Trade and effectiveness of unilateral CO_2-abatement policies: evidence from Green', *OECD Economic Studies* **19**, Paris.

OTA (Office of Technology Assessment), (1992), *Trade and Environment: Conflicts and Opportunities*, OTA, Washington DC.

Palmer, K., W. Oates and P. Portney (1995), 'Tightening Environmental Standards: the benefit–cost or the no–cost paradigm?', *Journal of Economic Perspectives*, **9**(4), Fall, 97–118.

Pearce, D. (1992), 'Should the GATT be reformed for environmental reasons?', CSERGE Working Paper GEC 92–06, CSERGE, University of East Anglia/University College London.

Pezzey, J. (1991), *Impacts of Greenhouse Gas Control Strategies on UK Competitiveness*, Department of Trade and Industry, HMSO, London.

Porter, M. (1990), *The Competitive Advantage of Nations*, Free Press, New York.

Porter, M. and C. van der Linde (1995), 'Toward a new conception of the environment–competitiveness relationship', *Journal of Economic Perspectives*, **9**(4), Fall, 97–118.

Proops, J., M. Faber and G. Wagenhals (1993), *Reducing CO_2 Emissions: a Comparative Input–Output Study for Germany and the UK*, Springer Verlag, Berlin.

Schmidheiny, S. (with the Business Council for Sustainable Development) (1992), *Changing Course: a Global Business Perspective on Development and the Environment*, MIT Press, Cambridge MA.

Smart, B. (ed) (1992), *Beyond Compliance: a New Industry View of the Environment*, World Resources Institute, Washington DC.

Solow, J. (1987), 'The capital–energy complementarity debate revisited', *American Economic Review*, **77**(4), (September), 605–14.

Wallace, D. (1995), *Environmental Policy and Industrial Innovation*, Royal Institute for International Affairs/Earthscan, London.

WIFO (Austrian Institute of Economic Reserach) (1995), *Makroökonomische und sektorale Auswirkungen einer umweltorientierten Energiebesteuerung in Österreich*, Vienna.

Yamaji, K., R. Matsuhashi,Y. Nagata and Y. Kaya (1993), 'A Study on economic measures for CO_2 reduction in Japan', *Energy Policy*, **21**(2), February, 123–32.

4. International competitiveness and carbon taxation

Terry Barker and Nick Johnstone [*]

1 INTRODUCTION

1.1 Global Warming, Greenhouse Gas Abatement and the Carbon Tax

The UN Climate Change Convention recognises the threat of climate change as a result of increases in greenhouse gases (GHGs) in the atmosphere. The Convention has over 150 signatories, including the UK and the European Union, who have agreed on the need for precautionary action to limit emissions of greenhouse gases, of which carbon dioxide is the most important. Under the convention, developed country parties are required to aim to return emissions to 1990 levels by the year 2000. The achievement of this aim is in doubt for many countries and a new agreement is to be negotiated in Kyoto, December 1997.

At the same time as the problem of global warming was emerging, there has been a marked change in the attitude of governments, especially in Europe, to environmental policy. There has been a move away from the idea of using the traditional policies to manage environmental problems, such as explicit technology-based regulations or enforcement of emission standards ('command–and–control' policies) towards that of using market based instruments, such as the tax differential in the UK in favour of lead free petrol. The use of market instruments is often a more efficient way of achieving environmental targets, and gives business more discretion in deciding how to produce goods and services. The move has generally been greatly welcomed by

* Please address any correspondence to Terry Barker. Nick Johnstone is now with the International Institute for Environment and Development, London.

business (Schmidheiny, 1992). Governments have therefore been considering how GHG abatement can be achieved through market based instruments and comparing these with other instruments. CO_2 emissions arise from many activities which are important to the workings of industrial and service economies, such as electricity generation and transportation. The emissions are associated with the burning of coal, oil and gas, activities which are readily measured and in many countries already taxed or subsidised. The environmental damages arising from CO_2 emissions do not depend upon the place or time of emission. These features imply that one particular market based instrument, carbon taxation, would be a highly efficient means of reducing the emissions. It would have a pervasive effect in encouraging the use of goods and services which are less carbon–intensive at all stages in the production process, from electricity generation to consumer spending. It would encourage producers to shift towards less carbon–intensive methods of production, often involving saving energy.

This strong *prima facie* case has led to many proposals to introduce carbon taxes, including the European Commission's (EC) carbon/energy tax (EC, 1992), but few of them have been successfully implemented. The EC tax has in particular failed to achieve unanimous agreement among EU Member States, despite being heavily modified to accommodate the interests of energy–intensive industries and of lower–income EU economies – Greece, Ireland, Portugal and Spain. This failure has partly been attributed to 'a concerted attempt (by the business sector) to kill the tax idea' (p.7 in Ikwue and Skea, 1994) which included a period of intense and emotional lobbying by special interest groups in Brussels. The reaction was similar, though more measured, from broad–based international and national business federations such as UNICE (European employers' federation) and the UK equivalent, CBI.

This may seem surprising given the apparent 'greening' of business in recent years and the approval by business leaders of the move to market-based instruments. The Precautionary Principle suggests that governments should act to abate global warming in advance of complete and reliable scientific evidence because of the possibility of significant and irreversible environmental damage. Business has accepted this Principle, but there has been an instinctive reaction against the tax and an apparent preference for regulation and voluntary agreements (pp.6–8 in Ikwue and Skea, 1994). Little credence has been given to independent economic analyses, excepting those that have provided particular criticisms of the tax for use in lobbying politicians and the public. Chief among these criticisms is that a tax would reduce the international competitiveness of the countries which introduce it. Furthermore, it is argued that it would be ineffectual because it would induce carbon–intensive activities to migrate to other parts of the world – the carbon leakage problem (for example Pezzey, 1991, 1992a).

Growth rates: Average growth rates are calculated as compound rates over the stated period, for example average growth of X over the five-year period 1990-95 is ([X(1995)/X(1990)]^(1/5)–1)*100

Carbon Tax Rates: These have been converted where necessary to $/boe in 1993 prices using the US wholesale price index and a fixed coefficient for the carbon content of a barrel of oil.

Initials Used for Geographical Areas

EC European Commission
EU European Union
OECD Organisation for Economic Cooperation and Development

Initials Used for Model Types

DGE Dynamic General Equilibrium
MACRO–A Aggregate Macroeconometric
MACRO–S Sectoral Macroeconometric
SGE Static General Equilibrium

CONVENTIONS ADOPTED IN THIS CHAPTER

1.2 The Purpose of the Chapter

This chapter identifies the relevant literature which considers, in an analytically rigorous fashion, the direct and indirect impacts of a carbon/energy tax introduced unilaterally at a national or world regional level. The chapter focuses on the price competitiveness effects estimated in this literature, and the extent to which these effects are the outcome of the assumptions and modelling approaches adopted. The chapter also sets out and evaluates the estimates of carbon leakage or 'environmental dumping' effects, which are closely associated with loss of competitiveness in particular sectors. The chapter concentrates on estimates of the effects of policies proposed by the EU, and to some extent similar ones for the US and other OECD countries. It also concentrates on the effect of policies such as carbon and/or energy taxes, although insights from studies which use other instruments are also discussed. Policies related to greenhouse gases other than carbon dioxide are not examined.

Few studies have been designed to tackle the competitiveness and leakage questions directly, and most report the relevant results in a summary fashion if at all. Competitiveness effects have been seen as incidental to other questions such as: the rate of tax required to achieve the target reduction in emissions; the effect of the tax on economic growth and inflation; or a comparison of the tax with other taxes or other methods of reducing emissions. This aspect of the literature means that caution is required in interpreting the results; if these are incidental to the main arguments and largely the effect of simplifying assumptions, the results should be given limited weight.

An analysis of the costs of climate protection for the USA (Repetto and Austin, 1997) which is based on 16 world and US models, demonstrates this point in that competitiveness effects were not considered an important factor in the effects estimated by the models of taxation on economic growth. In the analysis, 80 per cent of the differences in results for the US GDP costs of abatement (as measured from projections using the models) could be explained by assumptions relating to the 7 factors: backstop technology, model type, fuel substitution permitted in the model, availability of joint implementation, recycling of revenues, treatment of secondary benefits, and treatment of climate change effects. Many of these assumptions are also important in explaining the competitiveness and leakage results from the models, as discussed below.

A second *caveat* relating to the results is worth mentioning. Although the models and applications reviewed are often given equal weight, for example by being listed in tables and described in the text, each has absorbed different levels of resources. Some are off-the-shelf applications of a standard model by one researcher (Pezzey, 1992a); others, such as the OECD GREEN model, have involved a team of researchers over several years building and applying a much larger and more refined model (Burniaux et al., 1992b). Extra resources do not necessarily imply that the results are more reliable, or more 'right' in any sense, but they do allow for more detailed modelling and more accurate representation of economic behaviour and technological change.

Finally, since this chapter is intended to assess competitiveness, detailed results have not been reported from the model applications which simulate the EC's carbon/energy tax proposal **including** the exemptions, in one form or another, of the energy–intensive industries from coverage of the tax. The exemptions were proposed as a response to the concerns of the effects of the tax on competitiveness: this review of the literature is intended to assess potential effects of the tax on competitiveness, not the effects of measures and exemptions mitigating these effects in the expectation that they would prove to be adverse. Pearson and Smith (1991, pp. 23–5) set out reasons for being extremely cautious before introducing such exemptions; Oliveira–Martins (1995) presents empirical evidence of the ability of energy-intensive industries to reduce emissions in response to a carbon tax and argues that exemption will entail a serious efficiency loss (p. 111).

1.3 Competitiveness and Leakage Effects of a Carbon Tax

In this chapter, competitiveness is taken to mean 'the ability to compete in international markets by industries or nations as depending on the prices and qualities of the goods and services they produce'. Changes in price competitiveness are distinguished from those in non–price competitiveness depending on whether the changes arise from changes in prices or in qualities. Sectoral competitiveness means that of the goods and services of a particular industrial sector, assuming that exchange rates are constant. Also, national competitiveness is affected by the exchange rates. These definitions are similar to those used by Porter (1990) rather than those used by Pezzey (1991), which are more related to relative labour productivity performance. Competitiveness should be distinguished from comparative advantage, which refers to the relative competitiveness of different industries in an economy.

Carbon leakage would occur if a country or trading block takes unilateral action to reduce CO_2 emissions, and this action results in higher emissions elsewhere in the world. A net loss of competitiveness could also be the result of such unilateral action. The most widely quoted example is the loss of price competitiveness in carbon–intensive goods and services which arises from the introduction of a carbon tax. It is argued that the tax would raise costs of burning fossil fuels and hence the costs of goods for export; these exports would then lose price competitiveness, and hence market share; industries in other countries which do not face the increase in costs will take that market share, increasing their use of fossil fuels leading to carbon leakage.

The argument is persuasive, but it is incomplete. The effects of unilateral action also depend on the use of the revenues from the tax. If they are returned to the economy by way of reductions in taxes which bear on sectoral competitiveness, such as taxes on employers, the initial loss of price competitiveness would be reduced depending on each industries use of fossil fuels and labour. Although energy–intensive industries may still lose out, there may be a **net increase** in price competitiveness of labour–intensive industries. If all the tax collected from energy–intensive industries were to be recycled to those industries, in the form of direct subsidy or support for R&D and investment which results in energy savings, then their competitiveness may increase in relation to other industries, although the extent of reductions in other taxes would be lower and the efficiency of the outcome would be in doubt.

Furthermore there may also be an increase in more general non–price competitiveness. Three factors could give rise to such a result: firstly, the encouragement given to domestic industries specialising in technologies which generate energy savings or allow for fuel substitution may lead them to develop international markets in these technologies or improve their ability to compete in these markets; secondly, any associated improvements (for example reduced traffic congestion or reduced emissions of other pollutants) caused by the abatement policy could boost the attractiveness of the country; and thirdly, technological development and hence growth of exports may be stimulated by efforts to reduce CO_2 emissions. The scale of these improvements in non-competitiveness may be difficult to judge since it depends on the initial energy efficiency of the industries bearing the tax and the unexploited innovations available to them.

In summary, two fundamental questions arise from the application of a unilateral or regional measure such as the carbon/energy tax, aside from the question of the ability of the measure to meet the Climate Change Convention commitments. Firstly, what are the **international economic consequences** of unilateral/regional abatement policies relative to global abatement policies? More particularly, is there a national or sectoral competitiveness penalty associated with unilateral abatement? Do industries and firms lose market share and if so by how much? Secondly, what are the **global environmental consequences** of undertaking unilateral abatement? This refers to carbon leakage, the indirect effects of unilateral abatement on emissions from other countries.

The two questions are closely related. According to orthodox trade theory, if one country imposes a fiscal or regulatory constraint on the use of carbon in production then other countries would export relatively more goods which tend to be more carbon-intensive, and would employ production processes which are also more carbon-intensive. To some extent leakages are merely the environmental effects which follow from the economic effects of changes in competitiveness, although the two are conceptually distinct and may not co-exist. This chapter will analyse the causes and extent of these impacts of carbon taxation.

1.4 GHG Emissions and the Global Energy System

These questions cannot be adequately addressed without considering the main characteristics of the global economy which involve GHG emissions, particularly those from the burning of fossil fuels. Figure 4.1 shows the global emissions of CO_2 in 1987, the main GHG from human activity, divided into those from the burning of solid fuels (such as coal and coke), liquid fuels (mainly oil products), gas, the production of cement and finally from changes in land use (mainly the burning and clearing of tropical rainforest). The figure clearly shows the importance of burning fossil fuels and the large share of coal. Since burning coal, oil or gas generates rather different quantities of CO_2 for the same heat output, and since there are widespread possibilities of substituting between these fuels,

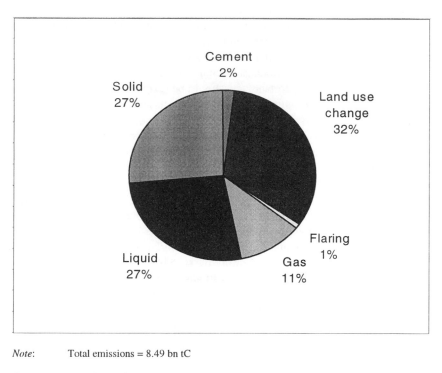

Note: Total emissions = 8.49 bn tC

Source: World Resources Institute, Washington DC

Figure 4.1 Anthropogenic sources of global CO$_2$ in 1987

especially in electricity generation, it is important in any modelling of GHG abatement through a carbon tax that these three fuels are distinguished.

Another feature of global emissions is their country or region of origin. The industrialised countries of Western Europe and North America are responsible for a large share of current emissions. However, the magnitude of the future abatement problem is demonstrated by the IPCC's (1991) reference scenario over 1985 to 2025. The huge increase expected in the developing countries' share of emissions, as India and China exploit their coal reserves, completely dominates the total of emissions from Western Europe. It is clear that without substantial action by all the main world regions, it will be difficult to stabilise emissions, let alone reduce them by some 60 per cent, the reduction estimated by the IPCC as required to stabilise GHG **concentrations** in the atmosphere and so eventually to slow global warming. Even if Western Europe were to cease emissions altogether this would make little difference to the long-term growth of total emissions.

The IPCC reference scenario is an example of a base case projection which is a feature of the methodology employed in the carbon tax literature. The base case is important because it shows what is to be expected without the carbon tax, and the differences between the carbon tax scenario and the base case show the effects of the carbon tax. Three important facts should be taken into account in the base case if it is to represent the future of the world's energy markets. The first is the ample global reserves of coal that will be available over the next few centuries. It appears unlikely that increasing demand for coal will force up real coal prices significantly in the foreseeable future; the problem is that it is expensive to move around in bulk, so the market is largely confined to particular regions. The second is the large proportion of world oil reserves held by OPEC countries. This implies that as world demand for oil grows, a higher proportion of supplies will come from OPEC. Therefore if growth in oil consumption slows as a result of carbon taxes in oil-consuming countries, the world oil price may stay constant when otherwise it would have risen as OPEC used its market power. The third feature of the world energy market is the limiting of trade in natural gas to a network of pipelines; only in the very long term could gas supply respond to extra demand for substitution into gas as a low–carbon fuel as a result of carbon taxes.

A further technological feature of the world's energy system is that much of the coal is used for electricity generation, especially in OECD countries. This makes it important to distinguish the electricity generation sector in the models as well as the possibilities of substitution between fuels for generation. Clearly in some regions there are substantial opportunities for low-cost substitution of gas for coal in generation.

1.5 Competitiveness and International Trade

The effects of a carbon tax on competitiveness must be put in context in order to understand the significance of the results in the competitiveness literature. There are many determinants of competitiveness in international markets, but different tax regimes, let alone the existence or otherwise of a carbon or energy tax, seldom enter the debate. Porter (1990) does not mention energy prices or taxes even as a minor auxiliary factor in determining competitiveness; what is important is the dynamic clustering of innovation and improvements in quality and active domestic rivalry. Indeed, Porter draws the important implication from his study that 'dynamism leads to competitive advantage, not short-term cost advantages... Policies that convey static, short-term cost advantages but that unconsciously undermine innovation and dynamism represent the most common and most profound error in government policy toward industry' (p. 621). The picture of modern economic growth which he paints seems much closer to likely developments over the next 100 years than that presented by the general equilibrium models described below. If he is right, the long–term improvements in sectoral competitiveness are more likely to come from an announced policy of rapidly rising carbon taxes, which lead to rapid product and process improvement, stimulating innovation, than from general resistance to change and protection of domestic industries from short term increases in costs.

Although it is often asserted that the unilateral application of environmental regulations in some countries has resulted in adverse competitiveness effects, there is little systematic evidence of widespread restructuring of production to escape environmental regulations (Stevens, 1993). Much of the formal evidence which exists is based on American and OECD trade patterns. For instance, Kalt (1988) and Tobey (1990) find that American abatement costs have not been found to be significant determinants of trading relations with other countries, including developing countries.

More recently, Han and Braden (1996) use American data to examine the effects of pollution abatement costs on next exports with the rest of the world. They find negative competitiveness effects, but that the effects have been decreasing over time. This would be consistent with a scenario whereby the United States has been the leader in terms of the adoption of environmental regulations, but that its main trading partners have been catching up. And finally, van Beers and van den Bergh (1996) examine the bilateral trade flows between 21 OECD countries for 22 sectors. They find that their derived index of environmental policy has ambiguous trade effects. However, if resource-based sectors are excluded from the subset of pollution intensive industries the trade effects are significant and negative. This would indicate that while environmental policy is not generally an important factor in determining trade flows, it may be significant for those sectors which are not bound by proximity to resource endowments. Even in such cases, the effects are small.

A number of general conclusions emerge from these studies. Firstly, only a few studies have found negative trade and investment effects from the unilateral application of environmental regulations. Secondly, in those cases where such effects have been found they are often temporary in nature and limited to a subset of sectors. And thirdly, even in those cases the magnitude of such effects is quite small. Thus, there is a general consensus that environmental regulations and taxes are not important determinants of national competitiveness (Beckerman, 1990; Smith, 1990; and Ekins, 1994; for surveys see Dean, 1992 and Adams, 1997). At the broad sectoral level, the effect of changes in environment–related costs of production has been but one small and usually insignificant item among many others, with long–term competitive advantage dependent on quality and innovation.

Despite these findings, in the global warming debate considerable weight is put on the expected loss of competitiveness following the introduction of carbon and/or energy taxes, as illustrated by the failure of the EC tax proposal. The reasons are threefold. Firstly, unlike other environmental regulations and taxes, which tend to be sector based, the effects of a carbon tax are pervasive throughout the economy. This puts the debate at a national rather than a sectoral level. Secondly, there is little question that the attainment of environmental objectives such as GHG stabilisation would necessitate a fundamental restructuring of the economy along lines which are not required for the attainment of many other objectives; this need is not yet generally accepted. Thirdly, the economic consequences of the policy are more obvious to the industries which face the prospects of higher costs or the need to become more efficient in the use of carbon-based fuels. The promulgation of a new tax at specific rates, such as $10/boe, on inputs which are used by every industrial sector is much more likely to attract attention than regulations which affect technologies or practices in a small subset of industries.

In summary, studies of the determinants of international trade are hard pressed to find significant relative price effects, and when they do so it is clear that changes in exchange rates, in labour costs and or even in raw material prices are more important than changes in taxes on energy. If national competitiveness of economies is considered, it is clear that high energy prices, brought about by high taxes or lack of domestic energy supplies, are no obstacle to industrialisation or rapid economic growth (witness the successes of Singapore, Hong Kong and Japan on a larger scale). Conversely the availability of ample reserves of low cost oil and gas, let alone coal, is not sufficient to provide a high degree of success in international trade (consider Nigeria, Iran, or indeed the UK). The root causes of competitiveness lie elsewhere.

1.6 The Organisation of the Chapter

The rest of this chapter is divided into four parts. First the models used in the carbon tax literature are surveyed, listing the main characteristics which are relevant to their treatment of competitiveness and leakage. In the next chapter, the studies using the models are reviewed, first with respect to their estimates of competitiveness effects and then to leakage rates. The results of the reviews are then brought together in an account of the determinants of both competitiveness and leakage in the models. This section evaluates the effect of the modelling framework on the results before assessing the contributions of the assumptions, the level of aggregation adopted and the treatment of the world oil market; each section of the chapter ends with a summary of conclusions. The last section presents some general conclusions.

2 SURVEY OF THE MODELS

The models which have been included in the review are those which address the issues of competitiveness and/or carbon leakages explicitly. This is significant since some of the best–known models of GHG abatement do not address these issues, either because the models are one-region (for example Nordhaus, 1991, 1993), thus precluding competitiveness and leakages, or they focus on the US (for example Jorgenson and Wilcoxen, 1993) or the EU (Bohringer et al., 1995) where such issues are less important due to the size of the domestic economy, or they are explicitly based on analyses of optimality (for example Barns, Edmonds and Reilly, 1992), in which international differences in policies are removed by assumption. However, insights from these models and other similar studies will be included to reinforce points which are relevant to the analyses of competitiveness and leakages.

Those models which are considered explicitly can be divided into four broad general categories: static general equilibrium models (SGE), dynamic general equilibrium models (DGE), aggregated macroeconometric models (MACRO–A) and disaggregated macroeconometric models (MACRO–S), whether national or global. They differ significantly not only in terms of basic methodology and parameter assumptions but also by sectoral and regional classification. The models considered below are grouped by model type; some of the main differences between them are listed in Table 4.1.

2.1 The Static General Equilibrium Models

Both the static CRTM (Carbon Related Trade Model, referred to as CRTM–1 in this chapter) and the dynamic CRTM (CRTM–2) have been derived from the Manne and Richels (1992) Global 2100 model which focuses on the world energy system. The former is a static general equilibrium model (Perroni and Rutherford, 1993). There are two non–energy goods (basic intermediate materials and other non–energy output). The former includes steel, plastics, chemicals and glass. On the energy side there are six electric energy sources (hydro, old coal, new coal, nuclear, gas, advanced), six non–electric energy sources (coal, gas, synthetic, renewable, low cost oil and high cost oil), and two types of natural gas (low cost and high cost). The world is disaggregated into four trading blocks: the US, Other OECD, Former Soviet Union and Eastern Europe, China and ROW. Exceptionally, the model is calibrated on values from a future year (2020), using the estimates of Global 2100.

A second static model is the general equilibrium model of Whalley and Wigle (1991) which has been adapted by Pezzey (1992a) to analyse the issues of a unilateral carbon tax and its effects on competitiveness and leakages. In the

Table 4.1 Summary of models discussed

Model	Type	Geographical Coverage	Sectoral Disaggregation
CRTM-1	SGE	USA, OECD, FSU&EE, China, ROW	2 Energy 2 Non–Energy
Whalley–Wigle	SGE	EU, NA, Japan, OECD, OilX LDCs/Planned	3 Energy 2 Non–Energy
12RT	DGE	US, Japan, OECD, FSU, CEECs OilX, China, India, DAEs, Brz, ROW	19 Energy 2 Non–Energy
CRTM-2	DGE	USA, OECD, FSU, China MOPEC/ROW	2 Energy 2 Non–Energy
GREEN	DGE	US, Japan, OECD, FSU, CEECs OilX, China, India, DAEs, Brz, ROW	8 Energy 3 Non–Energy
LEAN	DGE	Germany, EU-9, ROW	14 Sectors
EGEM	MACRO-A	EU, NA, Japan, Africa, LA, S&SE-A, F-CMN, OPEC, ROW	3 Energy Non-Energy NK
NERA/GEM	MACRO-A	NA, WE, CPs, ROW	NK
DRI-1	MACRO-S	EU-12 plus trade links	1 Energy 19 Non–Energy
DRI-2	MACRO-S	US plus trade links	4 Energy 60 Non–Energy
HERMES	MACRO-S	West Germany, UK, France, Italy Plus links with ROW	1 Energy 8 Non–Energy
MDM-E3	MACRO-S	UK plus trade links	4 Energy 45 Non–Energy
OWEM	MACRO-S	OECD-A, OECD-E, OECD-P, OPEC OXLDC, OMLDC, NICs, FCPE	5 Energy

Notes: The acronyms for geographical coverage are those used in the literature (see box text below). See the list of conventions for the explanation of the model types.
NK - not known

Sources: See the list of references

model total output is disaggregated by three forms of energy (carbon, non–carbon, and a composite of the two) and two other sectors (energy–intensive goods and other goods). Carbon energy is the aggregate of oil, solids and gas, while non–carbon energy is the aggregate of nuclear, solar and hydro. Those energy–intensive goods which have been distinguished from aggregate production are primary metals, glass, ceramics and other basic manufactures (Whalley and Wigle, 1991). There is final consumption of composite energy, energy–intensive goods and other goods, with trade in the latter two as well as carbon energy. Technology is assumed to be identical in all six regions: EU, North America, Japan, Other OECD, Oil Exporters, and Developing/Centrally Planned Economies. The model is calibrated on data for 1982 and has just one projection period, with either 1990–2030 or 1990–2100 being chosen in published studies.

2.2 The Dynamic General Equilibrium Models

The first of the dynamic models in Table 1 is a version of the Carbon Related Trade Model, CRTM–2. The three papers which employ CRTM–2 (Felder and Rutherford, 1993, Manne and Rutherford, 1994, and Rutherford, 1992) show that it is similar to CRTM–1 with two notable exceptions. Firstly, in one study (Felder and Rutherford, 1993) the rest of the world (ROW) group in Global 2100 is divided into Mexico and OPEC (MOPEC) and a residual ROW, which although slightly less heterogenous than before still includes India and most other developing countries. Secondly, in all three cases the model uses a dynamic structure, although the precise formulation differs; Felder and Rutherford (1993) and Rutherford (1992) use a recursive framework, while Manne and Rutherford (1994) is forward looking.

Another dynamic general equilibrium model is 12RT (Manne and Oliveira–Martins, 1994), also adapted from Global 2100. However, unlike the CRTM models there is no sectoral disaggregation in the non–energy sectors, although trade (but not production) by energy–intensive industries is distinguished. The energy supply industry is disaggregated into nine electric sources (including two backstop technologies) and ten non–electric sources (including one backstop technology). Backstop technologies are used in these models to provide terminal conditions so that the models can be solved; it is assumed that unlimited quantities of electricity or other energy sources can be supplied at a fixed high unit cost. The largest and most comprehensive of the dynamic general equilibrium models in the literature is the OECD's GREEN model (Manne and Oliveira–Martins, 1994; Oliveira–Martins et al., 1992; Burniaux et al., 1992a; Burniaux et al., 1992b and Nicoletti and Oliveira–Martins, 1992). Although it has undergone a series of modifications, in all cases there are eight energy sectors (coal, oil, gas, refined oil, electricity and three backstop sources – carbon electric, carbon-free electric and non-electric). Other production is disaggregated by energy-intensive industries (paper and pulp, chemicals, iron and steel, and non–ferrous metals), other industry/services, and agriculture. The world is disaggregated into twelve regions (US, Japan, EU–12, Other OECD, FSU, China, Oil Exporting LDCs, Central and Eastern European Countries,

Brz	Brazil
CEECs	Central and Eastern European Countries
Cps	Centrally Planned economies
DAEs	Dynamic Asian Economies
EC	European Commission
EU	European Union
EU-9	EU less Germany, Luxembourg and Greece
F-CMN	Former Communist Countries
FSU	Former Soviet Union
LDCs/Planned	Less Developed Countries and Former Planned Economies
LA	Latin America
MOPEC	Mexico and OPEC
NA	North America
OECD	Organisation for Economic Cooperation and Development
OOECD	Other OECD Countries
OilX	Oil Exporters
ROW	Rest of the world
S&SE-A	South and South-East Asia
WE	Western Europe
OECD-A	North American OECD Countries
OECD-E	European OECD Countries
OECD-P	Pacific Rim OECD Countries

REGIONAL ACRONYMS IN TABLE 3.2

Dynamic Asian Economies, India, Brazil and ROW). The model is calibrated on data for 1985 and usually simulated over five year periods from 1985–2010 and two 20–year periods to 2050.

2.3 The Aggregate Macroeconometric Models

The EGEM model is an econometric model of energy demand integrated with the GEM global macroeconometric model of the UK National Institute of Economic and Social Research and the London Business School (Boone et al., 1995; Mabey et al., 1997). The macroeconometric model treats each economy as a whole, with no sectoral differentiation. However, EGEM applies the historical proportion of energy-intensive industries in each economy to the forecast, in order to estimate changes in the sectoral grouping. The major OECD economies are modelled explicitly, supplemented by trade equations for six world areas. In the energy model aggregate energy use is estimated and then split into oil, coal and gas on the basis of fuel share equations. Within EGEM there is considerably more detail given to the nine major OECD economies than to the other regions (Africa, Latin America, South and Southeast Asia, China/LDCs, former Communist countries and OPEC).

The study by Horton et al. (1992) is also based on GEM, although complications in the application prevented full use of the model. Instead a number of simulations were run using the World Fuel Model which ensures energy balance in the full version of GEM. Documentation of the simulations is sketchy, but it appears that four regions were distinguished (OECD–North America, OECD–Europe, OECD–Pacific and ROW). In the aggregate scenario there is no sectoral disaggregation. However, in a further simulation a hypothetical imperfectly competitive industrial sector was distinguished.

2.4 The Disaggregated Macroeconometric Models

The most extensive applications of modelling to the carbon tax have been undertaken by Data Resources Incorporated (DRI). Only brief details of the DRI models are published, but the general methodology is clear. DRI have conducted two studies, one for the US and one for the EU. The US study (DRI/Charles River, 1994) was based on the DRI's integrated US macroeconomic and energy models. The economic model disaggregates industrial production by 60 sectors. The macroeconomic model generates relevant explanatory variables (for example industrial production, vehicle sales, fixed investment, and so on) for the energy model, which distinguishes between four fuels (coal, petroleum, natural gas and electricity). The EU study (DRI, 1992) was based on long–term forecasts generated by DRI's European national macroeconomic models, trade linkages across countries, and economy–industry–energy linkages within the national economies. The results are obtained by solving the suite of models repeatedly. All of the then twelve EU economies were included in the study. The level of sectoral disaggregation is quite high, distinguishing 20 industrial sectors and four fuels in the energy sector (solid fuels, oil, gas and electricity).

The HERMES model is actually a set of interlinked European neo–Keynesian macroeconomic models. For the analysis of environmental policies a version involving detailed models of the four major European economies (West Germany, France, Italy and the UK) is employed (Standaert, 1992). Trade linkages are modelled between the four, with the rest of the EU, and with the rest of the world. Nine sectors are distinguished, with a single aggregate energy sector. The HERMES model has also been used in conjunction with the MIDAS energy model to improve the analysis of energy supply through detailed treatment of electricity generating station load curves, plant utilisation, and scheduling of new investment (Karadeloglou, 1992).

MDM (Barker and Peterson, 1987) is a dynamic input–output macroeconometric model of the UK economy which has been developed into an integrated environment–energy–economy (E3) model. There are trade linkages with 26 regions of the world, all 15 EU economies, Switzerland, Norway, the US, Japan, other OECD, OPEC, Eastern Europe, Former Soviet Union, China, NICs and ROW. Production is disaggregated to a much finer degree than in the global models, with 49 sectors in total. There are five energy sectors: two for extraction (coal and oil/gas), two for supply (gas and electricity) and oil refining. The fine level of detail in manufacturing, services and the public sector is a distinguishing feature. The energy–environment submodel disaggregates 12 fuel–using sectors, 10 energy carriers and 10 air emissions (Barker, Baylis and Bryden, 1994; Barker, 1995a, 1995b).

The OPEC World Energy Model (OWEM) is a large–scale integrated econometric model estimated on annual data over 1973-92 with five modules (Walker and Birol, 1992). In addition to a Keynesian macroeconometric module, there are four separate modules for energy demand, energy supply, energy pricing and the environment. The model includes five energy users (industry, household/commercial, transport, electricity and marine bunkers) and four energy carriers (oil and other liquids, solid fuels, gas and electricity). Geographically the model is split into North America, Western Europe, OECD–Pacific, OPEC, oil exporting LDCs, oil importing LDCs, NICs and formerly centrally planned economies. It includes a detailed treatment of substitution between fuels by the fuel users in the OECD areas.

3 ESTIMATES OF COMPETITIVENESS EFFECTS AND LEAKAGE RATES

3.1 Introduction

Before proceeding to a discussion of the results generated by the studies listed in Table 4.2 it is worth emphasising that such results are not directly comparable. In addition to differences in the size of the coalition which imposes the emissions constraint and the stringency of the constraint, the models also differ in terms of their basic framework and a variety of further assumptions. Particular factors such as the extent of factor mobility, the means of exchange rate determination, the magnitude of trade elasticities, the means by which revenue is recycled, the treatment of the international oil market, and a number of other factors will affect

Table 4.2 Summary of Studies

Model	Studies	Target	Instrument
CRTM–1	Perroni & Rutherford (1993)	Toronto Toronto: only OECD	Carbon tax
Whalley –Wigle	Pezzey(1992a)	20–50% EU cut 20–50% in OECD–E & OECD–P 20–50% in OECD	Carbon tax
12RT	Manne & Olivera– Martins (1994)	FCCC target: Combinations of OECD, FSU & CEECs	Carbon tax
CRTM–2	Manne & Rutherford (1994) Felder & Rutherford (1993) Rutherford (1992)	Toronto target OECD reductions of 1-4% pa OECD reductions of 2-5% pa	Carbon tax Carbon tax Carbon tax
GREEN	Olivera–Martins (1995) Manne & Olivera– Martins (1995) Burniaux et al (1992a) Olivera–Martins et al (1992)	EU stabilisation FCCC target OECD stabilisation FCCC target: combinations of Japan, EU, NA, OOECD, OECD	Carbon tax Carbon tax Carbon tax &Energy tax Carbon tax
LEAN	Welsch & Hoster (1994)	Not specified	EU Carbon /Energy tax
EGEM	Smith (1994)	FCCC target: combinations of OECD, EU, NA, Japan	Carbon/ Energy tax
NERA/ GEM	Horton et al (1992)	FCCC: only OECD Toronto target	Carbon tax, Energy tax
DRI–1	DRI (1992)	N/S, but applies to the EU	Carbon/ Energy tax
DRI–2	DRI (1994)	N/S, but applies to the US	Carbon tax
HERMES	Karadeloglou (1992) Standeart (1992)	N/S N/S	Carbon tax, Energy tax Carbon tax
MDM–E3	Barker (1995a) Barker (1995b) Barker, Baylis & Bryden (1994)	FCCC target: UK FCCC target: UK FCCC target: UK	VAT on Domestic Fuels,Petrol Duty Escalator Carbon/ Energy tax
OWEM	Walker & Birol (1994)	FCCC: only OECD	Carbon tax

Notes: The Framework Convention against Climate Change (FCCC) target is return of emissions
             to 1990 levels by 2000 for OECD, FSU and CEECs.
             The Toronto target is 80% of 1988 emissions by 2005 for OECD and 150% for ROW.
             The acronyms are given in the boxed text below Table 4.1 above.
Sources: See the list of references.

Table 4.3 Summary of model assumptions

Study	Trade	Factor Mobility	Oil Market	Expectations	Adjustment	Revenue
CRTM–1	H–O		PC		Putty/Clay	Lump-sum
Whalley–Wigle	H–O		PC[1]			
12RT	H–O		PC	Perfect foresight	Putty/Clay	
CRTM–2	H–O	Mobile/ Immobile[1]	PC[1]	Perfect foresight	Putty/Clay	Lump-sum
GREEN	Armington	Mobile[1]	PC	Myopic	Putty/ Semi-clay	Income tax
EGEM	Est'd		TMS	Rational Expectations	ECM	Various[1]
DRI	Est'd	Mobile	Fixed	Adaptive		Various[1]
HERMES	Est'd	Mobile	Fixed	Adaptive	Putty/Clay	
MDM-E3	Est'd	Implicitly Mobile	Fixed	Primarily adaptive	ECM	Various[1]
OWEM	Est'd		Fixed	Adaptive		Indirect and direct taxes

Notes: 1. See text
              H-O Heckscher - Ohlin, PC Perfect Competition, TMS Target Market Share,
              Fixed Fixed Price, ECM Error Correction Model

Sources: See the list of references.

the estimates significantly (see Table 4.3). These effects, and many others, are discussed in Section 4 below. For these reasons the estimates cited, although illuminating, are not strictly comparable. Because of significant differences in methodology, assumptions and even policy scenarios the results can not be generalised in a satisfactory manner.

3.2 Competitiveness effects

The competitiveness effects of unilateral (or regional but non–global) abatement strategies have often been used as arguments to discourage unilateral efforts to address the problem of global warming. For example, it is argued that the imposition of a tax rate sufficient to reduce domestic emissions significantly will result in significant price increases relative to firms in non–constrained economies, resulting in a loss of price competitiveness and market share. Estimating competitiveness effects of a carbon or energy tax is, however, difficult not only in methodological terms, but also in more straightforward conceptual terms. On one hand it is important to distinguish between short run and long run changes in competitiveness. In the short run a number of factors such as exchange rate fluctuations can influence national competitiveness. However, in the long run, other factors such as innovation, R&D spending and changes in labour productivity are more important. On the other hand, it is worthwhile distinguishing between national and sectoral competitiveness. Changes in the fiscal regime (taxes and expenditures) which affect particular sectors adversely may also benefit other sectors, changing sectoral competitiveness significantly but leaving national competitiveness unchanged.

Competitiveness effects from the static general equilibrium studies

Using the static CRTM model Perroni and Rutherford (1993) simulate the effects of a tax sufficient to reduce OECD emissions by 20 per cent relative to 1990 levels. According to their estimates basic materials production (steel, plastics, chemicals and glass) in the US falls by 10.1 per cent relative to the base case in 2020 (this is a 0.4pp fall in the average annual growth rate). Production in other OECD countries falls by a smaller 7.4 per cent (0.3pp pa), while production in former Soviet Bloc countries rises by 5.5 per cent (0.2pp pa), in China by 4.6 per cent (0.2pp pa) and in ROW by 5.2 per cent (0.2pp pa) (see Table 7 in the study).

Pezzey (1991 and 1992a) uses the Whalley–Wigle model to examine the effects of the imposition of a tax sufficient to reduce CO_2 emissions in the EU and the OECD by 20 per cent relative to 1990 levels. Results are reported for 2100. In the EU case the overall terms of trade increase by 1.9 per cent relative to the base case (0.02pp pa) and production of energy-intensive goods falls by 8.1 per cent (0.07pp pa) relative to world production (see Table 2 in Pezzey, 1992a). In the OECD case the terms of trade increase by 8.5 per cent (0.07pp pa) and relative energy–intensive production falls by 5.4 per cent (0.05pp pa). A 50 per cent cut in EU emissions increases the terms of trade by 4.9 per cent (0.04pp pa) and energy–intensive sector production decreases by 23.6 per cent (0.19pp pa) relative to world production. Interestingly, in a study conducted by Whalley and Wigle (1991) they find that a **global** 50 per cent cut in emissions results in some trade pattern reversal for energy-intensive industries. With the 50 per cent cut in emissions, the EU and Japan change from net exporters to net importers of energy-intensive products, while the oil exporting countries change from importers to exporters, ie this implies major relocation of these industries from OECD to OPEC countries.

Competitiveness effects from the dynamic general equilibrium studies

None of the studies using the CTRM dynamic models report results on the competitiveness of international trade or the investment effects of carbon or energy taxes.

Using GREEN Oliveira–Martins et al. (1992) simulate the effects of stabilising

CO_2 emissions for subsets of OECD countries at 1990 levels through to 2050. When the US does so unilaterally, production of energy–intensive industries (pulp and paper, chemicals, iron and steel and non–ferrous metals) is on average 1.2 per cent below base case production over the period 1990–2050 (see Table 4 in the study). This implies that the annual growth in production is 0.02pp below that in the base case. The equivalent figure for Japan is 3.8 per cent (0.06pp pa), for the EU it is 2.4 per cent (0.04pp pa) and for other OECD it is 4.2 per cent (0.07pp pa). When the entire OECD stabilises emissions with a flat rate tax, production falls by 0.4 per cent (0.01pp pa) below the base case growth rate) in the US, 3.3 per cent (0.05pp pa) in Japan, 1.7 per cent (0.03pp pa in the EU and 1.6 per cent (0.03pp pa) in other OECD countries. Production rises by 1.0 per cent (0.02pp pa) above the base case growth) in former Soviet Union and eastern European economies, 0.5 per cent (0.01pp pa) in energy exporting LDCs, 0.3 per cent (0.01pp pa) in China and India and 1.5 per cent (0.02pp pa) in other LDCs. Simulating the EC carbon/energy tax Nicoletti and Oliveira–Martins (1992) find that production falls by an average of 3.5 per cent over the period 1990–2050 (0.06pp below the base case annual growth rate) in the energy–intensive industries in the EU (see Table 3 in the study). Production increases by 1.1 per cent (0.02pp pa) in other OECD and 1.4 per cent (0.02pp pa) in ROW. Production in the non–energy intensive sectors also falls in the EU, but only by 0.4 per cent (0.01pp pa).

Competitiveness effects from the disaggregated macroeconometric studies
The DRI (1992) study for Europe examined the effects of the introduction of the $10/boe EC carbon/energy tax. Detailed sectoral results are reported. In the case of the ores and metals sector the rate of growth in exports between 1992 and 2005 falls by 0.28pp from a base growth rate of 5.15 per cent pa (see Table 6.4 in the study). The growth in imports rose by 0.03pp from base growth of 5.39 per cent pa. Export growth of metal products fell by 0.02pp from 4.18 per cent pa, while imports rose by 0.12pp from 4.29 per cent pa (see Table 6.7 in the study). The rate of growth in exports of chemicals fell by 0.19pp from 5.65 per cent pa while the import growth rate fell by 0.05pp from 5.66 per cent pa (see Table 6.13 in the study).

The DRI (1994) study for the US examined the effects of a $100/ton ($8.79/boe in 1993 prices) carbon tax phased in over the period 1995–2000 on the US economy. They found that exports fell by 2.9 per cent (0.19pp pa) and imports fell by 1.9 per cent (0.13pp pa), resulting in an improvement of approximately $10bn (1993 prices) in the trade balance by 2010 (see Table 4–13 in the study). The only aggregate sector which suffers a deterioration in the trade balance relative to the base case is the consumer goods sector (see Table 7–5 in the study). The non-energy sectors which are most affected by the tax in terms of price effects are hydraulic cement (16.9 per cent higher relative to the base case in 2000), primary aluminium (10.9 per cent), state and local government enterprises (9.8 per cent), primary ferrous metals (8.5 per cent), iron ore (7.9 per cent) and paperboard mills (6.0 per cent) (see Table 3–4 in the study).

In an application of the HERMES model the effects of the imposition of the European Community carbon/energy tax is examined under two different revenue recycling scenarios (Standaert, 1992). Using the scenario whereby direct taxes are reduced, exports of consumer goods from the EU fall by 1.6 per cent relative to the base case in 2005. This represents a 0.13pp pa fall in export growth from 1993, when the tax is assumed to be introduced. Imports rise by 1.3 per cent (0.11pp pa). The results for equipment goods are –1.2 per cent (–0.10pp pa) and 1.5 per cent (0.12pp pa), and for intermediate goods –1.4 per cent (–0.11pp pa) and 1.1 per cent (0.09pp pa) (see Table 3/2 in the study). The results for the UK are –2.5 per cent (–0.21pp pa) and nil for consumer goods, –2.3 per cent (–0.19pp pa) and 1.1 per cent (0.09pp pa) for equipment goods and –2.2 per cent (–0.18pp pa) and –0.4 per cent (0.03pp pa) for intermediate goods (see Table A 4.C in the study). Overall the results improve when social security payments are reduced, the significance of which is discussed below. Using the integrated HERMES–MIDAS model Karadeloglou (1992) examines the effects of a carbon tax equivalent to $10/boe and an energy tax (value based) of equivalent magnitude initially, but with a 5 per cent annual escalator. In three of the four countries the current account improves, with Germany being the exception (see Table 4/2 in the study). The study finds that the difference between the carbon and energy taxes is small, presumably because most energy users have equipment which can only use one specific type of energy. Even in the longer term, it is only in electricity generation, where renewable, gas or nuclear alternatives are available, that large-scale substitution is feasible, so that a carbon tax would have larger effects than an energy tax.

A number of studies of the UK economy have been conducted using MDM–E3. The Cambridge Econometrics study (1991) of the EC tax also includes the proposed exemptions of energy-intensive industries, which have the effect of increasing their price competitiveness, so this study has not been considered further. Barker (1995a) uses MDM–E3 to examine the effects of a number of policies, including the imposition of a road fuel duty escalator at 5 per cent and 17.6 per cent and the EC carbon/energy tax (imposed only in the UK).[1] In the case of the 17.6 per cent escalator the balance of payments improves from 3.9 per cent of GDP in the base case in 2005 to 4.3 per cent. In the case of the carbon/energy tax scenario the balance of payments deteriorates to 3.7 per cent (see Table 3). Nearly all sectors improve their price competitiveness as a result of the reduction in employers' taxes. However, in the carbon/energy tax scenario, industrial costs for the most energy-intensive manufactures increase by 1.6 per cent for chemicals, 2.6 per cent for basic metals, 1.8 per cent for non-metallic mineral products (see Table 5). In a similar set of scenarios Barker, Baylis and

Bryden (1994) find that the effect of the imposition of both the VAT on domestic fuels and the petrol duty escalator is a deterioration in the balance of payments as a percentage of GDP by 0.2pp relative to the base case in 2000. The EC carbon/energy tax also reduces the balance of payments by 0.2pp (see Table 4 in the study).

Other estimated competitiveness effects
In addition to the models with the more detailed results some other more studies have also been conducted which do not report details explicitly. Using their LEAN general equilibrium model of the EC, Welsch and Hoster (1995) conducted a study of the effects of the imposition of the imposition of the EC carbon/energy tax and the imposition of an energy tax of equivalent magnitude on Germany. They find that the balance of payments improves in both cases, with imports falling further than exports. Another study of the German economy was conducted by DIW (1994). Using an aggregated business cycle model of the west German economy they find few competitiveness effects when an annual tax increase of 7 per cent (real terms) is imposed on energy.

3.3 Leakage Rates

Carbon leakages reflect the effects of unilateral (or regional but non–global) policies to reduce greenhouse gas emissions on emissions from countries which do not restrict their own emissions. The carbon leakage rate can be defined as the ratio of the difference between emissions from the rest of the world in the policy scenario and the base scenario over the difference between emissions in the regulating coalition in the policy scenario and the base scenario:

$$L_i = \frac{C_{w,p} - C_{w,b}}{C_{i,p} - C_{i,b}} * 100$$

where   L = the leakage rate, expressed in per cent
C = carbon emissions
I = the country/trading bloc
w = the rest of the world
p = the policy scenario
b = the base scenario.

If the rate is greater than 100, then the effects of the policy are environmentally perverse, increasing global emissions. If the rate is less than zero then the effect of the policy is to reduce emissions elsewhere, reinforcing its beneficial environmental effects. And if the rate is between zero and 100 then some, but not

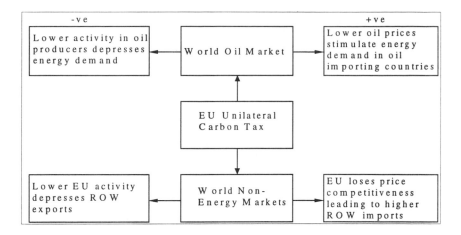

Source: Cambridge Econometrics

Figure 4.2 Channels for Leakage

all, of the effects of reduced emissions are negated by increased emissions elsewhere.

As shown in Figure 4.2, leakages take place through two principal channels: the relocation of trade in manufactures and the substitution effects arising from a fall in oil prices. When a set of countries restricts emissions by imposing taxes (or instituting an emission permit regime) this increases the relative cost of carbon–intensive production, potentially shifting the comparative advantage of non–constrained economies toward the production of those goods which tend to be carbon–intensive, thus increasing emissions by changing the composition of world output **across** sectors. Similarly, the constraint will also reduce the demand for oil, potentially lowering the world pre–tax price depending on the response of suppliers. Depending on fuel substitutability in individual economies this may increase the carbon intensity of production processes **within** individual sectors. There may, therefore, be increased emissions due to both sectoral composition and sectoral production processes. To some extent, these two may be counter-balanced by income effects if the effect of the demand reduction implied by the carbon constraint reduces emissions from oil exporters, and if the coalition which imposes the tax experiences a significant fall in income and its imports from the rest of the world are relatively income elastic.

Intuitively, leakage rates for a given policy constraint should decrease with the size, expressed in terms of energy consumption, of the regulating coalition. There are two reasons for this. On the one hand, there are fewer 'free riders' able to exploit a given change in relative prices of fuels and manufactured goods. On the

Table 4.4 Summary of estimated leakage rates

Model	Study	Coalition	Constraint	% leakage min	max
CRTM–1	Perroni & Rutherford (1993)	OECD	80% of 1990	NS	7
Whalley–Wigle	Pezzey (1992a)	EU	80% of 1990	NS	80
		OECD	80% of 1990	NS	70
12RT	Manne & Oliveira–Martins (1994)	ANNEX-1	return to 1990 levels	10	35
		ANNEX-1	return to 1990 levels[2]	7	30
CRTM–2	Manne & Rutherford (1994)	OECD	80% of 1990	7	35
	Felder & Rutherford (1993)	OECD	2% pa cuts	NS	35
	Rutherford (1992)	OECD	3% pa cuts	-45	30
GREEN	Oliveira–Martins (1995)	EC	return to 1990 levels	-2	6
	Manne & Oliveira–Martins (1994)	ANNEX-1	return to 1990 levels	-2	2
		ANNEX-1	return to 1990 levels[2]	0	3
	Oliveira–Martins et al. (1995)	EC	return to 1990 levels	2.2	11.9
		OECD	return to 1990 levels	-0.5	3.5
	Nicoletti & Oliveira–Martins (1992)	EC	C/E tax	0	11
EGEM	Smith (1994)	EC	C/E tax	12	30
		OECD	C/E tax	8	15
NERA/ GEM	Horton et al. (1992)	OECD	return to 1990 levels	NS	9
		OECD	80% of 1990	NS	17
		OECD	80% of 1990[2]	NS	22
OWEM	Walker & Birol (1992)	OECD	C/E tax	NS	-17
	OPEC (1996)	OECD	90% of 1990 by 2020	NS	-18

Notes: 1. Leakage rates are approximate.
                2. Uses either a uniform tax rate across regions or a tradeable permit system.
                NS - not stated or not relevant.

Sources: See the list of references.

other hand, since the demand shock will be relatively more severe with a larger coalition, relative prices will tend to change more significantly. Leakages should also increase as the constraint is made more stringent, that is the higher tax rates implied by a shift from the Rio targets to the Toronto targets. This also reveals the importance of distinguishing between average and marginal leakage rates. For instance, in order to include leakage rates in the determination of optimal policies by the regulating coalition marginal leakage rates, which may be considerably higher than average rates, must be subtracted from marginal emission rates in the coalition country.

Given these two points it is important to distinguish between the size of the coalition and the stringency of the constraint when discussing alternative estimates of leakage rates (see Table 4.4).

Leakage estimates from the static general equilibrium studies
The static CRTM–1 study (Perroni and Rutherford, 1993) simulates a 20 per cent cut in OECD emissions relative to 1990 levels by 2020. Leakage rates are less than 7 per cent (p.272 in the study). Estimating the leakage rate which arises strictly from trade in energy-intensive products it is found that rates are approximately 9 per cent for a 23 per cent cutback in global emissions (see Figure 6 in the study). This rises by approximately 8 per cent if the growth elasticity of basic materials production (the energy-intensive sectors) is increased from 0.6 to 0.8.

In Pezzey's study (1992a) 20 per cent cuts in EU emissions and OECD emissions by 2100 respectively are simulated using the Whalley–Wigle model. The results are considerably higher than those found in most other studies. In the EU case leakage rates are approximately 80 per cent, falling to 70 per cent when the larger OECD coalition introduces the tax (p.166 in the study). Horton et al. (1992) model a 1990 stabilisation scenario, using different regional configurations and policy scenarios. In the case where a non-uniform carbon tax is imposed leakage rates are 9 per cent (see Table 3.2 in the study). Although more efficient, the uniform tax scenario does not change the leakage rate. Leakage rates fall to 8 per cent (3 per cent for NA and 5 per cent for ROW) when North America is excluded. OECD emission reductions of 20 per cent relative to 1990 by 2005 are also modelled. In the non-uniform case leakages are 17 per cent, with a figure of 22 per cent for the non-uniform case. And finally, in a separate scenario which attempts to capture the effects of strategic behaviour on the part of firms much higher rates (100 per cent) are found, but this figure is more illustrative than predictive.

Leakage estimates from the dynamic general equilibrium studies
Using 12RT Manne (Manne and Oliveira-Martins, 1994) found that leakage rates were as high as 35 per cent when each of the individual Rio Convention Annex I countries (OECD, FSU and Eastern Europe) attempted to stabilise emissions at 1990 levels through 2050. Simulating a more efficient scenario by allocating emission permits within the Annex I grouping on the basis of 1990 emission levels reduced maximum leakage rates to 30 per cent (see Figure 19 in the study). Exceptionally, leakage rates rise throughout the simulation. The reasons for this will be discussed below. The most significant source geographically is China, with trade in manufactures being the most significant channel.

The various CRTM–2 studies find high leakage rates, close to those generated by 12RT. Assuming a 20 per cent cut in emissions in the OECD relative to 1990 levels leakage rates rise from less than 10 per cent in 2000 to almost 20 per cent in 2010, falling back to slightly more than 10 per cent in 2030 and then rising to almost 35 per cent in 2050 (see Figure 6 in Manne and Rutherford, 1994). A second study (Felder and Rutherford, 1993) modelled OECD cutbacks of 1 per cent to 4 per cent pa from 1990 levels. Marginal leakage rates for the 1 per cent scenario rise to approximately 50 per cent in 2030, and then fall. In the 2 per cent scenario average leakage rates peak at 35 per cent in 2030–40 and then decline, most of the leakages coming from ROW, with MOPEC and the FSU having negative rates for some periods (see Figure 8 in the study). A decomposition reveals that both channels of leakage are important (see Figure 11). In the third application of CRTM-2 (Rutherford, 1992) scenarios involving 3–5 per cent reductions in emissions are simulated. Similar leakage rates are estimated, with the marginal rate being almost 100 per cent for cutbacks greater than 3 per cent, implying that further reductions are counterproductive (p.22 in the study). The maximum leakage rate is 30 per cent in 2000 and the minimum is –45 per cent in 2070. Most leakage is driven by the oil market (see Figure 14).

Under a number of different scenarios GREEN consistently finds much lower levels of leakages. In one of the more recent studies Manne and Oliveira–Martins (1994) applied the same scenarios (and parameter assumptions) as 12RT and found that leakages were small (5 per cent) and sometimes negative. In a further paper reporting the use of GREEN to assess the effects of stabilising emissions in Annex I countries, Oliveira–Martins finds that leakage rates are virtually nil despite a large cut in Annex I country emissions. The negative leakages arise from income effects in oil exporting LDCs and fuel switching effects in China. In an earlier study Oliveira–Martins et al. (1992) present more detailed results for unilateral scenarios for Japan, the EU, the US and OOECD, as well as the OECD as a whole. The highest leakage rates for unilateral 1990 stabilisation regimes are 2.8 per cent for the US in 1995, 15.8 per cent for Japan in 1995, 11.9 per cent for the EU in 1995 and 8.4 per cent for other OECD in 2000. Rates decline significantly following the peak, becoming negative in the case of the US. The intra–OECD decomposition highlights the importance of intra–OECD trade in manufactures as a source. The estimate for the scenario for the OECD as whole reaches a peak of 3.5 per cent in 1995. In a modified scenario (Burniaux et al., 1992a) in which Japan stabilises at 1990 levels on a per capita basis while the rest of the OECD stabilises at gross emissions, leakage rates peak at 2.5 per cent in 2000, become negative in 2010 and then rise again to 1.5 per cent by 2050, with FSU being the biggest source of leakages. Another study (Nicoletti and Oliveira–Martins, 1992) modelling the effect of the proposed EC carbon/energy tax, leakage rates fall from 11 per cent in 1995 to negative rates by 2050. In the latest study, Oliveira–Martins (1995) has explored the carbon leakage results from GREEN in some detail in the context of assumed unilateral action by the EU to stabilise emissions using a carbon tax. In the base specification of the model, the net leakage is small, with a maximum of 6 per cent, with the rate declining throughout the period and becoming negative by 2030. However, sensitivity analysis of the effects of changing the model specifications show that it is possible to come up with high leakages, especially if the supply of fossil fuels is very inelastic (for example 40 per cent leakage if the oil–supply price elasticity of energy exporting LDCs is lowered from 3 to 0.5) or if a high elasticity of substitution is assumed between capital and energy (leakages peaking at 35 per cent when the long run elasticity is raised from 1 to 2).

Leakage estimates from an aggregate macroeconometric study
Relatively high leakage rates are also estimated by Smith (1994), when taxes equivalent to the proposed EC carbon/energy tax are simulated. In the case of Japan leakage rates peak at 80 per cent in the first year, falling and then rising again to 70 per cent just after 2000 and then falling to 10 per cent by 2030. Rates for the other countries are considerably lower. When the OECD as a whole imposes the tax, rates peak at just over 15 per cent in 2000 and fall steadily to just over 5 per cent by 2030. In a simulated decomposition of the OECD tax it is estimated that most of the leakage is a result of relocation of energy–intensive manufacturing, with the oil price effects and the OPEC income effects counterbalancing one another.

Leakage estimates from a disaggregate macroeonometric study
The study using OPEC's world energy model (Walker and Birol, 1992) examined the effects of introducing an OECD carbon tax, phased in between 1993 and 2000, such that it is sufficient to stabilise 2000 emissions at 1990 levels. They estimated that emissions in the non–OECD countries decreased from 5.0bn tonnes of carbon (tC) in the base case in 2010 to 4.8bn tC in the stabilisation scenario (see Table 4 in the study). In the OECD emissions fell from 3.5 to 2.3. This yields a leakage rate of –17 per cent, indicating that the income effect outweighs the combined oil price and manufactures trade effects. This leakage rate is confirmed in a later study using the same model but with an OECD carbon tax sufficient to reduce OECD emissions by 10 per cent below 1990 levels by 2020 (OPEC, 1996).

4 THE DETERMINANTS OF COMPETITIVENESS EFFECTS AND CARBON LEAKAGES

4.1 Introduction

As noted above the estimates of the competitiveness and leakage effects cited are not strictly comparable due to the importance of model assumptions and structure. Given this qualification it is vital to analyse the effects of such assumptions in detail. This will cast light on the reliability of the estimates and the likely direction of error in the individual studies.

4.2 Modelling Framework

Before proceeding to a discussion of some of the effects on leakages and competitiveness of the more specific assumptions made in the studies, it is worth looking at the more fundamental effects which arise out of the modelling frameworks themselves. In the survey above the distinction between static and dynamic general equilibrium models, and aggregate and disaggregate macroeconometric models was drawn. In this section it is the distinction between the first two and the latter two which is made.

General Equilibrium Models (GEM) have dominated the early literature on quantitative assessments of US and global CO_2 and other GHG abatement (Boero et al., 1991). The basic assumptions of such models are constant returns to scale, perfect competition in most if not all sectors (sometimes even in the world oil market), welfare maximisation by representative consumers and full employment. All the models exclude the primary and secondary benefits from the reductions of the costs of externalities, most notably those of global warming, from the welfare maximisation. This is often done implicitly because these benefits are so uncertain, but clearly the projection of the world economy over periods of 40 to 100 years on the basis of one year's data is itself fraught with uncertainties. The models, even if dynamic, are usually calibrated on one set of observations in a base year. The parameters which drive the models are imposed on the basis of literature searches, the requirements of functional forms, or frequently the intuition of the modellers. Jorgenson and Wilcoxen (1993) is a notable exception in that the general equilibrium approach is combined with econometric estimation of the main sets of relationships.

In such analyses CO_2 emissions arise as a consequence of the inclusion of fossil-fuel energy carriers as factors of production in aggregate (or disaggregated) production functions. Thus CO_2 emissions per unit of output depend crucially upon the degree of substitutability between energy and other factors of production and between fuels of different carbon-intensity within the energy bundle. With

suitable   supplementary   functions   (such   as   those   for   capital
accumulation/depreciation and consumer utility) as well as other exogenous
assumptions (such as those for population growth and the rate of social time
preference), the models can be run under different scenarios such that consumer
utility is maximised subject to the economic constraints implied by the production
functions and any policy constraints such as those associated with carbon
abatement.

For the most part such analyses have tended to find that the economic costs
associated with attempts to abate emissions of greenhouse gases are negative and
often considerable. For reviews see Boero et al. (1991), Cline (1992) and Ekins
(1995). To some extent, however, the negative results arise by definition. Given
the model structure, the carbon tax is introduced as a constraint on an economy
which is presently operating efficiently and at full employment. Any change,
other than changes in the values of some of the exogenous parameters, would
generate negative costs.[2] In effect the competitive losses estimated by GEM
models (GREEN, CRTM, 12RT, Whalley–Wigle) are merely incidental
manifestations of more fundamental characteristics of the models themselves.

Macroeconometric models come from quite a different tradition. For instance,
unemployment need not be assumed as voluntary, the economy need not be
assumed to be in a state of equilibrium, and firm and household behaviour need
not be assumed as optimal. The parameters which drive the models are typically
estimated on the basis of time series historical data using formal methods of
statistical inference and are not calibrated on a single year. On the demand side,
prices do not play the fundamental equilibrating role that they do in GEM models.
On the supply side the use of input–output techniques captures the importance of
production processes. CO_2 emissions arise out of the estimation of energy
consumption and the fuel mix. Usually output functions are estimated, either at
an aggregate or disaggregate level. Energy consumption within the sector is
determined on the basis of output and other relevant variables such as air
temperature and relative prices. The total demand for energy is divided between
electricity, coal, oil products and gas by means of a set of share equations. In
general the results indicate that the costs associated with attempts to abate carbon
dioxide emissions are considerably less than is implied by growth models and
general equilibrium models.

Such a modelling framework has its drawbacks. Welfare can not be estimated
directly, but can only be imputed from consumption, GDP or other activity
variables. The amount of data required usually restricts the scope of the models,
with global models tending to operate at an aggregate sectoral level and
disaggregated sectoral models tending to be restricted in geographical scope. The
nature of estimation can limit the relevant time-frame of the analyses to the short
run and medium run. And the use of fixed input–output coefficients restricts
potential substitutability.

In conclusion, for the analysis of competitiveness effects it is important to distinguish between the purposes for which the two types of models tend to be constructed. GEM models have dominated the field because the emphasis has been on developing models which are able to determine the *optimal* level of abatement in the very long run. The costs of reduction are estimated and compared with the likely benefits. Nordhaus (1993) even includes damage costs, and thus reduction benefits, directly in the model. Competitiveness issues are, however, short–run and medium–run phenomena which arise from the precise means by which a policy is introduced. The long–run nature of the problem of global warming is to a great extent irrelevant to the determination of competitiveness effects. A model which attempts to capture how the economy *actually* behaves may be more suitable than one which projects the economy over a century or more.

4.3 Price Elasticities of Trade in Manufactures

One of the most important factors behind the reported competitiveness and leakage effects is the assumed or estimated price elasticities of trade, usually those of energy–intensive manufactured goods. Most of the models discussed distinguish between energy-intensive manufactures and other manufactures and this distinction will be maintained by concentrating on the former in the following discussion. However, it should be emphasised that **all** price elasticities of trade, including those of trade in services and agriculture, are relevant to a full analysis. This is particularly important since those sectors which are energy–intensive may not be particularly tradeable, while those with high price elasticities of trade may not be energy-intensive. Figure 4.3 shows the trade intensity and energy intensity of UK industrial sectors in 1992.

In the general equilibrium models discussed, one of two assumptions is usually made. On one hand some models apply Heckscher–Ohlin methodology, treating domestic and foreign goods as perfect substitutes, thus implying price elasticities which approach infinity. Assuming zero transport costs this could result in complete specialisation following the imposition of a carbon tax, thus generating significant competitiveness effects and leakage rates.[3] The assumption of perfect substitutability is particularly unsatisfactory if the level of aggregation is significant, since it implies that goods and services within very broad industrial classes are indistinguishable irrespective of their origin (for example if manufacturing is the class adopted, motor vehicles are assumed to be perfect substitutes for shoes).

The Heckscher–Ohlin assumptions are employed in 12RT, CRTM, and Whalley–Wigle. However in the case of 12RT a quadratic penalty function is associated with deviations from base year trade patterns in energy–intensive manufactures (p.7 in Manne and Oliveira–Martins, 1994). Effectively this means that rapid adjustments in trade patterns are limited. This might reflect the effects of capacity constraints or capital adjustment. However, the consistency of this penalty function with the treatment of the aggregate non–energy production function is not clear. The dynamic CRTM studies do not discuss the treatment of trade beyond specifying that oil, basic materials, and non–basic manufactures are all tradeables. However, in the static model study, the authors do specify that all three are considered homogeneous, implying Heckscher–Ohlin assumptions (p.260 in Perroni and Rutherford, 1993). Whalley and Wigle also apply unrestricted Heckscher–Ohlin assumptions for trade in carbon energy, energy–intensive goods and non–energy–intensive goods (p.248 in Whalley and Wigle, 1991).

In the other general equilibrium models which have addressed the issues of competitiveness and leakages, the so–called Armington assumptions have been applied, implying finite price elasticities explicitly rather than implicitly through other types of restriction (Armington, 1969). This implies that the characteristics of goods vary by place of origin. This might reflect a number of factors such as product differentiation, qualitative characteristics and other non–price trade determination (Linder, 1961; Grubel and Lloyd, 1975; Barker, 1977), and helps to explain real-world phenomena such as intra-industry trade and international commodity price differences. With respect to competitiveness issues and leakage rates, the finite price elasticities will reduce the adverse economic and environmental effects of unilateral or regional abatement since the abating

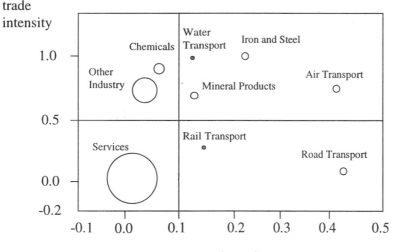

Figure 4.3 Trade intensity against energy intensity of industrial output in the UK, 1992

country is insulated to some extent from the trade effects of cost increases.

Although Armington assumptions are common in general equilibrium modelling, of the studies discussed in this chapter only those using GREEN employ them. GREEN has finite price elasticities for all goods except crude oil (Burniaux et al., 1992b), and in the central case the price elasticities of trade for manufactured goods are assumed to range between 2 and 3 (Oliveira–Martins et al., 1992). In Burniaux et al. (1992c) the figure is 3 for both energy-intensive manufactures and other goods (see Table 3 in the study). With their empirical basis, the aggregate (EGEM) and disaggregate (DRI, MDM–E3) macroeconometric models would necessarily employ finite price elasticities of trade. In the case of DRI (1994), price elasticities of demand for imports range from –0.42 to –1.70, while price elasticities of demand for exports range from –0.24 to –2.12 (see Table 7–1 in the study). Interestingly, and significantly, the energy–intensive sectors are not particularly elastic.

Comparison of the effects of alternative assumptions for the price elasticity of trade on estimates of leakage rates and competitive dislocation is complicated by the existence of more general differences in methodologies and assumptions employed in the models. Fortunately, a comparison of 12RT (Heckscher–Ohlin) and GREEN (Armington) was undertaken by Manne and Oliveira–Martins (1994) which casts light on this question. In their simulation of the imposition of unilateral OECD carbon emission stabilisation leakage rates are much higher when using 12RT than with GREEN, with most of the 12RT leakage attributable to trade in energy–intensive manufactures, while this source is relatively small with GREEN (see Figures 19–21 in the study). In a separate study using GREEN it was found that tripling trade elasticities in the non-energy sectors increased the leakage rate from 2.4 per cent to 6.8 per cent (p.136 in Oliveira-Martins et al., 1992). Felder and Rutherford (1993) use CRTM–2 to analyse the change in leakage effects when trade in the energy–intensive sectors is held constant (that is price elasticities of trade are small) and find that leakages decrease significantly (see Figure 11 in the study). Rutherford (1992) finds similar results (see Figure 14 in the study) but leakage becomes less important toward the end of the simulation period.

Surprisingly, using macroeconomic methodology Smith (1994) finds that leakage rates are primarily a function of the relocation of energy–intensive sectors rather than oil market effects (see Figure 2 in the study). However this is almost certainly attributable to the means of estimation, since a 'relocation elasticity' is assumed; decreases in emissions from OECD energy–intensive sectors are estimated on the basis of lagged emissions and the oil price. Equivalent increases are attributed directly to non–OECD countries, rather than being estimated on the basis of changes in industrial production. Unfortunately, neither the DRI model nor MDM has been estimated using alternative values for price elasticities of trade in energy–intensive goods.

The experiments using GREEN lead to the second conclusion of this study. If the model builders assume that price elasticities of substitution between domestic and foreign energy-intensive manufactures are high, they will find high estimates of competitive losses and leakage. However, this assumption is made without any supporting evidence; those studies which draw on the econometric evidence find that these elasticities are low and the competitiveness and leakage effects are small.

4.4 Exchange Rate

The effect of the treatment of the exchange rate is of fundamental importance to the analysis of competitiveness and leakage. In the event that the exchange rate is assumed to be fixed, the cost effects of a carbon constraint will be borne domestically by the carbon-intensive sectors with higher domestic prices fully reflected in a loss of their price competitiveness; depending on the method used to recycle the revenues, this loss may be compensated by a gain in price competitiveness of other sectors, for example labour-intensive sectors if taxes on employment are lowered. However, if the exchange rate is flexible then competitiveness effects may be exacerbated or diminished, depending on the methodology employed or assumptions imposed. In the event that the nominal exchange rate adjusts fully in the projection to reflect the change in relative prices, then the effects of the tax on competitiveness will be obviated. In all likelihood the outcome will be partial adjustment with other factors (for example interest rate differentials and capital flows) partially mitigating exchange rate adjustment. This will, however, depend upon the response of the monetary authorities.

The assumption of fixed exchange rates employed by many of the models discussed is valid, particularly if the country which is imposing the tax is part of a currency bloc (for example the ERM) and small in economic importance. However, if a significant number of economically powerful countries or trading blocs impose the constraint (for example the EU or the OECD) it is unrealistic to assume that the exchange rate will not respond if a significant fiscal reform, such as that associated with a carbon tax, is imposed. This would also be true of models of small economies which have flexible exchange rates.

The treatment of the exchange rate in macroeconometric models is generally more sophisticated than in general equilibrium models, but the treatment depends upon the scenario. In the case of the DRI (1994) study conducted for the US the exchange rate is treated as endogenous, a necessary assumption considering the importance of the US economy in trade flows. Following the imposition of the $100/ton ($8.79/boe) carbon tax the **nominal** exchange rate falls relative to the base case. However, the fall in the dollar does not fully reflect the change in relative prices since real interest rates rise, pushing up the exchange rate. The *real* exchange rate rises are 0.4 per cent in 2000 and 1.8 per cent in 2010, making exports less competitive than they would be with full adjustment, but more competitive than if the exchange rate is assumed fixed (see pages 4–22 and 4–23 in the study). Amongst the other macroeconometric models both MDM and HERMES use fixed exchange rates, while LEAN uses a flexible exchange rate.

In conclusion, if exchange rates are allowed to adjust, any overall loss of price competitiveness brought about by a carbon tax will be partially compensated by exchange rate movements. Studies which have found large changes in competitiveness have generally adopted a simplistic or inappropriate treatment of exchange rates.

4.5 Factor Mobility

The treatment of factor mobility is, like the treatment of the foreign exchange rate, rather straightforward in terms of its effects on competitiveness and leakages, but also profoundly important. In the pure theory of international trade factor immobility is assumed. Trade in goods is, in effect, a substitute for trade in factors of production. If however, factors of production are internationally mobile, leakage rates and competitiveness effects may increase. This is because the flow of factors from one country to another following the imposition of a measure which reduces factor productivity will raise the degree of international economic specialisation. In the case of a carbon tax, factor mobility allows the comparative advantage of countries which do not impose the tax to be reflected in sectoral composition and production processes to a greater extent than when factor immobility is assumed.

For the most part the models discussed tend to assume that labour is immobile and capital is either mobile or immobile. In the event that capital is perfectly immobile across countries the only means by which competitiveness effects will be felt is through commodity trade flows. However, in the event that capital is perfectly mobile, competitiveness can also be reflected in investment flows, potentially amplifying the effects.

However, in order to determine the full consequences of capital mobility in the models it is also important to examine the treatment of rates of return on investment. Whereas some models assume equal rates of return globally and use the interest rate to equilibrate savings and investment, other models allow for international differences in the real rate of return. In the former case capital flows will almost certainly be more significant than in the latter case. Therefore, if capital is mobile across countries and rates of return are equalised internationally through financial markets, competitiveness effects will be greater than if either of these two assumptions are violated.

The treatment of capital mobility in GREEN requires careful examination. The supply of capital in a given year is exogenous and determined by household savings, while rates of return are endogenous (p.7 in Manne and Oliveira–Martins, 1994). This capital is assumed to be internationally immobile (p.6 in Nicoletti and Oliveira–Martins, 1992). Net capital flows between regions are exogenous, being derived in the calibration of the model from current account imbalances in the benchmark year which are assumed to remain constant in nominal terms, thus to fall in real terms throughout the simulation period (p.12 in Burniaux et al., 1992b). In effect capital flows are merely the mirror image of current account deficits. This treatment may underestimate competitiveness and leakage effects (see footnote 5 in Oliveira–Martins et al., 1992).

In one of the CRTM studies capital is assumed to be strictly immobile across regions (p.165 in Felder and Rutherford, 1993). However, in a later study capital is assumed to be fully mobile (p.61 in Manne and Rutherford, 1994). Although this should result in quite different results the relative importance of the change is mitigated by the fact that rates of return are assumed to be approximately equal across regions.

The only other studies which explicitly mention the question of factor mobility are those conducted by the DRI (1994), Barker and Lewney (1991), and Horton et al. (1992). Indeed in the US study capital flows are the primary determinants of changes in the foreign exchange rate following the imposition of a carbon tax, significantly affecting commodity trade flows. Although capital flows are not given, in the scenario in which a $100/ton ($8.79/boe) carbon tax is imposed short-term rates rise by 118 basis points and long-term rates by 51 basis points by 2010 (Table 4–21 in DRI, 1994). In the first study of the carbon tax using MDM (Barker and Lewney, 1991) it is explicitly assumed that production would not move abroad following the increases in prices brought about by the tax, except in as much as the estimated price elasticities of trade allow for such movements in response to similar relative price changes in the data. The assumption of immobility of capital is justified if the risks of political instability or potential increases in trade barriers are high, as they may well be between the trading blocs distinguished in many of the models. The treatment of capital mobility in Horton et al. (1992) allows for scale economies and strategic behaviour (see Section 4.12 below).

The conclusion on the effects of the assumptions of capital mobility is that the loss of sectoral competitiveness brought about by a high unilateral carbon tax in one country within a trading bloc could lead to substantial relocation of industries within the bloc, justifying the concerns of particular industries. However, the estimates of high carbon leakage brought about by relocation of industries between one world trading bloc, such as the EU or the OECD, and another appear exaggerated and unlikely given the prevalence of non–tariff barriers to trade and the risks of relocation.

4.6 Market Power in the Oil Sector

There is, perhaps, no aspect of the question of competitiveness effects and leakage rates which has attracted more controversy and which is potentially more important than the question of market power in the global oil market. In the face of a significant decrease in the level of demand for oil due to the imposition of a carbon tax by a coalition of importing countries (for example the EU or OECD) the degree of market power in the oil sector will determine the magnitude (and perhaps direction) of the change in price. For example if there is a significant fall in the price of oil, demand may rise in untaxed countries, improving competitiveness in energy intensive sectors and increasing carbon emissions.

The foundations of much of the work on oil pricing can be attributed to Hotelling (1931), who showed that the price of a non-renewable resource will rise at the real rate of interest, assuming perfect competition, information and foresight. In the case of a monopoly, marginal revenue will rise at the real rate of interest. In effect market structure should then be evident from the price path. However, the actual price level is dependent upon the perception of user costs, which are by nature unobservable. Moreover, empirical evidence has not supported models which apply the Hotelling rule, irrespective of assumed market structure (for example see Pindyck, 1978). For this reason more recent work has concentrated on more detailed analyses of the institutional characteristics of the oil market (see Adelman, 1993; Rauscher, 1988; Jones 1990; Griffin, 1985). Some work has even been done on such questions in light of the discussions on taxation of energy and/or carbon in order to address global warming (see Berger et al., 1992, and Wirl, 1993).

At one extreme are theories which cite the inherent instability of cartels and assert that although the market is not strictly competitive, the price path of oil is not significantly different from a competitive solution, at least in the long run. At the other extreme are models in which OPEC is characterised as a pure swing producer, providing residual supply to meet a specified fixed price. Alternatively, numerous intermediate positions can be posited, such as market–sharing scenarios in which OPEC is able to respond to changes in market conditions with a degree of market power, but is constrained by non–OPEC supply and changes in demand from importing countries. Variants of all of these scenarios occur in the models surveyed.

Although the model can be designed to assume a fixed exogenous oil price, in most studies using GREEN the price of oil is determined endogenously and perfect competition is assumed. For a given demand the price is determined by the marginal costs of extraction in oil-exporting countries (Burniaux et al., 1992b). Despite the perfectly competitive market structure, the effect on oil prices of a demand shock caused by the introduction of the proposed EC carbon/energy tax is estimated to be quite small, falling by a maximum of 1.5 per cent relative to the business-as-usual scenario (see Figure 6 in Nicoletti and Oliveira–Martins, 1992). In the case of OECD stabilisation of emissions, the price of oil drops by a maximum of 6 per cent relative to the baseline (see Figure 1 in Oliveira–Martins et al., 1992).

The treatment of oil markets in CRTM is rather more complex since the different studies have made rather different assumptions. In the static case (CRTM-1) perfect competition is assumed for the oil market. A tightening by the OECD in **global** emission reductions from 15 per cent to 25 per cent would lead to a 20 per cent fall in the world price of oil (see Figure 7 in Perroni and Rutherford, 1993). In the dynamic models perfect competition is also assumed, but oil transport costs of $2/boe are assumed, generating international price differences. In both the global Toronto target scenario and the unilateral OECD scenario, the price of oil falls by as much as 10 per cent relative to the business–as–usual scenario by 2010. However, under the global scenario in the longer run, the lower carbon content of oil relative to that of the assumed coal–based backstop pushes the price above the baseline case in some years (see Figure 7 in Manne and Rutherford, 1994). In the study which assumes myopic expectations there are import and export quotas for oil. The quotas reduce competitiveness effects when annual OECD emissions cutbacks of 1–4 per cent are modelled since it constrains the extent to which other countries can exploit the fall in the world price of oil. The effect on leakage rates is also significant, with energy markets in China and the USSR partially insulated from changes in world prices (pp.173–74 in Felder and Rutherford, 1993). In the last study it is assumed that OPEC restricts exports to maintain a target international price. In the case of a 2 per cent pa OECD cutback this generates a large fall in the ROW domestic price of oil, increasing leakage rates and competitiveness effects in energy-intensive manufacturing (p.23 in Rutherford, 1992).

Unlike the Global 2100 model upon which it is based, in 12RT the price of oil is determined endogenously and the market is assumed to be perfectly competitive (see pp.137–8 in Manne and Richels, 1992, and p.7 in Manne and Oliveira–Martins, 1994). In both the global Toronto target scenario and the unilateral OECD scenario, the price of oil falls by as much as 10 per cent relative to the business–as–usual scenario by 2010.

As noted in section 2, Pezzey (1991 and 1992a) does not distinguish between the three primary fossil fuels. However, the market for aggregate 'carbon energy' is assumed to be perfectly competitive, with free trade. Following the imposition of a 20 per cent cut in emissions by the EU, the price of carbon energy falls by 1 per cent relative to the base case. With a cut of 50 per cent the price falls by 1.8 per cent. If the OECD cuts emissions by 20 per cent the price falls by 6.7 per cent (see Table 2 in Pezzey, 1992a).

EGEM assumes that OPEC has a 'target market share' of 50 per cent, which it achieves in the long run. This gives OPEC market power, but it is not a price setter in the traditional sense since the degree to which it is able to set the price is circumscribed by the price elasticities of supply for non–OPEC producers (pp.17–18 in Smith, 1994). Following the imposition of the EC carbon/energy tax the world price of oil rises initially and then falls, but never by more than 1 per cent relative to the base case (see Figure 3 in Smith, 1994).

DRI assumes that the world price of oil is fixed (page 3–8 in DRI, 1994). In the face of the carbon tax this is equivalent to the assumption that supply is perfectly elastic or that OPEC is a pure swing producer. In any event this has the effect of mitigating some of the potential competitiveness or leakage effects. This assumption is also made in the analysis conducted by OPEC (Walker and Birol, 1992) and the studies which employ MDM (Barker, 1995a and 1995b). Conversely, Standaert assumes that the nominal price of oil is constant, implying that the change in the real price is strictly a function of the inflationary effects of the tax (p.7 in Standaert, 1992). In the scenarios simulated, the GDP deflator in 2005 under the direct tax reduction scenario is 3.43 per cent higher, while in the social security variant it is 1.28 per cent higher (see Tables 3/1 and 4/1 in the study).

The conclusion here is that the treatment of the world oil market is critical in the estimates of carbon leakage. Behaviour in the world oil market will be increasingly affected by OPEC as a cartel producer since a high proportion of world oil reserves are owned by OPEC member states. The outcome of a reduction in OECD demand on the oil price is likely to lead to reductions in the real price of oil. However, the introduction of a carbon tax in the OECD, providing it is imposed on OECD exports of oil and coal as well as consumption, could lead OPEC to assert further market power so reducing leakage; if the OECD tax were purely on consumption with no associated reduction in OECD oil supply, the fall in world oil demand could weaken the cartel, leading to a lower oil price than otherwise and an increase in non-OECD demand. If the world oil price falls, there is the possibility that the fall will induce a switch from coal to oil in developing countries, such as India and China, offsetting the positive leakage effects.

4.7 Market Structure in Other Energy Sectors

The leakage rates and competitiveness effects arising from a change in the price of oil due to a demand reduction is determined not only by market power in the oil sector, but also the market structure for other fuels, principally gas and coal. There are three interrelated issues. Firstly, due to its possible use in a variety of ways, oil tends to be the swing fuel affecting the prices of coal and gas. Secondly, since coal and gas are less tradeable than oil due to infrastructure requirements and transport costs, markets in coal and gas tend to be regional rather than global. Thirdly, within individual regions the price elasticities of supply of coal and gas will affect interfuel substitution, with more inelastic supply implying bigger price changes. Therefore, depending on regional energy reserves, price elasticities of energy supply and energy price determination, changes in the price of oil will affect trade patterns and emission levels.

In the CRTM model there is no trade in energy carriers other than oil. In the static case this generates very large differences in regional prices of electric and non–electric energy when a constraint on CO_2 emissions from the OECD area is imposed (See Tables 9 and 10 in Perroni and Rutherford, 1993). For instance the price of non-electric energy becomes almost double that in the rest of the world, increasing competitiveness effects and leakage rates. In the dynamic studies, price elasticities of supply are assumed to be unity (p.11 in Rutherford, 1992). In addition, study–specific constraints are introduced. In one of the dynamic studies there are import and export quotas for oil, and no trade in coal and gas. The oil quotas reduce competitiveness effects when OECD cutbacks of 1–4 per cent are modelled, since it constrains the extent to which other countries can exploit the fall in the world price of oil. The effect on leakage rates is also diminished, with energy markets in China and the FSU insulated from changes in world prices (pp.173–4 in Felder and Rutherford, 1993). In the case of Manne and Rutherford (1994) further constraints are introduced: the rate of oil and gas depletion in the FSU is reduced; the share of natural gas in a region's non–electric energy supply is limited to 50 per cent; and there are limits on interfuel substitution. All of these factors reduce the impact of changes in the oil price on domestic energy markets. Finally, Rutherford (1992) places upper and lower bounds on production in all energy sectors. The effect on competitiveness and leakages varies regionally depending upon domestic gas and coal reserves.

In 12RT coal is non–tradeable, but gas is assumed to be tradeable with transport costs of \$2/GJ (Manne and Oliveira-Martins, 1994). In the Whalley–Wigle model there is trade in carbon energy, but not non-carbon energy and the composite energy source. The price elasticity of supply of the carbon based fuel is 0.5 in Pezzey (1992a), but sensitivity studies are conducted over the range 0.1–1.5 in Whalley and Wigle (1991). Not surprisingly the low elasticity scenario reduces welfare significantly, but results for competitiveness and leakages are not given.

In GREEN, international trade in both coal and gas is assumed. However, the existence of transport costs is captured through the use of Armington trade assumptions. There is a sophisticated resource depletion sub-model for oil and gas which distinguishes between potential supply and actual output. Coal reserves are assumed to be infinite. In the central case the upward price elasticity of coal supply is assumed to be between 4 and 5 in all regions, while the downward elasticity is infinite. For gas the upward price elasticities of supply are nil, while the downward elasticities are between 3 and 4 (see Table 16 in Burniaux et al., 1992b). The combined effect of the tradeability of oil and different regional reserves of coal on leakages is significant. For instance, in the OECD stabilisation scenario emissions from India and China fall since there is a large switch from coal to oil until 2030, at which point oil resource constraints push up the price of oil (p.130 in Oliveira–Martins et al., 1992). The same study examines the importance of supply elasticities. Changing the price elasticity of supply of coal from 4–5 to 0.1 increases the leakage rate from zero to 26 per cent in 2010 (see Table 6 in the study).

The macroeconometric models (DRI, MDM, EGEM, HERMES) do not restrict trade in any energy sources, although clearly flows will be low for those with prohibitive transport costs. Price elasticities of supply are not reported.

The conclusion is that the market structure of coal and gas in the different regions is important since it affects competitiveness and leakages by determining the degree of substitutability between fuels in response to changes in oil prices. This is particularly important for those models which do not disaggregate energy carriers, an issue which will be addressed in Section 4.11.

4.8 Expectations and Adjustment

The two issues of agent expectations and capital adjustment are treated together, as agent expectations will affect the degree and path of capital adjustment. To some extent, therefore, capital adjustment is a substitute for expectations. If capital is perfectly and instantaneously mobile across sectors, firms will not adjust to anticipated changes in the economy until they actually occur. Conversely, if capital is less malleable expectations about the future will be vital in determining the costs of adjustment. For these reasons, and since they play an important role in determining the degree of disruption following the introduction of measures such as a carbon tax, the treatment of agent expectations and capital adjustment will have a considerable effect on estimates of leakage rates and competitiveness effects.

The treatment of expectations in general equilibrium modelling can be best discussed by comparing two extreme positions: myopic expectations and perfect foresight. The former assumes that households and firms have no information about the future and base all their decisions on current and past values of variables. For this reason models based on myopic expectations are usually referred to as 'backward looking'. Perfect foresight assumes that households and firms possess all information about the future path of the economy when taking decisions. For this reason they are referred to as 'forward looking'. Neither are realistic descriptions of actual decision making, since firms and households will certainly know something, but not everything, about the future path of the economy. For example, the imposition of a carbon tax would be announced by the government in advance, but firms and households may know very little about future trends in the underlying pre–tax price of fuels. Some, but not all, information is available. Firms will adjust their capital stock to some extent, but the degree of inherent uncertainty will necessitate some degree of caution.[4]

The speed with which firms and households respond to changes (foreseen and actual) in the economy is determined by the flexibility of capital adjustment. If capital is perfectly malleable and fungible the speed of adjustment will be rapid and costless. If, however, capital is sector specific and long–lived the speed of adjustment may be slow and costly. In general equilibrium models the determination of capital adjustment arises out of the form of the production function and the imposed factor substitution elasticities. In econometric studies it arises out of the short-run and long-run elasticities either from estimated production functions or from estimated equations for the derived demand for different factors of production.

The importance of the treatment of expectations and adjustment is graphically illustrated through a comparison of 12RT with GREEN. In 12RT, firms and households are assumed to have an infinite planning horizon with perfect foresight. Rather more inflexible putty/clay assumptions are assumed in the aggregate non–energy sector. The nesting takes a different form with capital and labour bundled together and then bundled with energy (Manne and Oliveira–Martins, 1994). Leakage rates are much higher than under equivalent scenarios using GREEN, which assumes myopic expectations, but the path is quite different. In the 12RT study, leakage starts low and rises, whereas GREEN's highest rates occur at the beginning. This indicates that the role of expectations is significant in determining the path of adjustment, if not the long-run magnitude of costs. Moreover, the effects of the relatively more rigid production structure in 12RT appear to have been obviated by the perfect foresight of households and firms.

The various studies which employ CRTM also provide interesting comparisons since one of the dynamic studies uses perfect foresight (Manne and Rutherford, 1994) while the other two assume myopic expectations (Felder and Rutherford, 1993, and Rutherford, 1992). All three employ nested constant elasticity of substitution production functions for both energy–intensive and non–energy–intensive production, with putty/clay capital. Under a unilateral OECD cut in emissions of 20 per cent, leakage rates in the perfect foresight case are low initially, and then rise to 30 per cent (see Figure 6 in Manne and Rutherford, 1994). In a scenario using the myopic expectation assumption the opposite happens. For a 3 per cent pa reduction in OECD emissions, leakages start at 30 per cent and then fall, becoming negative by 2050 (see Figure 14 in Rutherford, 1992).

In GREEN production takes the form of nested constant-elasticity-of-substitution functions. The structure is many–tiered, but the most important characteristics are the bundling of energy with capital at one tier and aggregate capital/energy with labour. This allows capital and energy to be complements in the short run and substitutes in the long run. Capital adjustment is assumed to be putty/semi–putty. In other words, capital is subdivided into vintages and new capital is assumed to be more mobile across sectors than old capital. Expectations are myopic (backward looking) with no account taken of future values of variables (Burniaux et al., 1992c). The result of this treatment is rather high estimates of adjustment costs (and thus competitiveness effects and leakage rates) in the short run which fall in magnitude as time passes. For instance in the unilateral OECD stabilisation scenario leakages fall from 3.5 per cent in 1995 to 0.9 per cent in 2005, before becoming negative (see Table 2 in Oliveira–Martins et al., 1992).

HERMES also employs a putty/clay production function. Full adjustment following a shock is assumed to take ten years. The model is also backward-looking, implying that initial costs should be high. However, the results of the imposition of the EC carbon/energy tax do not bear this out, with competitiveness effects and gross costs rising through time (see Tables 3/1 and 4/1 in Standaert, 1992). This is almost certainly due to the policy implementation, which assumes that the tax rises gradually form $3/boe in 1993 to $10/boe in 2000 rather than being imposed suddenly.

These issues are less important for the static GEM and the other econometric studies. In the former case this is because the static GEM models usually estimate results for a year in which full adjustment has taken place (Pezzey, 1992a, and Perroni and Rutherford, 1993). In the case of the econometric results the rate of adjustment is captured by the short and long run estimated price elasticities and not imposed on the basis of intuition, literature searches or the requirements of functional form. However, the method of estimation may affect forecasts of adjustment. For example, the use of error-correction models in MDM (Barker, 1995a; 1995b) and EGEM (Boone et al., 1995) clearly distinguishes between short– and long–run effects, with adjustment, expressed in terms of changes in the dependent variable (for example energy consumption) in the face of changes in the explanatory variable (for example fuel prices due to a carbon tax), being much greater in the long run than in the short run.

In conclusion, expectations and adjustment affect competitiveness and leakages significantly. However, their effects might be manifest primarily in terms of paths over time rather than in terms of absolute magnitudes. Nonetheless, given the time scales involved the path may be as important as the level.

4.9 Revenue Recycling and the Double Dividend

The related issues of revenue recycling and the double dividend have received increased attention in recent years. The reason is simple: the revenues raised by a carbon and/or energy tax sufficient to meet any of the environmental objectives discussed in policy circles (for example Toronto or Rio) are of such a magnitude that the disbursement (or retention) of such revenue may have at least as significant an effect on economic and environmental performance as the tax itself. It is this fact which inspired Nordhaus to remark that 'the tail of revenue recycling would seem to wag the dog of climate-change policy' (p.317 in Nordhaus, 1993). In terms of competitiveness and leakages, the debate is important in both sectoral and national terms. In the event that revenue recycling reduces distortions in the economy it will have the effect of making the economy more competitive generally, that is evidence of a 'double dividend'. In addition, the means by which the revenue is recycled will affect sectoral competitiveness and trade–related leakages, generating quite different results than those implied by a study based purely on the tax impacts.

The double dividend in the literature is (1) an environmental dividend in the form of the economic benefit of reducing climate change or other environmental damages associated with the burning of fossil fuels (the benefit is brought about by the correction of prices for the global warming externality) and (2) an economic dividend in the form of some further improvement in economic performance, for example arising from a reduction in the rate of pre–existing distortionary taxes by the use of the revenues from a carbon tax or an increase in employment. The nature of the results for these dividends in the literature depends on the type of models being used.

The macroeconometric models generally do not value the environmental dividend as such, although they may provide estimates of reductions in CO_2 emissions, and they measure the economic dividend as the increases in employment and reductions in unemployment arising from the substitution of carbon taxes for employment taxes. The modellers generally do not attempt to measure the benefits in terms of increases in social welfare brought about by correcting prices for externalities.

The general equilibrium models rule out reductions in involuntary unemployment by assumption. They also often treat the inclusion of carbon taxes in prices (with the explicit purpose of correcting for the global warming externality) **as a distortion and cost to the economy** (eg Goulder, 1994) when in theory it is an economic benefit. This treatment arises because the initial position (without the carbon tax) is assumed to be at the economic optimum, apart from distortions from those existing taxes which do not correct for externalities (see Bohm, 1997, p.114 for a discussion). Most results from general equilibrium models, therefore, consider the only economic benefit from carbon taxes to arise from the use of revenues, for example the improvement in welfare arising from the reduction in the distortionary tax on labour or capital; if the revenues are used for lump sum payments to consumers, then (by assumption) there are no benefits at all.

The treatment of the carbon tax as a cost to the market economy rather than a benefit is a feature of the methodology of double dividends introduced by

Goulder (1994, 1995). He distinguishes between weak and strong forms of the double dividend arising in general equilibrium modelling by setting aside the environmental benefits of a carbon tax of including an external cost in prices. His strong form asserts that revenue can be recycled in such a way as to yield negative economic costs. He sets aside the primary (global warming) and secondary (for example damage from emissions of SO_x) externalities and assumes that the original optimum is being distorted by the carbon tax leading to economic costs. A strong double dividend exists if these costs are more than offset by economic benefits from the reduction in other taxes which are also distortionary. A strong double dividend is therefore one which is to be had if the carbon tax has no environmental effects; since the carbon tax is normally regarded as an environmental tax, this form of dividend is irrelevant. His weak form merely asserts that alternative forms of recycling will tend to have less adverse effects than lump-sum recycling, mitigating some of the so–called distortionary effects of the carbon tax on the economy.

However much of the theoretical work is highly restricted in scope, concentrating on perfectly competitive economies at full employment, with a representative consumer and a single production function, in which ideal (least distortionary) taxes are initially assumed and the non-monetary benefits of employment are ignored. In a situation in which taxes are not ideal and where the economy is not at full employment, a sensible reform seems likely to lead to a double dividend.

Taking the existing characteristics of the economy into account is therefore vital in the evaluation of the significance of the double dividend and the optimal means of recycling (Poterba, 1993). Shackleton et al. (1992) argue that in the US the optimal means of recycling (in terms of growth) is through investment tax credits, followed in order of preference by reduction in marginal corporate income tax and payroll tax rates, reduced public sector borrowing requirements (tax retention) and reduced labour or employee social security contributions. The least efficient is, of course, lump –sum recycling. The situation in Europe is somewhat different. Reductions in marginal income tax rates or national insurance contributions may be the most efficient means of recycling since labour is already heavily taxed and since (as a rule of thumb) deadweight losses associated with taxes tend to rise with the square of the tax rate. Given the relatively low level of taxation associated with energy, Horton et al. (1992) argue that taxes up to 25 per cent would reduce existing distortions.

GREEN is structured such that the (marginal) income tax rate is adjusted in order to ensure that there is revenue neutrality between the base case and policy scenarios (p.10 in Burniaux et al., 1992b). Lump–sum recycling is assumed both in the CRTM studies (p.62 in Manne and Rutherford, 1994) and in 12RT (Manne and Oliveira–Martins, 1994). These models are not designed to address domestic public finance issues and lump-sum recycling is chosen as simply a convenient assumption. The degree to which the relatively favourable results reported in GREEN (compared with those from the other GEM models) can be attributed to the means of revenue recycling is difficult to ascertain due to the very different model structures involved.

The DRI study of the US economy uses a complex means of recycling, with 47 per cent used to reduce personal income taxes (average not marginal), 17 per cent through transfer payments (due to higher unemployment rates), 20 per cent through transfers to consumers and businesses (due to higher interest rates), 4 per cent to businesses for federal purchases (due to higher inflation), 8 per cent retained, and 1 per cent due to falls in other taxes (page 4–21 in DRI, 1994). It is not clear, but it would seem that the recycling of revenue *via* reduced average income taxes is equivalent to lump-sum recycling to wage earners. A similarly complicated methodology is employed in the DRI EU study with 35 per cent recycled through reductions in personal income taxes and employee social security contributions, 40 per cent in employers' contributions, 10 per cent in corporate taxes, 10 per cent in investment incentives for energy conservation, and 5 per cent for property income tax relief for household conservation (see Table 3.5 in DRI, 1992). Walker and Birol (1992) implicitly assume that revenue is recycled through indirect taxes by holding the consumer price index constant.

Unfortunately in all of these studies the means of recycling is not varied in alternative scenarios so effects can not be compared. However, this is not true of the studies using HERMES and MDM. In the HERMES study the same scenario (an energy tax) is run using two different means of revenue recycling. In one case the revenue is used to lower direct taxes, with budget neutrality assumed. In the other case social security contributions are reduced. The effects of the latter formulation are significantly better, with GDP falling by 0.12 per cent relative to the base case, while the direct tax recycling variant results in a fall of 0.53 per cent (see Tables 3/1 and 4/1 in Standaert, 1992). In terms of the implications for competitiveness, the direct tax case results in a fall in the trade balance of 0.48 per cent, while in the social security case the fall is only 0.05 per cent.

In the MDM studies the revenue is recycled in a variety of ways: reducing employers' NIC contributions, expenditures on energy–efficiency measures, and compensation for pensioners (Barker, 1995a and 1995b, and Barker, Baylis and Bryden, 1994). In the case where the effects of the EC carbon/energy tax is analysed the scenario is run with reductions in employers' contributions. Changes in industrial costs are decomposed into increases associated with the tax and decreases associated with reductions in NIC contributions (Barker, 1995a). Overall, industrial costs increase by 0.3 per cent relative to the base case in 2000, but the results are also presented in sectoral terms (see Table 5 in the study). Although many of the energy–intensive sectors are among the sectors which are hardest hit, the correlation is by no means perfect. This casts doubt on the leakage and competitiveness estimates of models which examine the trade effects of a carbon and/or energy tax on energy-intensive sectors and which assume the unlikely scenario that the revenue is recycled via lump sum payments.

The conclusion regarding the effects of recycling is that the assumptions adopted do have significant effects on the estimates of competitiveness. Those studies which recycle the carbon tax revenues so that taxes on employers are reduced find that the national loss of competitiveness, assuming fixed exchange rates, is smaller. Indeed, for economies in which the carbon tax would be paid mainly by final consumers this form of recycling could increase national competitiveness (for example where electricity is generated by non-fossil means and the main export industry is employment-intensive tourism).

4.10 The Baseline and Income Effects

The inclusion of a base case or reference scenario in a study is important since most of the environmental objectives which are discussed in policy circles are expressed in terms of percentage reductions in emissions or stabilisation by some future date at current or past levels. As such the reference scenario results give an indication of the percentage reductions required to meet the stated objective. In this sense the estimation of the base is as significant as the imposition of the constraint in terms of the determination of the estimated costs.

It is, however, necessary to clarify what is meant by the reference scenario. Most usually it is defined as a business-as-usual scenario. This would imply that existing trends, institutions and tax structures remain in place. However, this is clearly unsatisfactory if existing policies are unsustainable. For instance, if subsidies are onerous and policy discussions are presently underway which indicate their imminent removal, it is perhaps misleading to use a business-as-usual scenario as the relevant reference scenario. More usually, particular assumptions are made, distinguished by region, fuel or sector. However, and more importantly, emissions in reference scenarios are frequently driven more by assumptions about the characteristics and timing of backstop technologies than by more sophisticated economic and institutional analysis.

What are the baseline or reference emissions forecast for those regions which are assumed to impose the tax? Manne and Rutherford (1994) predict that base case emissions in the US in 2020 will be 2.0bn tons and 2.1bn tons for the rest of the OECD. By 2050 the relevant figures are 3.0bn tons and 2.9bn tons (see Figure 1 in the study). In order to meet the 20 per cent cutback relative to 1990 levels it is necessary to stabilise emissions in each region at less than 1.2bn tons. Unfortunately no figures are given for the regional taxes required to meet this objective, but in the more efficient scenario where emission permit trading is allowed the price rises to \$140/ton (\$12.12/boe) in 2020, falls to \$80/ton (\$6.93/boe) in 2030 and then rises to over \$220/ton (\$19.05/boe) by 2050 (see

Figure 3 in the study). GDP losses rise to between 1.5 per cent and 2.0 per cent in 2050 (see Figure 2 in the study). Perroni and Rutherford (1993) forecast base case emissions of 2.08bn tons in the US in 2020 and 2.11bn tons in the rest of the OECD (see Table 7 in the study). In order to meet the Toronto target emissions would have to fall by more than 40 per cent, and hence tax rates of $362/ton ($32.03/boe) and $321/ton ($28.40/boe) are required (see Table 5 in the study). GDP losses are in the order of 1 per cent.

In one of the GREEN studies (Manne and Oliveira–Martins, 1992) US emissions in 2020 are approximately 2.0bn tons and total OECD emissions are approximately 3.8bn tons (see Figure 2 in the study). The tax required in order to stabilise emissions rises to approximately $150/ton ($13.29/boe) in the US and $200/ton ($17.72/boe) in the EU (see Figure 11 in the study). This contrasts sharply with the 12RT study which standardises parameter assumptions and the policy scenario. Emissions are approximately 20 per cent lower, although the tax required for the EU and the US is lower than in GREEN (see Figure 11 in the study). The US tax never exceeds $115/ton ($10.19/boe), and the EU tax never exceeds $135/ton ($11.96/boe). Under an efficient scenario, the tax falls to $7.97/boe in both areas. However, standardising the GREEN scenario to generate the same percentage reductions as in 12RT cuts the tax in half (see Figure 3 in the study). The relatively lower baseline in 12RT is largely attributable to a much higher penetration of carbon–free backstops. In the GREEN study by Oliveira-Martins et al. (1992) the tax required for stabilization in the EU rises from $2.30/boe in 1995 to $7.00/boe by 2050.

In the OPEC study base case, emissions in the OECD in 2010 are assumed to be 3.5bn tons while stabilisation requires reductions to 2.3bn tons (see Table 5 in Walker and Birol, 1992). In the European DRI study (1992) EU emissions are projected to rise from less than 2.7bn tons in 1990 to almost 3.1bn tons in 2005 (see Chart 1.1 in the study). Although the policy is not explicitly one of stabilisation, the imposition of the carbon/energy tax is sufficient to reduce emissions by 9.3 per cent compared with the base in 2000, 1 per cent above 1990 levels (p.21 in DRI, 1992). Horton et al. (1992) require taxes of $3.40/boe in the EU when the OECD stabilises 2000 emissions at 1990 levels, since base case emissions are 14 per cent higher (p. 22). A 20 per cent reduction necessitates EU taxes of $13.85/boe. The importance of technological and institutional assumptions are also illustrated in MDM. UK CO_2 emissions are predicted to drop from 158.6m tC in 1990 to 149.8m tC in 2000, before rising to 165.5m tC in 2005 (see Table 1 in Barker, 1995a). This removes the necessity for carbon reductions to reach stabilisation until after 2000. The reason for the drop in the absence of emission policies is almost certainly related to assumptions about the magnitude of the switch from coal to gas in electricity generation.

The importance of base case assumptions with respect to competitiveness effects is self-evident, with higher emissions necessitating higher taxes and potentially more adverse economic consequences including competitiveness effects. However, the consequences in terms of leakages are rather more complicated. On one hand the higher the base case emissions, the greater the required reduction in consumption of energy and the greater the reduction in exports from oil exporting countries. This has the effect of reducing income levels in OPEC and other oil exporting countries, thus reducing domestic emissions. In addition, and overlooked in most discussions, emission levels from other countries may also fall. For example, emissions from countries which are significant exporters of manufactured goods may be reduced due to decreased demand in OECD countries. Even if these demand effects do not outweigh the price effects associated with an increased comparative advantage in energy–intensive sectors, such effects may be significant. For example in the case of the US, DRI (1994) found that activity levels were three times more important than relative prices in the determination of import levels.

Numerous studies find evidence of negative leakages from non–constrained economies. In the case of Felder and Rutherford (1993) leakages from the MOPEC aggregation are negative in 2040 due to income-related effects (see Figure 10 in the study). In Rutherford (1992) leakages are negative after the middle of the century due to income-related effects in ROW (see pp.23–4 in the study). Such effects are also important in GREEN, generating negative leakages amongst the energy-exporting LDCs (p.15 in Manne and Oliveira–Martins, 1994). The EGEM study finds that reduced emissions from OPEC are almost sufficient to counter-balance the oil price effects (see Figure 2 in Smith, 1994). Finally, the OPEC study finds that emissions from non–OECD countries fall by 4 per cent in 2010 relative to the base case (see Table 4 in Walker and Birol, 1992).

Estimation of the baseline is significant in generating estimates of the costs (including potential negative competitiveness effects). This is particularly true for those studies which model stabilisation (or Toronto Target) scenarios.

4.11 Regional, Sectoral and Fuel Disaggregation

The degree of regional, sectoral and fuel disaggregation which exists in the models is a fundamental determinant of the estimated leakage rates. International trade is a set of bilateral relationships between specific pairs of countries in specific commodities using specific fuel mixes in production. Therefore, aggregating the world into broad regions, goods into broad aggregates and fuels into broad energy groups affects the extent of competitive dislocation and the degree of leakage estimated. Significant trading opportunities in manufactured goods and fossil fuels between countries are collapsed into intra-regional production structures. Broad categories of goods are effectively treated as being homogeneous. Finally, fuels with very different potential end uses are considered perfectly substitutable.

In terms of geographical aggregation it is important to emphasise that **any level** of aggregation above the level of the most likely policymaking unit will result in an underestimation of competitiveness and leakage effects if an inefficient scenario (that is non–uniform taxes or non–tradeable permits) is assumed. In effect, aggregation will implicitly make the scenario more efficient by allowing for marginal costs to be equated within the region rather than the country.

Nevertheless, some distinctions are more important than others. For non–OECD countries the most important distinctions are between OPEC, oil importing LDCs, oil exporting LDCs and newly-industrialised countries, since their roles as sources of competitiveness effects and leakage rates are very different. OPEC and other oil exporting LDCs are potentially significant sources of income-related negative leakages. Newly industrialised countries are potentially significant sources of leakages related to competitive relocation in manufactures. Oil importing LDCs are unlikely to play a significant role, but the carbon intensity of production processes may change in the face of changed relative fuel prices. Of the global models, GREEN, 12RT, and the CRTM study which distinguishes between OPEC (including Mexico) and ROW are satisfactory in this regard.

However, in the CRTM studies conducted by Rutherford (1992), Manne and Rutherford (1994) and Perroni and Rutherford (1993), ROW includes a heterogeneous grouping of oil importers, oil exporters, dynamic economies, and stagnant economies. This has significant repercussions. For example, in Rutherford (1992) OPEC restricts oil exports when the international price is below the target price. With different regional oil prices this drives the 'domestic' price well below the international price. Since regional aggregation places India, the East Asian 'tigers', and Latin America in the same regional market as OPEC it is not surprising that leakages are high and competitive dislocation likely. Whalley and Wigle also have an unsatisfactory level of geographical disaggregation with, for instance, the NICs and sub–Saharan Africa treated as part of the same region (Whalley and Wigle, 1991; Pezzey, 1992a). The suitability of the level of disaggregation employed in the non–global models depends upon whether or not the trade relationships with the country or region of focus is satisfactory. With the exceptions of LEAN (Welsch and Hoster, 1995) and NERA/GEM (Horton et al., 1992) they seem to be satisfactory.

Sectoral disaggregation is particularly important for the issue of competitiveness. For instance, some of the GEM models go to great pains to restrict the price-responsiveness of trade in manufactures by introducing Armington assumptions which allow for factors such as product differentiation and product quality. In effect, the country of origin becomes a determinant of trade. However, **within** the sectoral aggregation all goods are identical. Considering that disaggregation in the non–energy sectors is usually just between two broad groups – or in the case of GREEN three groups – this is significant.

The usual means of disaggregation is to distinguish between energy–intensive goods and a broad group of other goods. In GREEN agriculture is also disaggregated. The choice of a separate industrial classification for energy–intensive sectors such as steel, plastics and chemicals, is intuitively attractive. For instance in CRTM the energy-intensity of production is 14 per cent (in cost terms) in the disaggregated sectors relative to 6 per cent in the other sectors. Therefore one would imagine that an energy and/or carbon tax would increase costs relatively more in energy–intensive than in other sectors and result in more significant competitive dislocation. There are, however, two problems with this argument. Firstly, revenue recycling is unlikely to be sectorally neutral. This is discussed above. In addition the tradeability of the sector is at least as important in the determination of the competitiveness effects. To use energy intensity as the single criteria is misleading when examining such effects (see Figure 4.3 in Section 4.3 above). For instance, DRI classes plastics, some chemical products, glass, parts of the pulp and paper sector, and stone and clay in the least or second least most vulnerable sectors in terms of international competitive dislocation (see Table 3–8 in DRI, 1994). All of these figure strongly in the various definitions employed in the GEM models.

Amongst the macroeconometric models the primary distinction is between disaggregated and aggregated models. It is clear that the level of disaggregation employed by DRI (60 and 20 non–energy sectors in the two studies) and MDM (49 sectors) is more appropriate for the analysis of such questions, particularly if sector–specific trade restrictions apply and need to be modelled explicitly. The approach adopted in the EGEM model, estimating leakages associated with the relocation of energy–intensive sectors on the basis of historical sectoral importance and the relative price of oil, is necessitated by the aggregate formulation of the model (Smith, 1994). The OPEC and HERMES models fall somewhere in between the two, with a certain level of disaggregation but insufficient to capture some of the more detailed effects (Walker and Birol, 1992; Standaert, 1992).

The final issue – fuel disaggregation – is treated adequately by most of the models. In particular the distinction between oil, gas and coal is emphasised, with the different carbon intensities and potential end uses recognised. In the case of the GEM models the treatment is either through activity process flows (12RT and CRTM) or as standard factors of production (GREEN). In the macroeconometric models aggregate energy demand is usually estimated and then disaggregated on the basis of fuel share equations (EGEM and MDM). Detail in the supply side depends upon the degree of sectoral disaggregation. In the case of HERMES–MIDAS the two methodologies are combined with process flows on the supply side and fuel-share equations on the demand side (Karadeloglou, 1992). The one model which is clearly inadequate in terms of fuel disaggregation is Whalley and Wigle (1991) used by Pezzey (1991, 1992a). An aggregate carbon fuel (oil, coal and gas) is bundled together, with no account taken for substitutability in different end uses nor changes in carbon intensity as the fuel mix changes. The composite carbon/non–carbon energy sector is purely a theoretical construct, not referring to specific fuels. This model gave the 70 per cent leakage rate for OECD unilateral action, but Pezzey comments (personal communication, 1995) that he intended that the leakage results should provoke further investigation rather than to be treated as authoritative figures to guide policy.

The level of aggregation (regions, sectors, fuels), although apparently incidental, may have fundamental effects. In some cases the effects may be more significant than other more controversial assumptions such as the treatment of the oil market or trade elasticities.

4.12 Strategic Behaviour

The issue of strategic response is relevant for both firm behaviour and government behaviour. In the case of government behaviour it is important to analyse the political response of other countries to the imposition of a carbon or energy tax. If the imposition of a tax in one country has a 'demonstration' effect, encouraging other countries to follow suit, the effects estimated are overstated. However, for the most part in the models it is assumed that other countries do not undertake similar measures over the entire duration of the scenarios, irrespective of the levels of concentrations of GHGs in the atmosphere or domestic environmental damages.[5]

There are, however, good reasons to believe that other countries would follow suit. For example, since GHGs are stock pollutants and damages are disproportionately felt by LDCs their own policy stances will certainly change over time. In addition there are more subtle reasons, related to strategic behaviour, which also indicate that a non-cooperative outcome is unlikely. The assumption that some countries will not respond to abatement in other countries is dependent upon a belief that they will be indifferent to such measures. However, there is reason to believe that abating countries, by acting as leaders, may encourage abatement elsewhere. Firstly, if the relationship between abating and non-abating countries is not seen as a single 'one-off' event then abating countries may have greater leverage over potential non-abaters through their own behaviour, encouraging similar policy measures. Secondly, if the non-abating countries require cooperation from abating countries on other unrelated issues there will be some incentive for a degree of cooperation. Thirdly, if abating countries are willing to bear some of the costs of abatement in non-cooperating countries this will change the balance of costs and benefits in favour of abatement. The effect of all of these are to some extent dependent upon the precise relationship involved. However, the likelihood of such factors increasing abatement are improved by the fact that a negotiating framework, the Rio Convention, has been reached **before** unilateral abatement has been introduced at significant levels.[6]

Strategic firm behaviour may also affect the competitiveness effects arising from unilateral abatement policies. Horton et al. (1992) discuss two such cases: capacity decisions and location decisions. Through investment in increased capacity, firms in imperfectly competitive markets may be able to increase long-run profits by fighting for market share. Similarly, if markets are partially regionalised firms may choose to locate on the basis of the regional degree of competition, proximity to other markets, and the decisions of other firms. In a variant of the plant capacity model run by Horton et al. (1992), leakage increases relative to the perfect competition case. This occurs because it is assumed that relocation increases competition in non-abating countries, driving down prices and pushing up output. However, in general the impacts of such behaviour on the competitiveness effects of unilateral policies are ambiguous since they depend on a variety of further assumptions.

Strategic behaviour on the part of energy producers may also be relevant. For example, OPEC may see the proposed imposition of a carbon/energy tax as a threat to their rents and respond by restricting exports. The environmental objective would be attained, but the revenue would be captured in the producing countries rather than the consuming countries. It would also spread the effect of the price increase to all countries. Walker and Birol (1992) examine this issue in a scenario whereby OECD stabilisation is achieved through a combination of oil price increases and taxes within the OECD. Emissions from the rest of the world fall by just over 2 per cent relative to the tax case (see Table 4 in the study). Horton et al. (1992) report a study in which it is assumed that OPEC anticipates an OECD tax by bringing about full stabilisation through oil price increases. In this case, world emissions fall by 15 per cent relative to the tax case.

The effect of strategic behaviour (by governments and firms) on competitiveness and leakages is potentially important but necessarily uncertain.

4.13 Regulation and Technological Innovation

The final issue to be addressed among the effects of the introduction of a unilateral carbon and/or energy tax on leakages and competitiveness is the effect on investment and innovation. Although this issue is discussed in some of the theoretical literature (see Hung et al., 1993), it is not addressed directly in the studies surveyed and nor are quantitative estimates available from other sources. However, as remarked in the introduction above they may be the most important determinants of competitiveness and leakages in the long run.

The general equilibrium models implicitly assume that the investment required to meet the imposed constraint (for example a carbon tax sufficient to meet stabilisation objectives) is substituted from more directly 'productive' uses. Allowance is made for the effects of technological change on carbon emissions per unit of output through costless reductions in the amount of energy required for a given level of output. This process is captured through the use of coefficients which capture the effect of factor–saving technological progress. In some cases the effects are factor–neutral, reducing all factor input requirements equally, and in other cases they are biased, affecting some factors more than others. The effect of changing the parameter can be significant (for example see Burniaux et al., 1992b; Manne and Richels, 1992). However, the magnitude of the parameters is largely arbitrary and in no instance is the rate of technological progress explicitly related to institutional factors or even prices.

Some of the macroeconometric studies incorporate other factors into the determination of technological change. For instance, the EGEM analysis has been extended in an attempt to endogenise technological progress (Boone et al., 1995). A trend is estimated on the basis of energy prices and the share of manufacturing in output and included in the full equation for energy demand. Conversely, the DRI (1992) and MDM (Barker, 1995a) studies model the effect of institutional factors on technological change by using some of the revenue generated by the tax to improve energy efficiency in particular sectors. Such techniques would reduce the adverse effects of the tax by reducing energy requirements in ways which are not captured in orthodox estimation or modelling.

In addition, there is some evidence to indicate that a 'first–mover' country may reap other economic benefits from having done so. In the event that the required investment gives the country expertise in the production of goods which are associated with a low–carbon economy the country may develop a comparative advantage in the production of energy–efficient capital equipment, becoming a significant exporter of such goods to countries which imposed constraints rather later. This argument has been used for the regulation of some pollutants in some countries in terms of developing expertise in abatement equipment, but whether or not it would be true for policies which have effects as diffuse (in terms of industrial sectors and production processes) as a carbon tax is not clear.

Although very long run effects such as those related to technology and innovation are subject to a great deal of uncertainty their importance should be recognised. Indeed a comparison of orthodox economic methodology with more engineering–based bottom–up studies casts light on the potential for innovation and the role that it may play in reducing estimated costs (Wilson and Swisher, 1993).

5 CONCLUSIONS

The purpose of a carbon tax or duties on fuels in proportion to their carbon content is to reduce GHG emissions by raising the costs of burning fossil fuels in proportion to their CO_2 emissions. It is clear therefore that if the tax is introduced unilaterally in one country or world region and if the tax is successful in reducing GHG emissions, those industries using carbon–based products are likely to lose price competitiveness. However, the most carbon intensive sectors, electricity and road transport, are not traded in significant amounts so **international** competitiveness is not an issue for them; in addition, there are many opportunities for moving to low–carbon intensities in electricity generation via the use of gas or nuclear as a fuel instead of coal, so electricity prices may not rise as much as might be expected from the increase in carbon costs. Energy–intensive industries will face increases in costs, but these can be mitigated if they can switch to less carbon–intensive fuels, become more efficient in fuel use or switch output towards goods which are less carbon-intensive. The conditions under which this takes place varies over countries depending on their ability to adapt their technologies, the flexibility of their energy systems and the structure of their industrial output, so that the modelling of the competitiveness effects is inevitably complex if it is to capture even the rudimentary features of the process. Moreover, other industrial sectors are likely to improve their price competitiveness if revenues from the tax are recycled through reductions in other taxes.

The modelling of leakage also requires complex models, though with a different emphasis. There are three main channels which reduce or even counter the leakages arising from loss of competitiveness. First the lower demand for oil may depress the world price so that oil producers experience a substantial fall in real income: their economic activity and hence their CO_2 emissions will fall, as will those who export to the oil producers' home markets. Second if activity in the OECD is depressed by the carbon tax, the rest of the world will sell fewer exports to the OECD, so its activity will also be lower than otherwise and its emissions will also be reduced. Third, the lower price of oil will lead to substitution away from coal towards oil and gas in the major coal users such as India and China. For an OECD tax, these activity or income effects plus the substitution effect within the energy market are likely to be larger than the effects of changes in costs of energy using industries on relocation of output which are the basis of the leakage estimates in some of the literature.

Since the late 1980s, a number of models have been built or adapted to address the issue of CO_2 abatement through the use of a carbon tax. Some, such as Global 2100, began life as linear programming energy models which could be solved under a 'carbon constraint' (with an implicit carbon tax) but had an inadequate treatment of macroeconomic behaviour; they have been adapted to include effects on economic growth and carbon tax revenues by adding an economic growth component. Others, such as OECD's GREEN model were adapted from existing general equilibrium models (GREEN utilised a model of world agricultural protection). Finally a third group have developed from linked or integrated econometric macroeconomic and energy models. The estimates of competitiveness and carbon leakage in the literature using these models is inevitably affected by the assumptions and methods used.

This chapter has assessed the effects of these assumptions and methods on the results and the main conclusion to emerge is that many of the results are directly generated by assumptions which may or may not be justified by evidence. Although it is difficult to rank the importance of the assumptions in any strict sense, they are frequently interdependent and their effects will differ depending on the more general modelling framework. It is, however, significant that some of the apparently more incidental assumptions (for example the level of geographical aggregation) may be at least as important as more controversial issues (for example the magnitude of trade elasticities).

In much of the literature involving general equilibrium modelling, the treatment of evidence of the effects of changes in energy prices on competitiveness and therefore on carbon leakage appears to be at best 'informed' by consensus estimates of elasticities and parameters available in the literature or at worst imposed for mathematical or modelling convenience. Even if the effects of the assumptions are tested, as they are with GREEN, the model builders are still locked into a representation of an ideal world of perfect competition and constant returns to scale. These models are used for very long-term projections, often over 100 years, yet they are based on one year's data, 1985 in GREEN, and their treatment of economic growth processes or technological change is perforce extremely stylised, largely reflecting the outdated and discredited neoclassical growth theories of the 1950s.

The macroeconometric modelling has generally been less ambitious, looking ahead 10 or 15 years, with a full treatment of the dynamics of economic behaviour as the tax is introduced. However, it too is not without problems: inadequate data, lack of agreement as to the causes of growth, national rather than global coverage.

In global climate modelling, it is recognised that the models should be capable of representing the main features of climate behaviour relevant to climate change, such as the effects of the Mount Pinatubo eruption on global temperatures. A corresponding requirement for global energy–environment–economy models might be their capacity to represent dynamic reactions to the oil price shocks of the 1970s and 1980s. Annual data are available on economic performance and on the demand and supply of coal, oil and gas and their prices in considerable regional detail over the post–war period. However, to the authors' knowledge,

OPEC's World Energy Model is the only global model reviewed here to have been extensively tested and solved over a 20–30 year period to ensure that it captures the main features of the system. By their design, the general equilibrium models are not capable of simulating the dynamic effects on the global economy of the huge rises in oil prices 1973–74 or 1979–80, or their collapse in 1985, or such features as the effects of the corporate average fuel economy (CAFE) regulations on US gasoline consumption. Their capacity to simulate the long-term effects of a carbon tax is therefore subject to considerable reservations.

It is also true that the models have not been designed to analyse competitiveness or leakage effects; the results reported are largely incidental to the main purposes of the model and studies, which are to assess what rates of tax are required to achieve target emissions reductions, and what are the likely effects on inflation and growth. It is therefore too much to expect results to be reported in detail, or the assumptions and model structures to be designed to explore the causes of competitiveness changes. An ideal modelling exercise would include price and non–price effects in an historical estimation of sectoral production and trade by country and trading group in a global model, allow technical progress to respond to sustained price signals favouring low carbon/energy intensities in production and consumption, provide a credible reference scenario for the future, then introduce plausible carbon or energy taxes, with alternative assumptions about the use of the revenues. None of the studies reviewed comes close to this ideal.

However some conclusions on the quantitative estimates in the literature are worth making.

1) The high carbon leakage estimates of 80 per cent for EU and 70 per cent for OECD unilateral action which were given prominence following the DTI report on competitiveness (Pezzey, 1992a) and which have been quoted repeatedly in the literature, have not been confirmed by the other studies reviewed. The estimates arose from the mechanical application of an unsuitable model. One of the few studies for Annex 1 signatories to the Rio Convention (Oliveira–Martins, 1995, using the OECD GREEN model) concludes that substantial cuts in emissions can be achieved with virtually no leakage. Indeed, far from there being leakage, it seems likely that if the carbon tax reduces economic activity as the OECD area introduces the tax, as some of the studies suggest, then emissions in the rest of the world will fall ('negative leakage').

2) The effects of unilateral action in individual countries within a trading bloc, such as the UK in the EU, are likely to be larger than for a country outside of any bloc, because exchange rates are more likely to be fixed and barriers to trade smaller. However a series of studies on the effects of small unilateral taxes on national economies, on the lines of the EC's $10 proposal, have concluded that the macroeconomic effects and the general sectoral competitive effects would be very small.

3) The effects on the competitiveness of energy-intensive industrial sectors, such as chemicals or metal products, of unilateral action at the EU, NAFTA or OECD level appear to be very small in relation to the effects of exchange rate or wage rate fluctuations. The DRI studies estimate a change in the growth of EU exports of chemicals from 5.6 per cent pa to 5.4 per cent pa as a result of the EC tax. The reasons for the small response are transport costs and other barriers to trade, protection of domestic markets, especially in the case of iron and steel, and the relatively small increase in costs, especially when exchange rate changes, revenue recycling and carbon cost–saving at all stages in the industrial system (especially in electricity generation) are taken into account.

NOTES

1. These policies are imposed with different assumptions about revenue recycling, an issue which is discussed below.
2. Two points which have been brought up should be made in this regard. Firstly, Jorgenson and Wilcoxen (1993) find net benefits depending on the method of revenue recycling. Their benefits arise, however, from the replacement of a distortionary tax by a relatively less distortionary one. In practise this would mean that the tax should be advocated even if there are no environmental benefits. Secondly, Nordhaus's model (1993), which pioneers the inclusion of a climate change/output loss function, finds that the cost of abatement may be negative. However, it is not clear whether or not the costs would be negative in the absence of the loss function. In both cases, therefore, the benefits are a consequence of other factors and not of abatement *per se*.
3. It should be emphasised that Heckscher–Ohlin assumptions will not necessarily generate complete specialisation since marginal costs may differ across countries even if the goods are homogeneous and perfectly substitutable.
4. Expectations affect both the demand side and supply side of the economy. For example, if firms in non-renewable energy resource sectors believe that a policy will affect future demand, their perception of user costs will have changed, influencing their extraction profile. The discussion will concentrate on the demand side.
5. The only exceptions are those models which approximate the attainment of the Toronto Targets by restricting non-OECD (including Eastern Europe) emissions to 150 per cent of their 1990 levels.
6. For discussions of the circumstances in which unilateral abatement is likely to lead to increased abatement elsewhere see Cornes and Sandler (1983 and 1984), Barrett (1990 and 1994) and Mäler (1991). It should be recognised that abatement in some countries may reduce abatement in other countries in some circumstances. For example, if it is felt that future abatement policies are to be achieved through 'grandfathered' emission permits, some countries may increase emissions in order to improve their permit allocation.

DISCUSSANT: Rolf Iten

The main theses

The theses of the excellent and comprehensive paper presented by Terry Barker with regard to the models conventionally applied for the analysis of the competiveness effects of carbon taxes can be summarised as follows:

1.   General equilibrium models (GEM) are not an adequate modelling framework for the analysis of competitiveness of carbon taxes.
2.   Usually too high price elasticities of trade in manufactures are introduced in the models.
3.   Changes of exchange rates are treated inappropriately.
4.   Mobility of capital: relocation of industries is exaggerated.
5.   Market power in the oil sector: the behaviour of OPEC may offset positive leakage effects.
6.   The role of the market structure in other energy sectors is not analysed.
7.   Assumptions regarding expectations are crucial for the path and level of estimated adjustment costs.
8.   Revenue recycling by reducing taxes on labour reduces losses due to competition.
9.   Net costs depend on assumptions on the base line scenario.
10. Level of aggregation (regional, sectoral and fuel) has fundamental effects on the results.
11. Strategic behaviour of governments and firms is important but uncertain.
12. Long–run technology and innovation effects are neglected but may reduce adjustment costs significantly.

In the following we will present two selected illustrations related to the theses summarised above, based on a study carried out by INFRAS/ECOPLAN within the 3rd European Commission Framework Programmefor R&D and published recently (INFRAS/ECOPLAN 1996). The study contains a systematic comparison of current international models applied for the analysis of economic impacts of Ecotax proposals. We here present two complementary illustrations regarding the effects of revenue recycling and strategies offsetting negative impacts on international competitiveness and the effects of environmental regulation on innovations.

Illustration I: The role of revenue recycling and offsetting strategies

The impact of such offsetting policies has been analysed by INFRAS, in two separate case studies for the energy–intensive industries – cement as well as pulp and paper (see INFRAS/ECOPLAN, 1996). The starting point is an estimate of the tax burden of a 40 per cent energy tax in Switzerland: The simple – and static – estimate shows that there are winners and losers of a revenue–neutral energy tax. Even if no responses to the tax are considered, the additional net costs seem to be in an order of magnitude which can be interpreted as moderate, for example for the industries most affected, the additional net costs are below 3 per cent of the total production value (that is also for those industries, the resulting price increase due to such a tax will be below 3 per cent). If dynamic responses in terms of energy–saving measures are allowed for, the net effect of the tax burden will be even lower. The borderline between winners and losers follows, all in all, the energy intensity of the industries. But there are some interesting exceptions. The energy tax favours not only services but also industrial branches as, e.g. machinery, electronics and construction. The impact of offsetting measures is illustrated by Figure 4.4. The most important results are:

–   The net effect of general revenue recycling is relatively low because of the low labour intensity of the two industries compared to other industries.
    If revenue recycling is carried out separately for the industry (manufacturing) and the service sector (separate I–S–recycling), a slight additional reduction of the tax burden is achieved. No cross subsidies from the manufacturing sector to the service sector occur in this case.
–   Effective buffering effects can be achieved with two offsetting measures: the introduction of Border Tax Adjustments (BTAs) or of a sectoral recycling system ('protection bubbles') are able to eliminate the negative impacts on – international competitiveness and the relative tax burden remains at the same level for the cement and for the paper and pulp industry.
–   The rebate scheme admitting a maximal net cost increase of approximately 2 per cent of the total production value (PV) is less effective than the two incentive–oriented offsetting strategies. For a more effective offsetting impact, the rebate payments have to be extended by lowering the threshold for the access to rebate payments and decreasing the level of the maximal allowable tax burden.

Illustration II: Innovation and regulation

Although there is much literature on technological innovation in general, relatively little attention has been paid to the problem of the effects of (environmental) regulation on innovation. Figure 4.5 shows a mental model of how various factors determine environmental innovations (Hemmelskamp 1995). Energy and/or environmental prices (charges and taxes) are but one category among these, but an important one. Hemmelskamp concludes – on the basis of a systematic and relatively broad based analysis – that 'direct regulation (command

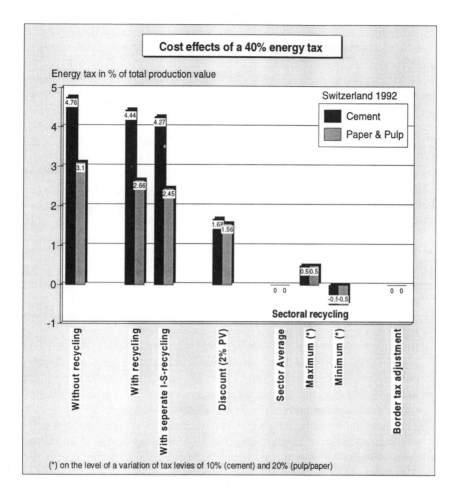

Figure 4.4 Impact of offsetting policies in the cement and the paper and pulp industry

and control) ... provide little incentives for dynamic effects and that emission taxes and permits are better instruments to promote innovations'.

Although it seems quite obvious that market–based environmental regulaion favours innovation and technical progress (some empirical evidence is already available, see Porter and van der Linde 1995), more precise conceptual models should be developed as a precondition for better quantitative understanding of the innovation offsets of static costs of good environmental regulation.

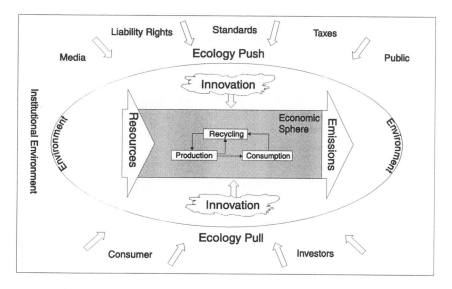

Source: Hemmelskamp 1996

Figure 4.5 Factors determining environmental innovations

Conclusions

1. It is important to distinguish short– and long–term impacts.
2. Conventional models (Top down models) overestimate economic costs and competitiveness effects, mainly because of the following reasons:
   - Neglection of transitional and dynamic phenomena, such as innovation effects and induced technical progress
   - Neglection of low–cost energy–saving potentials
   - Various model–internal assumptions, such as price elasticities, transformation elasticities between imports and exports, full capital mobility, and so on.
3. Simulation models need to be developed towards a more pronounced incorporation of dynamic effects.
4. It is possible to deal with potential negative effects, the focus being on two strategies:
   - adequate design of revenue recycling
   - effective offsetting strategies

DISCUSSANT: Najma Rajah

One of the main conclusions of the study is that the impact of a carbon tax on competitiveness and leakage is not perhaps as adverse as might be expected. This finding hinges partly on the potential existence of a 'double dividend', where the introduction of a new environmental tax, accompanied by a revenue neutral reduction in more distortionary forms of taxation could lead to two separate welfare improvements. The first arises from the improvement to the environment, and the second as a result of reducing the rates of taxation on those taxes which tend to be associated with relatively high welfare costs.

However, although there may be some circumstances where a double dividend might arise, it should not automatically be assumed that one will be obtained. There may be no second welfare improvement accruing from reduction in taxes on labour, if the reform leaves the real wage rate unchanged. This could occur if the increase in the nominal wage resulting from a reduction in labour taxes is offset by a corresponding increase in the price level due to the introduction of a new environmental tax levied on energy products. Moreover, the potential welfare costs resulting from the introduction of a new environmental tax should not be ignored, since nearly all forms of taxation lead to distortions to varying degrees. In the case of environmental taxes, if their introduction leads to a narrowing of the tax base, then this could potentially lead to increased compliance and enforcement costs.

The chapter also suggests that there might be some scope for increases in general 'non–price competitiveness'. For example, the encouragement given to domestic industries producing CO_2 abatement technologies might cause them to develop in international markets along the lines of the Porter First Mover Advantage hypothesis. Alternatively a reduction in some forms of pollution (most notably congestion) could lead to a stimulation in economic activity, again leading to an improvement in general non–price competitiveness.

But, again as with the fiscal double dividend related arguments, it is not evident that these wider non–fiscal benefits might occur. In particular, the Porter First Mover Hypothesis relies heavily on the assumption that firms will innovate in response to tightening of environmental policies. However, environmental policy is only one of a number of considerations which firms take into account when making R&D decisions, and other issues such as market structure, access to credit markets and the extent to which there might be a patenting system may also be significant. It is also not clear why the tightening of environmental policies should be assumed to generate efficiency improvements than would have otherwise have been delivered in a competitive market, nor why they should exceed compliance costs even if they do exist.

Finally, it would be useful to consider whether the same conclusions would hold if a different definition of competitiveness, based say on labour productivity rather than that adopted in the report based on market share and exports, were used?

General Discussion

It is necessary to establish the importance of competitiveness. Are there leakage effects or structural adjustment costs and would taxes induce other countries to follow the OECD/EU? Competitiveness is an important issue because it is perceived to be a problem by policy makers and is often used by industry as an argument against environmental policies. However, structural adjustment will occur with or without for example a carbon tax and the competitiveness effects of an OECD tax would be slight, as non–OECD countries are relatively small. Studies also indicate that the difference in effect between an OECD carbon tax and an EU tax would be small.

It is important to note that 'Industry' is not a single homogeneous entity, but consists of many different groupings. Although the energy industry is generally against environmental policies, other sectors are more positive. It is still necessary to look at the results from different types of models, as they give widely differing results. Finally, even with the globalization of industry, a distinction can still usefully be made between the competitiveness of countries and of firms, for example the Japanese government had directed the course of development of their multinational firms.

REFERENCES

Adams, J. (1997), 'Environmental policy and competitiveness in a globalised economy: conceptual issues and a review of the empirical evidence', Chapter 4 in *Globalisation and Environment: Preliminary Perspectives*, OECD, Paris.

Adelman, M.A. (1993), *The Economics of Petroleum Supply*, Cambridge, Massachusetts, MIT Press.

Armington, P.S. (1969), 'A theory of demand for products distinguished by place of production', *IMF Staff Papers*, **16**, 159–78.

Barker, T.S. (1977), 'International trade and economic growth: an alternative to the neoclassical approach', *Cambridge Journal of Economics*, **1**(2), 153–72.

Barker, T.S. (1995a), 'Taxing pollution instead of employment', *Energy and Environment*, **6**(1), 1-28.

Barker, T.S. (1995b), 'UK Energy price elasticities and their implications for long–term CO_2 abatement' in T.S. Barker, P. Ekins and N. Johnstone (eds),

Global Warming and Energy Demand, Routledge, London.

Barker, T.S., S. Baylis and C. Bryden (1994), 'Achieving the Rio Target: CO_2 abatement through fiscal policy in the UK', *Fiscal Studies*, **15**(3), 1–18.

Barker, T.S. and R. Lewney (1991), *Green Futures for Economic Growth: Britain in 2010*, Cambridge Econometrics.

Barker, T.S. and W. Peterson (eds), (1987), *The Cambridge Multisectoral Dynamic Model of the British Economy*, Cambridge University Press.

Barns, D.W., J.A. Edmonds and J.M. Reilly (1992), 'Use of the Edmonds–Reilly model to model energy–related greenhouse gas emissions', *Working Paper No.113*, OECD Economics Department.

Barrett, S. (1990), 'The problem of global environmental protection', *Oxford Review of Economic Policy*, **6**(1), 68–79.

Barrett, S. (1994), 'Self–enforcing international environmental agreements', *Oxford Economic Papers*, **46**, 878–94.

Bartik, T.J. (1988), 'The effects of environmental regulation on business location in the US', *Growth and Change*, **19**(1), 22–44.

Beckerman, W. (1990), 'Pricing for pollution', *Hobart Paper 66*, 2nd ed, p.73.

Berger, K. et al. (1992), 'The Oil Market and International Agreements on CO_2 Emissions', *Resources and Energy*, **14**(4), 315–36.

Bergman, L. (1991), 'General Equilibrium Effects of Environmental Policy: A CGE–Modelling Approach', *Environmental and Resource Economics*, **1**(1), 43–61.

Boero, G., R. Clarke, and A.L. Winters (1991), *The Macroeconomic Consequences of Controlling Greenhouse Gases: A Survey*, Department of Environment, London, HMSO.

Bohm, Peter (1997), 'Environmental taxation and the double dividend', in T. O'Riordan (ed), *Ecotaxation,* Earthscan, London.

Bohringer, Christoph, Michael Ferris and Thomas F. Rutherford (1995), 'A multi–sectoral framework for the analysis of carbon emission restrictions and bilateral trade in the European Union: model formulation and a sample application', *Discussion Papers in Economics*, 95–9, University of Colorado at Boulder.

Boone, L., S. Hall, D. Kemball–Cook and C. Smith (1995), 'Endogenous Technological Progress in Fossil Fuel Demand' in T.S. Barker, P. Ekins and N. Johnstone (eds), *Global Warming and Energy Demand*, Routledge, London.

Bovenberg, A.L. and F. van der Ploeg (1992), 'Environmental policy, public finance and the labour market in a second–best world', *Working Paper 30.93*, Fondazione Eni Enrico Mattei.

Burniaux, J.–M., et al. (1992a), 'The Costs of reducing co_2 emissions: evidence from Green', *Working Paper 115*, OECD Economics Department.

Burniaux, J.–M., et al. (1992b), 'Green: A multi–sector, multi–region general equilibrium model for quantifying the costs of curbing co_2 emissions: a technical manual', *Working Paper 116*, OECD Economics Department.

Burniaux, J–M, et al. (1992c), 'Green: a global model for quantifying the costs of policies to curb CO_2 emissions', *OECD Economic Studies 19*, 49–92.

Cambridge Econometrics (1991), 'The effects of the european commission's carbon/energy tax on the UK economy', *Industry and the British Economy*, Autumn Report, 31–44.

Cline, W.(1992), *The Economics of Global Warming*, Institute of International Economic Affairs, Washington.

Cornes, R. and T. Sandler (1983), 'On commons and tagedies', *American Economic Review*, **73**, 787-92, September.

Cornes, R. and T. Sandler (1984), 'Externalities, expectations and pigouvian taxes', *Journal of Environmental Economics and Management*, **12**(1), 1–13.

Data Resources Incorporated (1992), 'Impact of a Package of EC Measures to Control CO_2 Emissions on European Industry', Report Prepared for the European Commission by DRI.

Data Resources Incorporated (and Charles River Assocs), (1994), *Economic Impacts of Carbon Taxes*, EPRI, Pleasant Hill CA.

Dean, J. (1992), 'Trade and environment: a survey of the literature', Prepared as Background Paper for the *World Development Report 1992*, Washington, World Bank.

DIW (1994), 'Ecological tax reform even if Germany has to go it alone', *Economic Bulletin*, **31**(7), 3–10.

Ekins, Paul (1994), 'The Impact of carbon taxation on the UK economy', *Energy Policy*, **22**(7), July, 571–580.

Ekins, Paul (1995), 'Rethinking the costs related to global warming a survey of the issue', *Environmental and Resource Economics*, forthcoming.

European Commission (1992), *Proposal for a Council Directive Introducing a Tax on Carbon Emissions and Energy*, COM(92), No. 226 final, June.

Felder, S. and T.F. Rutherford (1993), 'Unilateral CO_2 reductions and carbon leakage: the consequences of international trade in oil and basic materials', *Journal of Environmental Economics and Management*, **25**, 162–76.

Goulder, L.H. (1994), 'Environmental Taxation and the 'double dividend': a reader's guide', mimeo, Department of Economics, Stanford University.

Goulder, L.H. (1995), 'Effects of carbon taxes in an economy with prior tax distortions: an intertemporal general equilibrium analysis', *Journal of Environmental Economics and Management*, **29**(3), November, 271-297.

Goulder, Lawrence H., Ian W. H. Parry and D. Burtaw (1996), 'Revenue–raising vs. other approaches to environmental protection: the critical significance of pre-existing tax distortions', Resources for the Future, Discussion Paper 96-24 Washington DC.

Griffin, J.M. (1992), 'OPEC and world oil prices: is the genie back in the bottle', *Energy Studies Review*, **4**(2), 27–39.

Griffin, J.M. (1985), 'OPEC behaviour: a test of alternative hypotheses', *American Economic Review*, **75**(5), 954–63.

Grossman, G.M. and A.B. Krueger (1992), 'Environmental Implications of a North American free trade agreement', *Discussion Paper 644*, Centre for Economic Policy Research.

Grubel, H.G. and P.J. Lloyd (1975), *Intra-Industry Trade: The Theory and Measurement of International Trade in Differentiated Products*, London, Macmillan.

Han, Ki-Ju and John B. Braden (1996), 'Environment and trade: new evidence from US manufacturing', University of Illinois, Department of Economics, mimeo.

Hemmelskamp, J. (1996), *Environmental Policy Instruments and Their Effects on Innovation*, Zentrum für Europäische Wirtschaftsforschung (ZEW), Mannheim.

Hoel, M. (1989), 'Global environment problems: the effects of unilateral actions taken by one country', *Journal of Environmental Economics and Management*, **20**, 55–70.

Hoeller, P., A. Dean and M. Hayafuji (1992), 'New Issues, New Results: The OECD's Second Survey of The Macroeconomic Costs of Reducing CO_2 Emissions', *Working Paper 123*, OECD Economics Department.

Horton, G.R., J.M.C. Rollo and A. Ulph (1992), 'The Implications for trade of greenhouse gas emission control policies', *Working Paper*, Department of Trade and Industry and Department of the Environment.

Hotelling, H. (1931), 'The economics of exhaustible resources', *Journal of Political Economy*, **39**(1).

Hung, V.T.Y., P. Chang and K. Blackburn (1993), 'Endogenous growth, environment and R&D', *Working Paper 23.93*, Fondazione Eni Enrico Mattei.

Ikwue, T. and J. Skea (1994), 'Business and the Genesis of the European Community Carbon Tax Proposal', *Business Strategy and the Environment*, **3**(2), Summer.

INFRAS/ECOPLAN (1996), Economic Impact Analysis of Ecotax Proposals, Comparative Analysis of Modelling Results, Final report in the EU 3rd Framework Programme Project 'Greenhouse Gas Abatement through Fiscal Policy', Zurich/Bern.

IPCC (1990), *Formulation of Response Strategies*, IPCC Working Group III, June.

Jones, C.T. (1990), 'OPEC behaviour under falling prices: implications for cartel stability', *The Energy Journal*, **11**(3), 117–29.

Jorgenson, D.W. and W.W. Hogan (1991), 'Productivity trends and the cost of reducing CO_2 emissions', *The Energy Journal*, **12**(1), 67–85.

Jorgenson, D.W. and P. Wilcoxen (1993), 'Reducing US carbon emissions: an econometric general equilibrium', *Resource and Energy Economics*, **15**(1), 7–25.

Kalt, J. P. (1988), 'The impact of domestic environmental regulatory policies on US international competitiveness', in M. Spence and H. A. Hazard (eds), *International Competitiveness*, Harper and Row, Cambridge, MA.

Karadeloglou, P. (1992), 'lCarbon tax vs energy tax: a quantitative analysis' in F. Laroui and J.W. Velthuijsen (eds), *The Economic Consequences of an Energy Tax in Europe: An application with HERMES*, Amsterdam, SEO.

Laroui, F. and J.W. Vethuijsen (1992), *The Economic Consequences of an Energy Tax in Europe*, Amsterdam, SEO.

Linder, S.B. (1961), *An Essay on Trade and Transformation*, New York, Wiley.

Mabey, Nick, Stephen Hall, Clare Smith and Sujata Gupta (1997), *Argument in the Greenhouse*, The International Economics of Controlling Global Warming, Routledge, London.

Mäler, K.–G. (1991), 'International Environmental Problems' in D. Helm (ed), *Economic Policy Toward the Environment*, Oxford, Blackwells, 156–201.

Manne, A.S. and J. Oliveira–Martins (1994), 'OECD Model Comparison Project (II), on the Costs of Cutting Carbon Emissions. Comparison of Model Structure and Policy Scenarios: Green and 12RT', *Working Paper 146*, OECD Economics Department.

Manne, A.S. and R. Richels (1992), *Buying Greenhouse Insurance*, Cambridge, Massachusetts, MIT Press.

Manne, A.S. and T.F. Rutherford (1994), 'International trade in oil, gas and carbon emission rights: an intertemporal general equilibrium model', *The Energy Journal*, **15**(1), 31–56.

Nicoletti, G. and J. Oliveira–Martins (1992), 'Global effects of the European carbon tax', *Working Paper 125*, OECD Economics Department.

Nordhaus, W.D. (1991), 'To slow or not to slow: the economics of the Greenhouse effect', *Economic Journal*, **101**, 920-37.

Nordhaus, W.D. (1993), 'Optimal Greenhouse gas reductions and tax policy in the 'DICE' model', *American Economic Review*, **83**(2), 313–17.

Oliveira–Martins, J., (1995), 'Unilateral emission control, energy-intensive industries and carbon leakages', Annex B 107–124 in *Global Warming Economic Dimensions and Policy Responses*, OECD, Paris.

Oliveira–Martins, J, et al. (1992), 'Trade and the effectiveness of unilateral CO_2 abatement policies: evidence from green', *OECD Economic Studies 19*, 123–40, Winter.

OECD (1996), *Implementation Strategies for Environmental Taxes*.

OPEC Secretariat (1996), 'The impact of climate change policies upon OPEC', *OPEC Bulletin*, Vol. XXVII, No. 5, May, 14-19.

Pearson, Mark and Stephen Smith (1991), *The European Carbon Tax: An*

Assessment of the European Commission's Proposals, Institute for Fiscal Studies, London.

Perroni, C. and T.F. Rutherford (1993), 'International trade in carbon emission rights and basic materials: general equilibrium calculations for 2020', *Scandinavian Journal of Economics* **95**(3), 257–78.

Pezzey, J. (1991), *Impacts of Greenhouse Gas Control Strategies on UK Competitiveness: A Survey and Exploration of the Issues*, London, HMSO.

Pezzey, J. (1992a), 'Analysis of unilateral CO_2 control in the EU and OECD', *The Energy Journal*, **13**.

Pezzey, J. (1992b), 'Some interactions between environmental policy and public finance', *Discussion Paper 92/340*, University of Bristol, Department of Economics.

Pindyck, R.S. (1978), 'Gains to producers from the cartelisation of exhaustible resources', *The Review of Economic and Statistics*, **60**(2), 238–51.

Porter, M.E. (1990), *The Competitive Advantage of Nations*, Macmillan, London.

Porter M. and van der Linde C. (1995), 'Toward a new conception of the Environment–Competitiveness Relationship', *Journal of Economic Perspectives*, **9**(4), 97–118.

Portney, P.R. (1981), 'The macroeconomic impacts of federal environmental regulations', *Natural Resources Journal*, **21**(3), 459–88.

Poterba, J.M. (1993), 'Global warming policy: a public finance perspective', *Journal of Economic Perspectives*, **7**(4), 47–63.

Proops, J.L.R., M. Faber and G. Wagenhals (1993), *Reducing CO_2 Emissions*, Berlin, Springer-Verlag.

Rauscher, M. (1988), 'OPEC behaviour and the price of petroleum', *Journal of Economics*, **48**(2), 59–78.

Repetto, Rober and Duncan Austin (1997), *The Costs of Climate Protection: A guide for the perplexed*, World Resources Institute, Washington DC, USA.

Richardson, J.D. and J.H. Mutti (1976), 'Industrial displacement through environmental controls: the international competitive aspects' in I. Walter (ed), *Studies in International Environmental Economics*, New York, Wiley.

Robison, H. (1988), 'Industrial pollution abatement: the impact on the balance of trade', *Canadian Journal of Economics*, **21**(1), 187–99.

Rutherford, T. (1992), 'The welfare effects of fossil carbon restrictions: results from a recursively dynamic trade model', *Working Paper 112*, OECD Economics Department.

Schmidheiny, S. (1992), *Changing Course: A Global Business Perspective on Development and the Environment*, MIT, Cambridge, Massachusetts.

Shackleton, R. et al. (1992), 'The Efficiency Value of Carbon Tax Revenue', mimeo, US Environmental Protection Agency.

Smith, C. (1994), 'Modelling carbon leakage in incomplete CO_2 abatement treaties', *Discussion Paper DP 26-94*, LBS, Centre for Economic

Forecasting.

Smith, C. (1995), 'Carbon leakage: a review and empirical assessment', Fondazione ENI Enrico Mattei *Working Paper 10.95*, Milan.

Smith, Stephen (1990), 'Environmental Policy: Implications for Taxation', conference paper, Institute for Fiscal Studies, London.

Standaert, S. (1992), 'Simulating an energy tax (with HERMES–LINK),' in D. Ulph, 'A Note on the "Double Benefit" of Pollution Taxes', *Discussion Paper 92/317*, University of Bristol, Department of Economics.

Stevens, Candice (1993), 'Do environmental policies affect competitiveness', in *The OECD Observer*, August/September.

Tobey, James A. (1990), 'The effects of domestic environmental policies on patterns of world trade', in *Kyklos*, **43**(2), 191–209.

Van Beers, C. and Jeroen C. J. M. van den Bergh (1996), 'The Environmental Impact of Environmental Policy on Trade Flows: An Empirical Analysis', in *Rijks Universiteit Leiden*, Department of Economics WP 96.05.

Walker, I.O. and F. Birol (1992), 'Analysing the cost of an OECD Environmental tax to the developing countries', *Energy Policy*, June, 559–67.

Welsch, H. and F. Hoster (1995), 'A General-Equilibrium Analysis of European Carbon/Energy Taxation: Model Structure and Macroeconomic Results', *Zeitschrift Für Wirtschafts und Sozialwissenshaften*, **115**(2).

Welsch, H. (1995), 'Joint vs. Unilateral Carbon/Enery Taxation in a Two–Region General Equilibrium Model for the European Community', Institute of Energy Economics, University of Cologne, February.

Whalley, J. and R. Wigle (1991), 'The international incidence of carbon taxes' in R. Dornbusch and J. Poterba (eds), *Economic Policy Responses to Global Warming*, Cambridge, Massachusetts, MIT Press.

Whalley, J. and R. Wigle (1992), 'Results for the OECD comparative modelling project from the Whalley–Wigle model', *Working Paper 121*, OECD Economics Department.

Wilson, D. and J. Swisher (1993), 'Exploring the gap: top–down versus bottom–up analyses of the cost of mitigating global warming', *Energy Policy*, March, 249–63.

Wirl, F. (1993), 'Energy Pricing When Externalities are Taxed', *Resource and Energy Economics*, **15**(3), 255–70.

World Resources Institute (1990), *World Resources 1990–91: A Guide to the Global Environment*, in collaboration with the UN Development and Environment Programmes, Oxford University Press.

PART TWO

Macroeconomic Simulations

5. Carbon leakage: an empirical assessment using a global econometric model

Clare Smith

1 INTRODUCTION

The establishment of the UN Framework Convention on Climate Change in 1992 was a milestone in international environmental policy, representing wide agreement on the need for coordinated and cooperative action to reduce greenhouse gas emissions. However the level of abatement targets agreed, and developments since Rio, have failed to reduce these emissions or to agree longer term targets that will tackle the problem effectively in terms of stabilising atmospheric CO_2 concentration. There are several reasons for this inaction – lack of certainty, doubts over the economic merits of carbon abatement, inertia, free–riding – but two major factors are competitiveness and carbon leakage (Barrett, 1994a; Mabey et al, 1997). In the EU, the 1992 proposal for an energy/carbon tax was abandoned by 1994, despite amendments, due principally to concerns over industrial competitiveness.

Carbon leakage and competitiveness are related but separate concerns. Leakage refers to the increase in carbon emissions in non–signatory countries as a direct result of measures to reduce emissions in the OECD or Europe; while competitiveness stems around more general economic loss in favour of non–signatory countries. Thus while a decline in competitiveness would be likely to lead to carbon leakage, the converse is not always true. Both leakage and competitiveness share their impact of reducing the incentive to participate in an international treaty.

There are three main routes for carbon leakage: via downwards pressure on world oil prices; via shifts in energy intensive industries away from signatory countries in the OECD, and more general income effects, whereby GDP changes in non–signatory countries affects their energy usage. This last could contribute negative leakage, as reduced income in energy exporting countries and reduced demands for imports into the OECD would tend to decrease their energy usage and emissions.

A possible additional effect suggested by Barrett (1994b) is that a successful reduction in carbon emissions would reduce the marginal environmental damage, thus reducing the incentive to abate. At present this route appears to be more applicable to other more soluble global environmental issues (such as CFC's perhaps) rather than carbon, where the marginal environmental damage is so uncertain and the current level of abatement so low, hence this effect has not been considered here. However the negotiating stance taken by some less developed countries (LDCs), that the OECD caused the problem and the OECD should therefore pay to clear it up, suggests that this argument is not irrelevant. LDCs have little incentive to abate at present, and if OECD action is successful their incentive may not increase in the future, unless and until their own emissions increase substantially.

In this chapter, the use of the model EGEM to study leakage will be described. EGEM is based on the London Business School Global Econometric Model (GEM), with additional equations added to describe the energy sector and carbon emissions. A more thorough description of the model including estimation of the energy sector equations and a study of the impacts of carbon taxes is given by Smith et al. (1995). The model consists of detailed macroeconomic models of nine OECD countries[1], including the G7 group plus Belgium and the Netherlands, that together make up 88 per cent of OECD emissions. The remaining countries of the world are dealt with in country groupings, with models of decreasing sophistication according to their economic significance. Developing countries exist as trading blocks with their trade flows determined by import and export goods prices.

Estimation of emissions and responses to carbon taxes in EGEM concentrates on the nine major OECD countries. For these countries, an aggregate model of energy demand has been econometrically estimated, together with fuel share models for gas, coal and oil that represent substitution effects between the three as functions of their relative prices. The aggregate fossil fuel demand depends on price and GDP, with a term for technical innovation induced by price changes. This form of model differs from a standard elasticity model, in that high fuel prices cause an endogenous increase in the rate of improvement of energy efficiency, equivalent to endogenizing the AEEI used in some other models. In a standard elasticity model, if prices later return to their original level, energy consumption will also return to its original level (apart from any exogenous time trend), with high prices having had no long term effect. Endogenizing the trend gives a better fit to observed data, and allows the irreversible aspects of technical improvements to be taken into account. An intuitive example is that the price shocks of the 1970s have had a long term impact in improving energy efficiency, despite energy prices now being back to, or less than, their real 1970 levels.

The three country groups (Europe, North America and Japan) may be designated as being 'in' or 'out' of an agreement to allow analysis of carbon taxes in different areas and their impact on competitiveness. In this study, the model is used to study carbon leakage from the three different routes, according to policy scenarios for carbon taxes in each of the three regions acting unilaterally or in unison.

Estimates of carbon leakage can be expressed as a leakage rate, the percentage by which reductions in the OECD are neutralized by increases elsewhere. The studies that have been done to quantify expected leakage rates have produced a wide range of results, and are heavily dependent on the modelling techniques and assumptions used (Table 5.1). At one end of the modelling spectrum lies Pezzey (1992), who used the Whalley–Wigle CGE model to forecast leakage rates of up to 70 per cent from an EC unilateral reduction of 20 per cent in carbon emissions from the base case. These very high estimates are indubitably due to his rather simplistic assumptions of a single energy good and 'free trade and perfect competition in world energy markets'. At the other extreme, Felder and Rutherford (1993) in one scenario using the Carbon–Related Trade Model (CRTM) quote a marginal leakage rate (leakage caused by a further 1 per cent cut in OECD emissions) of up to –180 per cent. This strong negative leakage is principally due to fuel substitution effects, with overall average leakage rates being positive and in the range 0–40 per cent. The updated version of CRTM used is based on Global 2100 (Manne and Richels, 1992), while two other versions (Perroni and Rutherford, 1993; Manne and Rutherford, 1994) gave leakage rates of around 10 per cent and up to 35 per cent respectively. The OECD model GREEN has been used by Oliveira–Martins et al. (1993) and Burniaux et al. (1992) to forecast modest leakage rates in the range 1.4 to 2.4 per cent for EU stabilisation.

There appears to be no consensus on the magnitude, the relative contributions of oil price, trade and income effects, or even the sign of leakage rates from these studies, although all agree that leakage will be higher if fewer countries participate in the agreement. There are many important differences in model structure and in the abatement scenarios used. Important model features include supply and demand elasticities, trade assumption, sectoral disaggregation, interfuel substitution and backstop fuels.

In his review paper Winters (1992) stresses that both GREEN and CRTM have strong product differentiation between OECD and non–OECD countries which could lead to underestimates of leakage. It is in this key area of how both price and non–price factors affect trade flows between OECD and non–OECD countries that most uncertainty lies. There is little empirical evidence available, and

international markets have shown structural changes over shorter time periods
than those being modelled. The very long timescales involved in models of
climate change policies, 100 years into the future or even more, present an almost
philosophical problem. How much can we truly predict with any certainty about
the world of 2100, in terms of technological options, market structure, political
processes or economic behaviour? How much could have been predicted in 1897

Table 5.1 Summary of carbon leakage studies

Study	Model and solution type	Industrial disaggreg–ation	Treatment of fuel markets	Policies simulated	Leakage rate and date
Pezzey (1992)	Whalley–Wigle GE model	Energy intensive/ non–energy intensive	Free trade; no distinction between fuels	20% cut in OECD 20% cut in EU	60% (2100) 70% (' ')
Oliveira–Martins et al. (1993)	GREEN	Energy intensive/ non–energy intensive	International market for oil only; inter-fuel substitution considered	OECD stabilization EU stabilization	1.4% (2050) 2.2% (2050)
Perroni and Rutherford (1993)	CRTM, based on Global 2100; static GE	'Basic materials' + other industry	International for oil, regional markets for oil, gas and electricity	OECD stabilization	5–15% (2020)
Felder and Rutherford (1993)	CRTM, based on Global 2100; recursive dynamics	'Basic materials' + other industry	International for oil; regional markets for oil, gas and electricity	OECD cut of 2% pa OECD cut of 4% pa	0–40% (1990-2100) -30 to +35% (' ')
Manne and Rutherford (1994)	Global 2100; full forward-looking inter-temporal dynamics	None	Competitive international oil market; gas trade bet. ex–USSR and OECD; some limits on fuel substitution	OECD cut of 20%	incre-asing to 30% (2050)

about energy use in today's world, at a time when the motor car was barely
invented, Middle East oil lay undiscovered, and it would be a further 60 years
before the discovery of either nuclear power or natural gas? Some fairly heroic
assumptions must be made in any model, and to have any confidence that at least
the changes in the different scenarios have any real validity these assumptions
must be examined in detail. All the above studies are based on computable

general equilibrium (CGE) models, unlike the present study using the macroeconomic model EGEM. There are certain advantages and disadvantages to each approach, summarized in Table 5.2. In general, macroeconomic models have a stronger empirical basis, with equations estimated econometrically from time series data, while many CGE models rely on their theoretical structure and are recalibrated from a single point in time. Assumptions about backstop energy forms and prices, and the rate of technological improvement or AEEI may be incorporated into CGE models, while in macroeconomic models the econometric relationships dominate with technology being implicit rather than explicit – if prices are high enough, technologies will be found that can supply a demand. CGE models have a more closely defined long–term equilibrium while macroeconomic models may be unstable in the long term although their short term dynamics are more realistic, a major reason for their use in short– to medium– term economic forecasting. However this strength in CGE models is also their major flaw, as real economies are not in equilibrium, more a state of 'dynamic disequilibrium', where market distortions and real life behaviour are more important than theoretical economic optima.

Table 5.2   Essential features of macroeconomic and CGE models

Macroeconomic models	**CGE models**
Time series data, econometric estimation – strong empirical basis	More theoretical structure, calibrated from existing equilibrium
Good for short term dynamics	Dynamics weak
May be unstable in longer term	Long term new equilibrium, rely on AEEI and backstop energy assumptions
Assumes 'dynamic disequilibrium'	Assumes economy in equilibrium
Based on data from real, distorted markets	Assumes markets clear and distortions minor

The aim of this chapter is to analyse some of the processes that affect leakage through the three channels and to assess the evidence for quantifying these processes. Given that all existing work on leakage has relied upon CGE models, it appears reasonable to assume that use of an entirely different modelling methodology will at least produce a rather different emphasis, and highlight some issues which have not previously been brought out.

Results from EGEM for a number of scenarios are presented, intended to illustrate the processes involved.

2   SOURCES AND MAGNITUDE OF CARBON LEAKAGE

While quantitative estimates vary, qualitative examination of leakage processes can shed considerable light on the possible magnitude of the different effects. The three main routes for leakage are discussed below: via changes in trade, via world oil prices, and income effects.

Trade and Energy Intensity

Trade leakage is the issue of most relevance in terms of competitiveness. High energy costs and the environmental regulatory burden are seen by some as being major disincentives to inward investment, encouraging European firms to relocate elsewhere, and favouring consumption of imported goods while reducing markets for high priced exports. However, others see the effect of general environmental regulation on competitiveness as quite small (Jaffe et al., 1995), especially when compared with such factors as access to markets, labour supply and exchange rate fluctuations. Indeed, some authors suggest that regulation can have a beneficial effect by stimulating innovation, as well as providing a boost to firms providing environmental goods and services (Ekins and Jacobs, 1994).

Leakage through changes in trade patterns can be divided into two categories. There may be a reduction in overall trade volumes, with a shift towards non–constrained countries in comparative advantage. In addition there is likely to be a shift in the composition of trade, with the more energy intensive sectors predominating in non–constrained countries where energy costs are lower.

The first category depends upon the impact of carbon abatement measures on overall costs, plus certain non–price factors. In the case of a revenue neutral carbon tax it is not clear whether there would be any impact on overall costs, as carbon tax revenue would be recycled back into the economy, reducing the tax burden in other ways. For the case of a tax that accurately reflects the external environmental cost of emissions, it is likely that there will be a long term net gain to the economy – firstly, from reduction of these environmental costs, and secondly from a reduction in the tax distortion caused by taxes on employment that could be reduced accordingly. This is the basis of the double dividend hypothesis (Barker et al., 1993). In the short term however, the environmental benefits are not likely to be significant (or visible), and there may be inflationary consequences from the transitional costs of adapting to a new tax structure.

Of perhaps more importance is the second category, the shift towards less energy intensive industries. Those industries where energy represents a high proportion of costs would be hard hit by a carbon tax (or by regulation to limit emissions), while less energy intensive industries would see a net benefit, from the revenue recycled as reduced taxes on employment or consumption (Pezzey,

1991). It is the manufacturing sector that is affected by this shift, as service, transport and domestic sectors are less prone to migration. Manufacturing consumes around 30 per cent of primary energy use in OECD countries. The main industries at risk are iron and steel, chemicals and other metals (the so–called 'big three'), which together account for typically 10–15 per cent of primary energy use (UN, 1992), with cement, paper/pulp mills and glass also important. Thus this type of leakage is essentially limited to this 10–15 per cent of carbon emissions.

A carbon tax that doubled energy costs, for example, would increase costs in the 'big three' by slightly less than 10–15 per cent, as they would reduce their energy use accordingly. The implication of revenue neutrality would be that the rest of the economy would see a benefit of 2–3 per cent, depending on how revenue is recycled. This would tend to lead to a zero–sum shift away from energy intensive industries, towards those that are less carbon dependent. In economic terms, there may be little overall effect on the trade balance from this shift, although transitional costs may be significant. In terms of emissions, however, it may be significant, allowing energy intensive industries to continue unconstrained in countries outside the OECD and import goods for consumption, avoiding any carbon tax.

Wyckoff and Roop (1994) give figures for the proportion of carbon emissions in six OECD countries that is embodied in imported goods. Overall, 13 per cent of carbon emissions was embodied in manufactured imports, with almost half of this coming from chemicals and metals alone. However, a very large proportion comes from neighbouring countries – between Canada and USA and between EU countries – with less than 20 per cent of imports coming from outside the OECD, implying an overall percentage of 2.5 per cent of carbon emissions coming from imports of goods from outside the OECD. Given this perspective, it appears that it would certainly require very large changes in trade patterns in these goods to have a large impact on carbon leakage, at least for an OECD–wide treaty.

In the case of an EU only agreement, there is the possibility of leakage within OECD. This may exacerbate the problem, as it would allow countries that are similar in terms of development of labour force, industrial infrastructure and technological expertise (such as the USA, Canada, Japan, Australia) to compete with European industry under the added advantage given by a tax. It would appear likely that leakage would be higher, and the few studies that have taken this into account confirm this (Pezzey, 1991; Oliveira–Martins et al., 1993).

Energy costs are certainly only one factor among many in a company's decision to invest or to relocate. Competitiveness and relocation in fact depend to a much greater extent on factors such as labour costs, quality of product, proximity to markets, increasing capital and technological mobility, existing trade links and barriers to trade in the form of protectionist import restrictions or tariffs. The energy intensive industries are often those that are under pressure and in decline in the OECD in any case, with increasing production in the newly industrialized countries of South–East Asia of steel, other metals and chemicals. However the development of steel production outside the OECD appears to be linked strongly to domestic demand for steel, much of it for heavy structural uses, as well as lower wage costs and new technologies. Keeling (1992) points out that steel use per unit of GDP tends to increase during a certain phase of development connected with industrialization, buildings and infrastructure, and level off as growth in the economy comes more from services and less steel-intensive sectors. Thus steel consumption in the OECD has declined since 1973, while developing country demand continues to grow – and production has followed the same pattern.   In both steel and chemicals, OECD industries have survived by diversifying into more specialized, high value products such as alloys and high–grade steels or pharmaceuticals, rather than the most energy intensive bulk products that are more cheaply produced elsewhere. Protectionist policies, productivity improvements and redundancies have also been important in maintaining these industries.

It is not clear to what extent the situation will be exacerbated by energy taxes, although these primary industries are already a sensitive sector in which for social and political reasons any further damage would be unpopular. The concern over rising environmental costs is evident in the vocal opposition to the 'Btu tax' by American chemical manufacturers, who claimed it would cost 10,000 jobs in the USA (Storck, 1993). As energy is still a relatively small part of costs, it will be less important than labour costs or technological expertise. World steel prices tend to be fairly volatile, as demand varies cyclically with capital investment throughout the economy, and for this reason as well as others, levels of trade are relatively low at 26 per cent of world output with most industries relying greatly on their domestic markets. Transport costs are often high and markets restricted – Keeling (1992) considers steel to be amongst the most protected industries in the world, with most OECD countries trying to keep their often monopolistic and nationalized industries going. Whether or not this situation changes, the extent to which developing countries can penetrate Western markets will depend on them producing the appropriate steel products of sufficient quality to compete, and suffering the problems of fluctuations in demand and world prices.

A possible policy to alleviate the economic impact on these industries is to exempt them from the tax, but to implement regulation or energy advice and support measures to improve energy efficiency, as the proposed amendment to the EU carbon tax suggested. It is likely that energy intensive industries are already more aware of energy efficiency for cost reasons, and the greatest energy savings from the tax may actually be in the non–intensive sectors. However the effectiveness of a tax depends on its representing the environmental cost of products throughout the economy. Exemption prevents the tax being passed on in increased prices of energy rich raw materials, acting as a signal to secondary producers and consumers. Much of the decline in energy intensity over the last two decades can be attributed to this kind of raw material efficiency, for instance reducing steel use in cars by lighter design, the use of less energy intensive alternatives such as plastics and the growth of recycling of energy intensive materials such as glass and metals. In addition a tax would be expected to shift the consumption function away from energy intensive goods and services, as prices start to favour goods produced using less raw materials, reduced use of agrochemicals, use of recycled materials, or buying goods produced locally. Exemption will hinder all these impacts, making the tax far less effective. Additionally, exemption will reduce the revenue available for recycling, leading to a situation where the 'second tier' of industries lose out while the majority do not gain as much from the double dividend effect. At best, exemption should only be advocated as a temporary measure designed to reduce the transitional costs of a tax.

A further possibility is to tax carbon embodied in imported products, to prevent their comparative advantage. To be effective, this would mean not only taxing raw materials such as metals, chemicals, glass and cement at an appropriate rate according to the energy used in their manufacture, but also taxing the raw materials embodied in other products. A car imported from Korea to Europe would be subject to taxes on the steel, glass and plastics used in its manufacture. This would be practically impossible to implement in terms of measuring the energy inputs to different products, in addition to being politically impossible under the terms of GATT and other trading agreements.

As industrial energy intensity is currently considerably higher in low–cost developing countries, the migration of these industries could result in higher overall energy use as the more efficient OECD plant is replaced. However if one looks at *new* plant in developing countries efficiency is more comparable with OECD; the lower overall efficiency seen in developing countries is generally a result of older and badly maintained plant. In the context of carbon leakage we are considering the early retirement of the least efficient (and hence higher energy cost) OECD plant, and its replacement by new growth elsewhere. Hence it appears a reasonable assumption that efficiencies are at least similar between the two despite the difference in energy prices.

Oil Market Responses

The fuel price effect arises from decreasing demand in countries imposing CO_2 abatement measures having a depressionary effect on world fuel prices, which leads to increases elsewhere. This effect is assumed to be limited to oil, as world markets for coal and gas are currently small compared with total demand, with prices chiefly being set domestically. Gas and coal markets within the OECD would not affect leakage if all the OECD were included in the treaty (or markets within the EU or from US–Canada in the case of unilateral treaties). For the case of oil, the major trade is between OECD and non–OECD countries, that is OPEC and LDC oil producers, and it would be expected that any significant decline in demand would affect the world price. This form of leakage could never exceed the reduction in oil use in the abating countries, as it is dependent on decreasing world demand.

Oil currently accounts for just under 40 per cent of world primary commercial energy (BP, 1996), a figure that has gradually declined with the growth of natural gas. Any change in the price of oil will not only affect oil demand but also demand for gas and coal. As the carbon content of oil is mid–way between the other two, this will have an ambiguous impact on leakage, dependent on cross–price elasticities and fuel substitution behaviour. Lower world oil prices could promote substitution away from coal, especially in large users such as China and India, decreasing CO_2 emissions. But low prices could also inhibit the development of natural gas, which would mean more CO_2 and increased leakage. Despite their potential importance, these interactions are not included in the model EGEM, which only allows for inter–fuel substitution within OECD. Non–OECD behaviour is much less well understood, essentially due to the lack of reliable data and the distorted and changeable nature of fuel markets in these countries.

In the future, markets for coal and gas could develop and internationalise, as trade in these fuels becomes more common. This would increase the potential for leakage by this route.

The issue of OPEC's market power is vital to understanding world oil markets. In 1970, OPEC had a market share of 50 per cent, compared with a current figure of 41 per cent, which has been rising since 1985 when it reached a low of 29 per cent (BP, 1996). Gately (1984) considers the underlying supply–demand balance to be the main driving force, with the OPEC cartel merely a short term anomaly. Certainly non–OPEC producers have grown and have considerable significance in determining supply and prices, as discussed by Bacon (1991), although it is OPEC that acts as swing producer. OPEC no longer wields the power it had in the 1970s (Gately, 1984; Parra, 1994) as now any increase in prices will cause growth in non–OPEC production and a loss in OPEC's market share.

World oil demand is currently depressed by the reduction in demand from the former Soviet Union, whose demand continues to fall albeit at the slower rate of 5.9 per cent in 1995 compared with 10 per cent per year over the last few years (BP, 1996). This appears to be keeping the market very slack and prices low, with world demand only increasing very slowly. However this rate of decline is rather more than would be envisaged from any carbon abatement measures, which would initially only apply to the OECD and be unlikely to do more than keep demand level.

Any effective carbon dioxide abatement policy has to ensure that a substantial amount of oil stays in the ground – reliance on physical resource scarcity increasing the price cannot be effective until too late. Oil (and other fossil fuel) producers must be forced into seeing lower prices to reduce supply, while at the same time the tax wedge between supply and consumer prices must increase to decrease demand. An important corollary of this is that, unless OPEC can restrain production and increase prices, there will be a transfer of wealth from oil producing to consuming countries, as the economic rent from consuming less than the free market equilibrium level of oil is taken more in the form of consumer taxes rather than above–cost producer prices. This process is already occurring as high excise duty on petrol has not passed on to the consumer the fall in the world oil price since 1980, and thus reduces the demand response. It is to be expected therefore that OPEC will do anything in its power to prevent a carbon tax being successful.

Income Effects

Income effects are often neglected by carbon leakage studies despite their overwhelming importance. Any change in GDP, either within the OECD or outside, is likely to have an immediate impact on energy use and therefore CO_2 emissions. These are probably the most complex effect to quantify, being dependent on relationships between prices, energy use and economic growth throughout the world macroeconomy.

One important contributor is the transfer of wealth away from OPEC and other oil exporting countries. A carbon tax within the OECD will cause significant reductions in GDP growth for oil exporters, which will lead to a reduction in their domestic energy demand. As the OPEC countries are among the most energy intensive economies in the world, this could reduce global emissions considerably, having a negative leakage effect.

Other than the energy exporters, the impact on non–OECD countries' economies is ambiguous. Within the OECD, there lies speculation over revenue recycling and the double dividend, with estimates of GDP impacts varying from large negative effects to small positive benefits (Boero et al., 1991; Winters, 1992; Weyant, 1993; Barker et al., 1993; Mabey et al., 1997). Non–OECD countries may see some benefits in terms of competitive advantage, providing a boost to certain sectors of industry. However if GDP growth within the OECD were to be curtailed by any significant amount, this would have knock–on effects on the economies of many other countries. In particular, many LDCs rely on export markets to the OECD for their economic growth, and any contraction of these markets would have a recessionary effect. This would affect some of the fastest growing developing countries, reducing their export revenues and hence having a multiplier effect as imports are reduced from other developing countries. For instance, 24 per cent of exports (by value) from South and South East Asia go to other countries in the same group, but 58 per cent go to OECD countries (EGEM data). Reducing OECD imports thus reduces exports, which then reduces imports as they are constrained by export revenues, reducing exports further. The sectors of the economy affected would be those using commercial fuels and driving the shift away from traditional biomass fuels, potentially leading to a decline in fossil energy intensity and large reductions in carbon emissions (albeit by this undesired route of reduced economic growth), which could contribute a large, negative carbon leakage.

3 USE OF THE EGEM MODEL TO MODEL CARBON LEAKAGE

The energy sector models in the nine OECD countries allow fairly detailed representation of the impact of price changes or taxes on overall energy consumption and CO_2 emissions, and also investigation of interfuel substitution effects in these countries. As an example, Figure 5.1 shows the impact of a

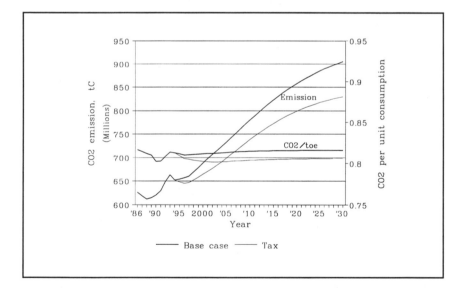

Figure 5.1   Impact of $10/bbl carbon tax in Europe on CO_2 emissions and CO_2/energy ratio

carbon tax of $10/bbl on CO_2 emissions and on the ratio of CO_2 to energy for five European countries (France, Germany, Italy, Netherlands and UK) while the impact on coal, oil and gas consumption is shown in Figure 5.2. The tax promotes considerable fuel switching away from coal and into natural gas, which together with overall reduction in energy use leads to a reduction in emissions of 8 per cent by 2030. Oil use initially increases very slightly due to substitution, then decreases. In order to 'globalize' the model, it was necessary to include models of CO_2 emissions for the rest of the world. EGEM divides the rest of the world into a number of regions: OPEC; the remainder of the OECD not modelled explicitly; South and South East Asia; Latin America; Africa; and the remaining less developed countries including China. Each of these regions is modelled as a trade block, with equations representing import and export volumes, value and prices (with slightly more detail for the OECD). The latter four are grouped together as the LDCs.

Carbon dioxide emissions are modelled for LDCs on a basis of export goods volume, on the assumption that this is an indicator of the commercial energy use in the economy. An elasticity of 0.8 is assumed, as trade has grown more rapidly than GDP, and energy intensity (with respect to GDP) in most countries has remained fairly constant, unlike in the OECD where it is decreasing. Current

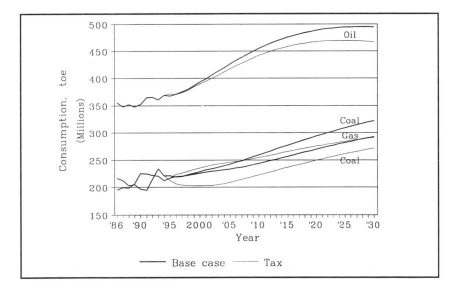

Figure 5.2   Impact of $10/bbl carbon tax in Europe on consumption of coal, oil and gas

emissions are from World Resources Institute data for 1987. An elasticity with respect to world oil price is included weighted according to the share of oil in energy use, as shown in Table 5.3. OPEC countries are modelled similarly but with respect to export value rather than volume with an elasticity of 0.6, as exports being predominantly oil there is a difference due to variations in the oil price. The equation is written in error correction form, to allow a long lag in response, analogous to the equations estimated for the nine countries modelled explicitly. For other OECD countries, consumption is assumed to be proportional to consumption in Europe, as these countries are mainly either current or future EU members, with the exceptions of Switzerland, Norway, Australia, New Zealand, Iceland and Turkey. The equation for carbon dioxide emissions for LDCs is thus given by:

$$D\ln(CO_{2\ t,r}) = 0.8D\ln(CO_{2\ t-1,r}) - 0.1(\ln(CO_{2\ t-1,r})$$

$$- 0.8\ln(XGI_{t-1,r}) + s_r D\ln(P_t) + k) \tag{5.1}$$

where
$CO_{2\ t,r} = CO_2$ production for region r at time t,
$XGI_{t,r}$ = exports goods index,
s_r = oil price elasticity,
P_t is the real world price of oil,
k is a constant derived from the region's current CO_2 emissions.

Table 5.3 Elasticity of CO_2 production with respect to the real price of oil

Region	Elasticity
Africa	–0.24
Latin America	–0.22
South and Southeast Asia	–0.13
China and rest of LDCs	–0.06
Former communist countries	–0.09
OPEC	–0.17

Modelling of the world oil market is on a supply/demand balance with OPEC as the price setter, under a target market share assumption (Baldwin and Prosser, 1988; Greene, 1991). The model assumes that OPEC retains considerable market power, and adjust the price to aim to keep their long–term market share stable at 50 per cent. Non–OPEC producers are assumed to act as price takers, adjusting their supply according to a price elasticity. The figure for elasticity is adapted from Al–Sahlawi (1989), whose empirical study estimated non–OPEC long–term supply elasticities of 0.6 for pooled world data, including the Soviet Union. The figure has been revised upwards, to 0.8, for this study to reflect greater market forces now prevalent in this region. Oil demand within the nine OECD countries is modelled explicitly, elsewhere it is assumed to be proportional to CO_2 as estimated above. No estimates of resource depletion are made, as over the time horizon of the forecast (2030) it is not thought that resources will reach critically low levels; similarly there is no explicit backstop energy source. However the structure of the model forces the real price up if and when demand increases. This model is chosen as a relatively simple form that can replicate long term market trends, although it cannot forecast instability or shocks that may be of great importance.

Oil supply is given by:

$$Dln(S_{ROW, t}) = 0.8 * Dln(P_t) + 0.5Dln(S_{ROW, t-1}) \qquad (5.2)$$

$$S_{OPEC} = D_{TOT} - S_{ROW} \qquad (5.3)$$

where S_{OPEC} = supply from OPEC,
            S_{ROW} = supply from the rest of the world,
            D_{TOT} = total world demand (including stock changes),
            P_t = world oil price, given by:

$$Dln(P_t) = 0.6Dln(P_{t-1}) - 0.2 \times (0.5 - S_{OPEC}/(S_{OPEC} + S_{ROW})) \qquad (5.4)$$

The model as detailed above will estimate the oil price effect on carbon leakage, under the assumption that international coal and gas markets are not developed enough to have a significant impact. The key parameters are the non–OPEC supply elasticity and oil demand elasticity for LDCs. These can be tested by comparison with other forecasts of oil price and LDC energy demand. Interfuel substitution in LDCs is not taken into account, as it is implicitly assumed that fuel mix remains the same as at present.

Trade leakage is divided into that caused by any overall changes in trade volumes and shares, including income effects, and that from the structural shift away from energy intensive processes within the OECD economies. The overall trade changes are made at an aggregate level, dependent on overall producer prices, income and markets. Likewise, income effects depend on changes in GDP within the OECD, and in export volumes or value elsewhere. GDP changes in the OECD may be made exogenously to clarify the impacts.

It is implicit that if the overall impact is small, some industrial sectors will benefit from the reductions in existing taxes, while others pay through the energy tax. For the countries modelled, the proportion of the energy intensive industries to relocate is estimated from the percentage increase in energy costs. For each of the G9 countries, the proportion of energy used in manufacturing is known, as is the proportion in the 'big three' industries of iron and steel, other metals and chemicals. From these the reduction in G9 of these sectors can be estimated, and the CO_2 emission reduction then attributed to other countries.

For each of the nine countries modelled, the proportion of CO_2 arising from heavy industry, allowing for relocation is:

$$Dln(CO_2H_t) = 0.7Dln(CO_2H_{t-1}) - 0.05(ln(CO_2H_{t-1}) - a.C_e.dln(RP) + k \qquad (5.5)$$

where CO_2H = proportion of CO_2 from heavy industry,
             $dln(RP)$ = change in real price of energy from the base case,
             a   = the 'relocation elasticity' (from 2–4 depending upon the number of countries participating in the treaty),
             C_e = the share of industrial costs going to energy (=0.15) and
             k   = a constant derived from the current proportion of energy from the 'big three'.

This change in CO_2 emissions becomes an increase in emissions from non–signatory countries which is added to the total CO_2 for the rest of the world, under the assumption that emissions per unit of goods produced is the same as in the OECD. This does not affect overall trade volumes or prices, as it alters only the net energy intensity of production, as represented by the proportion of energy consumed by the 'big 3'.

Once the total leakage from an OECD policy has been estimated, the results of leakage within the OECD (for example an EC only emissions reduction scenario) are assessed. The 'size' of the treaty is taken into account by adjusting the trade elasticity, allowing the stronger intra–OECD leakage effects to be accounted for. This accounts for the greater possibilities for relocation, and freer markets in fuels and basic materials between OECD countries.

4   RESULTS FROM EGEM

In order to assess the magnitude of the different leakage effects, several model simulations were run. Initially, the income effects arising from changes in OECD GDP are excluded, allowing identification of the oil price and industrial relocation effects brought about by carbon/energy taxes within the OECD. The final simulation endogenizes the macroeconomic impact of the tax, incorporating changes in GDP within the OECD and their knock–on effects on world trade and hence carbon emissions elsewhere.

Figure 5.3 shows the leakage rate brought about by a $10/bbl tax split 50:50 between carbon and energy, phased in from 1995–2002. The figure shows four scenarios for a tax applied throughout the OECD, and in three constituent regions alone: the European Union, North America and Japan. The rate is expressed as a proportion of the total carbon abatement in the region(s) to which the tax applies. This fairly modest tax level is sufficient to reduce carbon emissions within OECD by 14 per cent from their base case level in 2030, which does not achieve stabilization as in the base case OECD emissions rise by 48 per cent from 1990 to 2030.

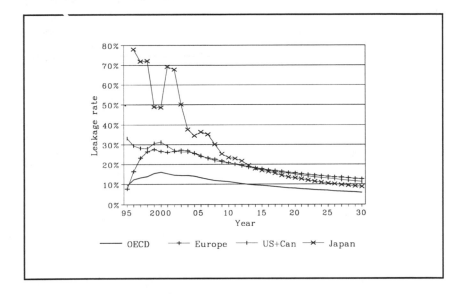

Figure 5.3   Leakage rates for taxes in three regions

For the case of the OECD tax (the solid line), the leakage rate reaches about 16 per cent at its height and later declines to around 6 per cent. The rate declines as abatement continues to increase while the leakage losses stabilize after around 10 years. For a tax in any one of the three regions, the rate is higher, as they will face competition from other OECD countries without the tax, increasing the industrial relocation element of leakage relative to overall abatement. Oil price effects will depend upon the characteristics of the country(ies) with the tax, that is the share of oil in energy consumption and the price elasticities of oil and total energy. The figure shows fairly similar rates for Europe and North America, with rates up to 30 per cent but declining to around 12 per cent. For Japan the initial rate is much higher, at up to almost 80 per cent in the first year, but again declines to under 10 per cent in the long term. The initial high rates in this case are due to Japan's high share of oil – the initial carbon abatement is almost entirely in reduced oil use, which then reduces world price and other countries consumption increases to compensate for Japan's reduction. After some fluctuation, the market then adjusts to a lower oil consumption level so the leakage rate declines.

Figure 5.4 shows for the case of the OECD–wide tax, how the leakage is broken down into the three effects, namely the oil price effect, trade relocation and OPEC–income effect, brought about by a reduction in OPEC's oil revenues and hence own energy use. The data show difference from the base case in GtC, and to put the figures in perspective abatement by the OECD increases to 484 GtC by the year 2030.

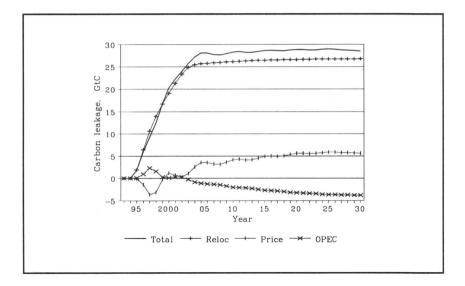

Figure 5.4   Leakage through different channels

It can be seen that the trade effect (crossed line) is the greatest contributor to the total (solid line), but after adapting to the new price the amount levels out. This comes about as the tax causes OECD countries to lose a proportion of their heavy industries, but once they have adapted to the altered price this proportion then remains constant. The oil price effect is significant but smaller, and fluctuates over time as the market comes to a new equilibrium. The lost OPEC revenues and concomitant reduction in emissions from OPEC's own consumption reduces the

overall leakage significantly, virtually cancelling out the positive leakage from
the oil price reduction. The oil price from 2000 to 2030 is maintained at about 1
per cent less than the base case, sufficient to depress production to a lower level
as oil demand overall continues to decrease from its base case level.

A comparison was made to assess the effect of the size of the tax on the leakage
rate. Figure 5.5 shows the forecast leakage rate in 2030, again as a proportion of
abatement, for four different carbon tax rates throughout the OECD. The smallest
is the tax of $10/bbl in 2002 already simulated; the three further scenarios
represent a tax of $10/bbl in 2002 increasing at $1 p.a. thereafter, and taxes of
$20/bbl and $30/bbl increasing at $2 and $3 p.a. respectively. The first of these
is sufficient to stabilize OECD emissions until 2007, resulting in a 10 per cent
increase by 2030 over 1990 (compared with 48 per cent for no tax), while the two
higher rates reduce emissions by 6 per cent and 15 per cent from their 1990 levels
by 2030.

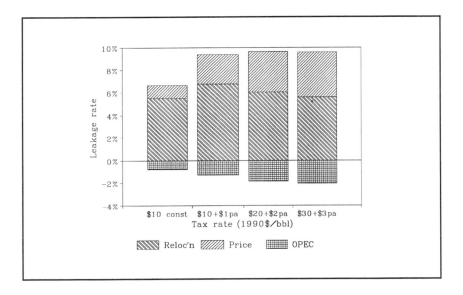

Figure 5.5   Variation in leakage rate with size of tax

It can be seen that the overall leakage rate increases only slightly with the larger
taxes, that is the amount of leakage in tonnes of carbon is increasing at a similar
rate to carbon abatement. The component of leakage from industrial relocation
does not vary greatly remaining at 5–7 per cent. The oil price effect however does

increase with the larger taxes, although this is mitigated by the reduction in emissions from OPEC countries brought about by the depressed oil market.

In order to assess income effects, an exogenous decrease of 1 per cent in consumption (that is total consumption in the economy, as opposed to energy consumption) for all OECD countries was imposed, scaled in over the period studied. This magnitude of decrease is broadly in line with that predicted by a number of studies referred to above, including EGEM, brought about by the decrease in disposable income and increase in prices due to the tax. Imposing the effect exogenously allows the leakage income effect to be clearly analysed, whereas simulations show variations from –3 per cent to +1 per cent in the actual effect depending on country and policy assumptions. The results for this simulation are shown in Figure 5.6, showing the change in carbon emissions in GtC from the base case.

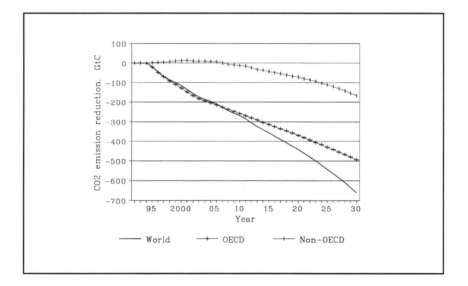

Figure 5.6 Carbon abatement under a 1 per cent reduction in consumption

The income effects are negative, and totally outweigh the positive leakage effects from trade and oil prices: a comparison with Figure 5.4 shows an **increase** of 25 GtC without income effects is now replaced by a **drop** in non–OECD emissions of around 150 GtC . This reduction is brought about solely by the world recession caused by the imposed reduction in consumption, as opposed to any improvement in energy efficiency. Emissions from OECD also decrease further than in the earlier simulations due to the decline in GDP.

5 CONCLUSIONS

The leakage rates estimated here of around 6 per cent by 2030 for the OECD carbon tax represent a fairly small proportion of abatement, indicating that the issue is not sufficiently serious to prevent a carbon tax or other emission reduction policies being worthwhile in terms of the impact on climate. Leakage will be higher if fewer countries participate in a treaty, at around 12 per cent for the case of an EU carbon tax. The rate is also higher initially, as imposition of the tax causes a rapid increase in emissions elsewhere, while the emission reductions in Europe continue to accrue over a longer timescale. This longer term reduction is due to the functional form used in the model, with the endogenous technical efficiency term described above.

Leakage is important in terms of climate change mitigation, as a large leakage rate would negate the efforts of those countries reducing emissions. It is also important in terms of treaty stability and acceptability. High leakage reduces the incentive for any one country or group of countries to abate, as the benefits in terms of climate are less; perhaps more importantly, the related concerns over competitiveness and loss of industrial development are a major barrier to agreements. It is these concerns that have thwarted the establishment of carbon taxes both in Europe and the United States.

It is quite possible that a carbon tax could cause leakage without any loss in competitiveness. The tax would promote a shift towards less energy intensive industries, but the benefits from revenue recycling to the majority of industry would balance the costs to the fairly small proportion that would be hard hit. Reductions in taxation could be used either to reduce taxes on employment and thus reduce manufacturers' costs in addition to helping to reduce unemployment; or to reduce income tax or indirect taxes, which would contribute to economic growth via increased consumer spending. The same processes that govern the relationship between carbon taxes and GDP also apply to competitiveness, and in broad terms it is not self-evident that there would be any net effect.

More crucially, costs may be incurred in the short term from adapting to the new tax regime; the industries affected may be of particular strategic significance or be major employers; or the political impact of damaging these industries may be greater than the small and 'invisible' benefit to the rest of the economy. Transitional costs could be real and severe. Any tax or other abatement regime needs to be introduced gradually, with the maximum of advance notice to allow forward–looking investment to adapt, and to obviate the need for premature retirement of plant. Certain countries or regions are more dependent on energy intensive industries, and these may require additional regional assistance to weather the changes, which could be funded through the tax.

In the longer term however, any carbon reduction strategy to be successful will require reductions in use of energy intensive raw materials, hence contraction of these industries is inevitable and must be accepted as such. There are many longer term benefits to be gained from diversification into alternatives, whether this means designing for recycling, development of new materials, or producing innovative new technologies to reduce energy use. Once these trends are recognized, it will become increasingly attractive to businesses to be at the forefront rather than surviving on existing, outmoded technologies.

More clear cut is the impact on energy exporting countries. As carbon taxes create a wedge between production and consumption, exporters will face an unambiguous loss in revenues as both world prices and consumption fall, and more of the economic rent is taken as consumer taxes. This may affect not only OPEC but also producers in higher cost areas such as the North Sea. Exporters of coal could also be severely affected, while natural gas demand will tend to be maintained while resources allow.

It is evident that more evidence is needed on some of the economic systems underlying carbon leakage, in particular empirical data on the impact of taxes and regulation on industries' decisions to invest in a certain country. More dialogue is needed between academic economists and policy makers, such that the reality of the political environment is reflected in the questions investigated, and that once consensus is reached amongst the academic community, this can be effectively communicated to inform policy. At present this dialogue is tenuous, although partly as a result of the lack of consensus. At best any quantitative model will be an approximation, but important insights can still be made and should be passed on.

The income effects simulated in the final scenario here demonstrate that these could be the most important form of leakage by far, with any significant change in GDP leading to large changes in energy use worldwide. The 1 per cent drop in consumption was assumed for the sake of clarity of analysis; however it is possible that rather than a drop, more efficient taxes could lead to an increase in GDP, which when multiplied worldwide could cancel out the carbon savings from abatement. Any overall loss of competitiveness in the OECD could also provide a boost to non–OECD countries, allowing them to expand developed country markets, and having an increased leakage effect through their increased income. As the non–OECD countries develop their economies they are likely to seek entry into the OECD, and could be encouraged to join international environmental treaties as a condition of doing so. While the industrialized countries practically and morally must bear the brunt of any costs of climate change policy today, in the future the LDCs too must develop in a sustainable way, and not just take over the polluting and energy intensive industries rejected by us.

The carbon taxes considered here represent fairly marginal changes, and are not sufficient to stabilize climate in the long term. There is still valid debate about the potential costs and benefits of climate change mitigation, but it apppears probable that to meet the Rio objective of stabilizing atmospheric CO_2 concentrations at a safe level, much more stringent measures will be required at some future date. There are no easy solutions and the problem will not just go away. Economic policy across the board needs to consider these issues and implement policies to promote the carbon–free economy. This may mean not just developing non–fossil energy sources, but expanding growth worldwide in the low energy activities of the service sector, leisure industries and financial services, rather than material goods and manufacturing. In welfare terms as well as conventional economic growth, consumer satisfaction can come from high value, low material input goods and services rather than purely from material goods – a fundamental change in consumption patterns that underlies sustainable development.

NOTES

1.   France, Germany, Italy, UK, Belgium, Netherlands, USA, Canada and Japan.

DISCUSSANT: Paul Ekins

Carbon leakage is an important issue, not least because its possibility can significantly reduce the will to tackle the issue of climate change. There is little point, it is argued, in even quite large groups of countries acting to reduce their emissions if this simply causes emissions to rise elsewhere.

However, the issue is a complex one, as Clare Smith's paper makes admirably clear and it is extremely difficult to model the various complexities satisfactorily. This is doubtless one explanation why the extant estimates of carbon leakage differ so much. It also means that any new modelling attempt needs to be very clear about its structure and assumptions, as they relate both to other modelling attempts and to the intractable realities of the real world. In some respects, the value of a new modelling attempt is not so much in the actual numerical results it generates, which are almost bound to be hedged round with ifs and buts, but in the opportunity it gives to revisit and worry again at all the various issues which are important in this area. One of the values of this paper is that it seizes this opportunity effectively.

It is necessary to distinguish clearly, as this paper does, between the three possible routes to leakage: via relocation of energy–intensive industries from taxed to untaxed countries; via price responses in the world markets for oil and other fossil fuels; and via income responses from the various effects of imposing energy taxes and of price changes. Each of these three areas is characterized by uncertainty, which is compounded by the fact that the areas are also interlinked. Thus relocation may amplify the (downward) income responses in taxed countries, which may reduce imports from untaxed countries. Lower world prices for oil will obviously affect (reduce) the incomes of oil producers. The responses of OPEC and non–OPEC producers to the price changes, and to each others' reactions to them, are a further source of unpredictability.

Models inevitably simplify and abstract from such complexities, and EGEM, the model described in the paper, is no exception. Some important linkages are left completely out of account, such as effects on the fuel choice (especially between oil and coal) in LDCs and the possibility of modernization effects during relocation leading to emission reductions. The means of treating LDC countries' CO_2 emissions (weighting their CO_2 elasticity with regard to the oil price by the share of oil in their energy consumption) results in China and India, for example, having very low CO_2 elasticities. Yet it may be either that a lower oil price encourages oil–using investment in these countries which is unrelated to the current share of oil in their energy use (thereby increasing emissions more than the model suggests); or that it encourages a switch away from coal without greatly increasing overall energy use (thereby reducing them).

The EGEM results fall within the range of other modelling results and seem reasonable. Of the unmodelled effects noted above, a shift from oil to coal would reduce the (modest) oil price effect, while greater investment would increase it; and modernization with relocation would reduce the much more substantial relocation effects. A more remarkable result is the fact that the long–term leakage rate does not vary with the size of the tax applied, even when it is more than trebled, remaining at under 10 per cent. This implies that a carbon tax in OECD countries alone could produce a substantial effect on global emissions.

One of the most controversial issues in the literature is whether a carbon tax imposed unilaterally in one country or a group of countries would negatively affect their economic performance in terms of GDP and its growth. The paper notes this as an issue, and the importance of how the tax revenues are recycled, in its discursive section, but sidesteps it when coming to the modelling. Instead it imposes a 1 per cent drop in consumption on OECD countries as a result of the carbon tax to assess the effects on carbon leakage. The result is a reduction in carbon emissions in non–OECD countries (because of trade effects) that is about six times the leakage calculated earlier. OECD emissions are reduced even more. On these figures a double dividend (which would prevent such a drop in consumption occurring) might be economically attractive, but certainly reduces the environmental benefits of the tax.

Finally, an issue which is often not mentioned in leakage studies is also omitted here. There are currently great disparities in per capita carbon emissions between OECD and non–OECD countries. This is recognized in the Framework Convention on Climate Change by the fact that only high per capita emitters (Annex I countries) are currently expected to undertake any carbon abatement. It is clear that until per capita emissions are substantially narrowed, low per capita emitters will be unwilling to undertake carbon abatement, even though they may be, or will soon become, high absolute emitters (like India and China). Leakage amounts to a transfer of emissions from high to low per capita emission countries. Undoubtedly it represents a diminution of the environmental effectiveness of any particular environmental measure. But if it aids the development of LDCs, and serves to narrow the gap between high and low per capita emitters, it may bring closer the day when all countries will agree to some carbon reduction commitments, which is what is ultimately required if the challenge of climate change is to be effectively addressed. Thus, even if leakage is a more significant phenomenon than this paper, among others, suggests, it should not prevent high per capita emission countries from taking the necessary steps to reduce their carbon output.

Discussion

Effects on GDP are ambiguous in the analysis. Taxes might recycle wealth from the OPEC to Europe and the market power of OPEC has decreased, largely due to the collapse of the Soviet Union.

Substitution of oil for coal was not examined outside the OECD as there were insufficient data and resources. It is possible that there would be relocation with a resulting introduction of plant with a higher energy efficiency, but if there were low local energy prices there would be lower energy efficiency in relocated industries.

REFERENCES

Al-Sahlawi, Mohammed A. (1989), 'Oil price changes and non–OPEC oil supply: an empirical analysis', *OPEC Review*, Spring, 11–19.

Bacon, Robert (1991), 'Modelling the price of oil', *Oxford Review Of Economic Policy*, **7**(2), 17–34.

Baldwin, Nick and Richard Prosser, (1988), 'World Oil Market Simulation', *Energy Economics*, July, 185–98.

Barker, T., S. Baylis and P. Madsen (1993), 'A UK carbon/energy tax: the macroeconomic effects', *Energy Policy*, March, 296–308.

Barrett, S. (1994a), 'Self-enforcing International Environmental Agreements', *Oxford Economic Papers* 46: 878–894.

Barrett, S. (1994b), 'Trade restrictions in international environmental agreements', *The Globe*, Issue 19, June, 6-7, UK Office, ESRC, Swindon.

Boero, G., R. Clarke and L.A. Winters (1991), *The Macroeconomic Consequences of Controlling Greenhouse Gases: A Survey*, DOE Environmental Economics Research Series, HMSO, London.

BP (1996), *Statistical Review of World Energy*.

Burniaux, J., J.P. Martin, G. Nicoletti and J. Oliveira–Martins (1992), 'The costs of reducing CO_2 emissions: evidence from Green', OECD *Economics and Statistics Dept. Working Paper* 115, Paris, 73.

Ekins, Paul and Michael Jacobs (1994), 'Are environmental sustainability and economic growth compatible?', *Energy–environment–economy Modelling Discussion Paper* 7, June.

Felder, S. and T.F. Rutherford (1993), 'Unilateral CO_2 reductions and carbon leakage: the consequences of international trade in basic materials', *Journal of Environmental Economics and Management*, **25**, 162–176.

Gately, Dermot (1984), 'A ten–year retrospective: OPEC and the world oil market', *Journal of Economic Literature*, **XXII** (Sept.), 1100–14.

Greene, D.L. (1991), 'A note on OPEC market power and oil prices', *Energy Economics*, April, 123-129.

Jaffe, A., S. Peterson, P. Portney and R. Stavins (1995), 'Environmental regulation and the competitiveness of us manufacturing: what does the evidence tell us?', *Journal of Economic Literature*, **XXXIII** (March), 132–163.

Keeling, Bernard (1992), 'Structural change in the world steel industry: a north–south perspective', in: G. Van Liemt (ed), *Industry On The Move: Causes and Consequences of International Relocation in the Manufacturing Industry*, Ilo, Geneva, 149-178.

Mabey, N., S. Hall, C. Smith and S. Gupta (1997), *'Argument in the Greenhouse: the International Economics of Controlling Global Warming'*, Routledge, London, 1997.

Manne, Alan S. and Thomas F. Rutherford (1994), 'International trade in oil, gas and carbon emission rights: an intertemporal general equilibrium model', *Energy Journal*, **15**(1), 57-76.

Manne. Alan S. and Richard G. Richels,(1992), *Buying Greenhouse Insurance: The Economic Cost of CO_2 Emission Limits*, MIT Press, Cambridge MA.

Oliveira–Martins, J., J. Burniaux, and J.P. Martin (1993), 'Trade and the effectiveness of unilateral CO_2 abatement policies: evidence from Green', Fondazione Eni Enrico Mattei, *Nota Di Lavoro* 47.93, Milan, 20.

Parra, F.R. (1994), 'OPEC and the price of oil in 1993', *Energy Journal*, **15**(1), 17-30.

Perroni, C. and T.F. Rutherford (1993), 'International trade in carbon emission rights and basic materials: general equilibrium calculations for 2020', *Scandinavian Journal Of Economics*, **95**(3), 257-278.

Pezzey, John (1991), '*Impacts of Greenhouse Gas Control Strategies on UK Competitiveness*', DTI, HMSO, London.

Pezzey, John (1992), 'Analysis of unilateral CO_2 control in the European Community and OECD', *The Energy Journal*, **13**(3), 159-171.

Smith, C., S. Hall and N. Mabey (1995), 'Econometric modelling of international carbon tax regimes', *Energy Economics*, **17**(2), 133-146.

Storck, William (1993), 'CMA says energy tax will cut jobs, increase costs'. *Chemical and Engineering News*, **71**, Iss. 14, 5 April, 21.

United Nations, (1992), *Annual Bulletin of General Energy Statistics for Europe*, xxiii, 1990.

Weyant, J.P. (1993), 'Costs of reducing global carbon emissions', *Journal of Economic Perspectives*, **7**, 27-46.

Winters, Alan L. (1992), 'The trade and welfare effects of greenhouse gas abatement: a survey of empirical estimates', in: Kym Anderson and Richard Blackhurst (eds), *The Greening of World Trade Issues*, Harvester Wheatsheaf.

Wyckoff, Andrew W. and Joseph M. Roop (1994), 'The embodiment of carbon in imports of manufactured products', *Energy Policy,* **22**(3), 187-194.

6. Effects of national, OECD–wide and world–wide energy taxes on the environment and on competitiveness

Carl C. Koopmans[*]

1 INTRODUCTION

In recent years, environmental problems have become increasingly serious. Consequently, the environment is on the political agenda in many countries, and environmental policy is developing rapidly. The incidence of environmental deterioration is closely linked to the scale and nature of production and consumption, especially that of physical goods. Along with the economy, fossil energy use, road traffic and waste production tend to grow as well. The main task of environmental policy is to curb these unwanted side effects.

In Section 2, the instruments available for environmental policy are compared. Section 3 presents empirical results obtained in extensive Dutch research on introducing energy taxes on different geographic scales. Special attention is given to the crucial influence of assumptions regarding the labour market and firm behaviour. In Section 4, the previous results are used in order to construct energy tax proposals for different geographic scales. Also, a perspective is described in which 'environmental diplomacy' is used to increase the scale. Section 5 concludes.

*   Many ideas in this paper were conceived in co–operation with Dirk J. Wolfson (see Wolfson and Koopmans, 1996).

2 INSTRUMENTS

Environmental problems arise because environmental values are not articulated in the choices made by producers and consumers. This view is visualized in Figure 6.1 (see Scientific Council, 1994).

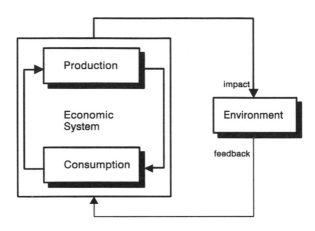

Figure 6.1 Lack of feedback

The resulting allocation is sub–optimal because there are insufficient feedbacks from environmental effects to (economic) behaviour. In public administration, therefore, the question is how to best exploit the potential of different instruments by making them reflect environmental values in the behaviour of individuals and organizations.

Until recently, regulatory bans and permits were the main type of instrument used in environmental policy. This preference for legal coercion was due to the high degree of precision and effectiveness this type of instrument was expected to achieve. The legislature prescribes a certain behaviour, making government responsible for monitoring, compliance and enforcement. The instruments involved, however, are heavily reliant on the availability of information and enforcement is often very difficult (Scientific Council, 1992). It became recognized that the size and nature of environmental problems require a sustained effort on the part of policymakers to incorporate incentives in the economic system, instead of adding more instruments of coercion to the system.

Charges and taxes are an efficient way of internalizing negative external effects, increasing private costs to the level of social costs (Pigou, 1932). Unlike coercion, charges and taxes offer a choice; only the parameters in that choice are changed to incorporate environmental values. People and institutions can still optimize. Consequently, reductions of damaging emissions are achieved at the lowest possible total cost (Baumol and Oates, 1988). Subsidies may seem to be a more friendly way to influence behaviour, but they are at odds with the polluter–pays–principle. Furthermore, subsidies may increase pollution, as they stimulate extra growth of polluting industries (Baumol and Oates, 1988).

Instruments based on persuasion (covenants, information campaigns) also aim at incorporating environmental values into economic behaviour. However, the effectiveness of this instrument type is doubtful.

Price Elasticity

It is often believed that a low price elasticity is a particular drawback when it comes to using regulatory charges. However, a low elasticity indicates that environmentally friendly behaviour entails high opportunity costs for the target group. In such cases, **any** instrument will be faced with an inelastic response. Considerable enforcement problems can be expected if coercion is used. Charges and taxes are also hard to enforce, but at least they keep the costs to a minimum, directing change to the points of least resistance. Persuasion will simply not work. Therefore, a low elasticity is a drawback with any instrument.

Geographic Scale

The ideal geographic scale for environmental policy depends on both the geographic scale of the environmental problem involved, and the geographic scale of the markets in which the polluters operate. If the policy scale is smaller than the scale of the environmental problem, total pollution will only be partly reduced. If the policy scale is smaller than the market scale, there is a strong risk that polluters will move their business to other areas within the market, where regulation is less strict or absent.

The main environmental problems caused by energy use are global (greenhouse effect, depletion) or continental (acidification) in nature. This would call for global policies, with continental policies as a next best alternative. The polluters involved are diverse: some are households or small businesses operating on a regional or national market, others are big firms that compete globally. Again, the ideal policies would be global, with continental policies as second best.

3 ENERGY TAX RESEARCH

In 1991 the Dutch Government initiated extensive research into energy taxes (Steering Committee, 1992; CPB, 1992). Three main types of taxes were considered: an OECD–wide tax on all fossil fuels, a national tax on all fossil fuels, and a national tax on energy use in which large users (over one million cubic metres of natural gas per year, or equivalent amounts of oil or electricity) are exempted. I will not describe all the lengthy and tedious steps made to assess the effects of these taxes. Instead I will report on some matters of interest encountered: which type of base line scenario was used? how are elasticities to be computed? which displacement effects are important? how do energy taxes affect the international distribution of rents? do energy taxes yield a 'double dividend'? are one–country–taxes feasible?

Base Line Scenario

As a base line, the 'European Renaissance' scenario (CPB, 1992a, 1992b) was selected in which European integration continues steadily. In macroeconomic policy, a 'coordination perspective' remains dominant, reflecting Keynesian views on short sightedness (excessively high rate of time preference) and uncertainties, requiring active government intervention. Energy taxes are appropriate in this context.

Elasticities

Although elasticities are not very important in choosing between instruments (see Section 2), they do indicate the effect of taxation. Therefore, estimates of elasticities were needed. This requires a choice between revealed preference (time series) and stated preference (polls). Time series data of past responses to high energy prices during the oil crises of 1973 and 1979 may underestimate the potential of regulatory taxation, as technical innovations lag behind and preferences might have changed since then. It was decided to specify elasticities primarily retrospectively, to avoid the risk of socially desirable stated preferences undermining the credibility of the results. In some cases where the econometric evidence was lacking, selected imputations were made on the basis of technical possibilities. We may conclude that the elasticities used may be somewhat conservative. The computed effects on energy use imply long–term price elasticities for the Netherlands of about –0.2, –0.3 and –0.7 for households, firms and transport, respectively.

Effects on world energy consumption were estimated on a region–by–region basis. With respect to displacement effects, imputations were made on a sector–by–sector basis, using information on relative cost levels and profit margins in the baseline scenario.

Results: One–Country Taxes

Not surprisingly, a national, all–user energy tax of 50 per cent in the Netherlands only is not an attractive option. Despite the recycling of the revenues towards labour costs, massive displacement of (energy intensive) industry results, leading to a GDP which is 6 per cent below the base after the first ten years. Later on, this is partly compensated by extra growth in labour intensive sectors, but the total effect in 2015 is still unfavourable (see Table 6.1, first column).

However, if 'large users' (together responsible for about half of Dutch energy use) are exempted, the growth loss is only 0.1 per cent, while employment may rise by 0.2 per cent. Energy use of 'small users' would eventually be reduced by 7 per cent (3.5 per cent for the Netherlands as a whole). It is important to note here that the Netherlands have a very open economy (about half of our national production is exported), with an energy intensive structure. For less open or less energy intensive economies, the negative effects (if any) of energy taxes will probably be smaller (see Table 6.1, second column).

We conclude that one–country taxes are feasible, if energy intensive industry is exempted. Also, the economic effects confirm the notion that one instrument cannot reach two goals (environment and employment). One–country taxes should be considered an environmental instrument; accordingly, they should be shaped as regulatory charges, aimed at substitution, not at revenues.

Results: International Taxes

An all–user OECD–wide energy tax of 50 per cent, modelled without compensating trade restrictions, would displace energy intensive industries to non–OECD countries. The loss in OECD income would be 7 per cent. Non–OECD countries would suffer from the unfavourable effects on the OECD economies, despite the displacement: non–OECD income would be reduced by 3 per cent by 2015 (see Table 6.1, third column). World income would be reduced by 6 per cent. The effect on world wide energy consumption is 16 per cent. It is important to note that, under the ceteris paribus conditions maintained, no trade policies were assumed to counter displacement effects; if such policies were implemented, the results would be better, of course.

In other research, CPB (1992b) has estimated the effects of an all–user worldwide carbon tax. The baseline for this tax was the 'Balanced Growth' scenario. This scenario is dominated by a market perspective. Not surprisingly, a worldwide tax would not cause substantial displacement. The effects on world income and world energy use are comparable to the results of the OECD tax

Table 6.1 Main effects of energy taxes, 1990–2015, in real terms

	percentages as differences from the base			
	Netherlands all users tax	Netherlands non–tradeables tax	OECD tax	World tax
Assumptions				
Tax level	50 [a]	50 [a]	50 [a]	70 [b]
Exemptions	none	cars, large users	none	none
Trade measures	none	none	none	yes
Oil prices	+ 3 p.a.	+3 p.a.	+3 p.a.	+3 p.a.
Recycling of revenues	labour costs	labour costs	labour costs	other taxes
World				
GDP			−6	−6
GDP (OECD)			−7	na
GDP		negligible	−3	na
Effect on oil prices at source			−1 p.a.	−1 p.a.
Energy consumption			−16	−16
CO_2 emission			−21	−43
Netherlands				
GDP	−6	0	−14	na
Employment	−1	0	+1	na
Energy	−36	−3	−29	na

Notes: a Of Netherlands end–user prices in 1993. Half of the tax is based on energy content, the other half on carbon content. Renewables are exempted. The tax is introduced in 1993

  b Of world end–user prices in 1990. The tax is based on carbon content only. The tax is increased gradually over the period 1990–2015; its end level is given.

  c Excluding not only the CO_2 tax itself, but also its effect on oil prices at source

Source: CPB (1992a, 1992b, 1993)

described above (see Table 6.1, fourth column). The average tax level of the world tax is higher, but the OECD tax is introduced in one step in 1993, while the world tax is introduced very gradually over the period. Moreover, the pure carbon base of the world tax strongly promotes substitution from coal to oil, from oil to natural gas, and from fossil fuels to renewable sources. As a result, the effect on world CO_2 emission is much larger than the effect on energy use.

Terms of trade

The demand reduction caused by our OECD tax would shift up to 25 per cent of the tax backward on producer prices of energy exporters; for a global tax this would be about one third. This implies a substantial gain in the terms of trade of net energy importers (all OECD, except Mexico, The Netherlands, Norway and the United Kingdom). Effectively, part of the rent on energy production would go to energy consuming countries. Clearly, such a welfare gain makes a big difference in determining the feasibility of energy taxation. Much depends, therefore, on our ability to deal with prisoners' dilemmas in getting a worldwide system in place, a matter to which we will return in Section 4.

Double Dividend?

An important matter in the debate on the regulatory taxation of energy is the question whether substituting suboptimal taxes on wages by optimal taxes on energy might create a double dividend in terms of both employment creation and sustainability, as suggested by among others, Pearce (1991) and Repetto et al. (1992). The results presented here suggest that we cannot have it both ways. We may note that this depends on the empirical specification of the models used.

Recognizing that, in tax design, we need a separate instrument for every single target, we have to come clear on our goals: do we want to (1) optimize the tax structure by replacing suboptimal taxes with 'normal' taxes on energy, with some substitution as a side effect, or do we want to (2) optimize sustainability with as much substitution as possible, and forget about the revenue as a structural source? We cannot have it both ways, without compromising on targets. In the next section, we will assume that the environment is the primary goal of energy taxes.

4 SOLVING PRISONER'S DILEMMAS

The International Context

Agreement regarding the objectives and instruments of greenhouse emission policy is not easily reached because the circumstances of countries differ considerably. Three general divisions exist (CPB, 1996):

1.   North versus South. Less developed countries tend to be primarily interested in securing economic development. These countries would consider it unfair if they were denied the right to consume as much energy per capita as the developed world.
2.   Energy producing versus energy consuming countries. As energy taxes allow consuming countries to take a share of the rent on energy production, energy consuming countries have an economic as well as an environmental interest in pressing for energy taxes.
3.   Vulnerable versus less vulnerable countries. Countries in low–lying coastal areas have a greater interest in securing international action to curb greenhouse gas emissions than other countries. This division is likely to become more sharply defined as research or experience makes it clearer exactly what the potential consequences of global warming are for individual countries.

Because of these divisions, it is very hard to secure international agreement on a common policy.

All in the Game

Countries that advocate an international greenhouse emission policy are in a classic 'prisoner's dilemma'; they know that, in global terms, collaboration is the best way forward, but most choose to wait and see what happens, because they fear the negative economic consequences of going it alone. Many countries, especially in the northern part of Europe, would like to introduce energy taxes, but are afraid of displacement effects. As a result, every country waits for others to start. A well known fact in game theory is that prisoners' dilemmas only persist if the parties involved do not cooperate, for instance because communication is impossible, or because they do not trust each other. Another important characteristic of this particular game–theoretic situation is that it is not a zero sum game.[1] Energy taxes can reduce environmental problems, partly replace other taxes (for instance on labour), and they can improve the terms of trade for energy importing countries. Therefore, the northern European countries can do themselves and others a favour by first communicating, and then cooperating, in getting energy taxes underway.

Using Exemptions

The major problem in this process is how to control displacement effects. For this aim, we can use exemptions. The Scientific Council (1992) proposed not to tax 'unavoidable use' (inelastic demand, for example the first 80 per cent of the energy used by each household or firm). This would reduce the amounts of money raised, making displacement smaller while maintaining the environmental effect. In view of the research results mentioned above the Netherlands have decided to follow this proposal: a small user tax will be introduced in 1996. In this tax, part of the energy use of each household or firm is exempted.[2]

We may note that this implies progressive tax rates, as opposed to the (failed) proposal of the European Commission (1992), in which rates were regressive. The regulatory tax proposed here is aimed mainly at the elastic part of energy use. The European Commission proposal, on the contrary, had many characteristics of a 'normal' tax, aimed mainly at raising revenues.

Southern Europe

The next step is to increase the geographic scale of the tax proposed here to include other European countries; this would make it possible to increase rates and/or reduce exemptions without risking displacement effects. The northern countries can propose a tradeoff between support for energy taxes and support for the fiscal budgets of southern countries in the European Union. Once at the EU level, most exemptions can be dropped and replaced by external trade policies.

And then?

After that, the future becomes hazy. The United States may well support the introduction of equivalent tradeable permits. Japan may cooperate as well, under trade policy pressures from EU and US, but is not absolutely essential, as Japan's prices of fossil fuels are already at 80 per cent above the OECD average. Trade–and–aid policies might help to bring the rest of the non–OPEC world into the coalition as well.[3]

Note that the regulatory element in the tax weakens gradually, as decreasing exemptions (and gradual broadening to areas where exemptions won't work, such as motor fuels) make it look more and more like a 'normal' tax on energy. However, the primary impact on controlling energy use and emissions remains, as the tax rates are set for this goal.

5 CONCLUSION

Energy taxes appear to be worthwhile. The northern European countries could make a joint effort to carefully introduce such taxes, meanwhile making great efforts to persuade other countries to join them. These taxes should be shaped to maximize the environmental effect (not employment), and to minimize displacement of industry. Well–designed exemptions can reach both goals.

NOTES

1. Carraro and Siniscalco (1994) also describe environmental taxes in game–theoretical terms.
2. The first 800 cubic metres of natural gas and the first 800 KWh of electricity is untaxed.
3. Displacement of energy intensive industries to oil producing countries can be discouraged by levying equivalent taxes on energy intensive goods imported from these countries.

DISCUSSION

The Prisoner's Dilemma problem can be solved if communication between the players is possible; a theoretical underpinning is provided by the Folk Theorem.

The result of a 6 per cent change in world GDP (Table 6.1) might seem surprisingly large, but this translates into 0.25 per cent per year, which is reasonable given the high tax rate used. Furthermore, the benefits of a tax may have been underestimated, as the model did not incorporate all dynamic effects.

One problem with macroeconomic models is that they are based on historical data. Since short or long term elasticities may be changing, this could lead to inaccurate predictions. Given the uncertainties associated with these models, it would be undesirable to try to reduce the number of different models. As a minimum, such models should include both energy producers and consumers and should distinguish between oil, gas and coal.

REFERENCES

Baumol, W.J. and W.E. Oates (1988), *The Theory of Environmental Policy*, Cambridge University Press,Cambridge.

Carraro, C. and D. Siniscalco (1994), *International Co–ordination of Environmental Policies and Implementation of International Environmental Agreements*, paper presented at the 50th Congress of the International Institute of Public Finance, 22–25 August, Harvard University.

CPB (Netherlands Bureau for Economic Policy Analysis) (1992a), *Regulating Energy tax: Working Paper*, Ministry of Economic Affairs, The Hague.

CPB (Netherlands Bureau for Economic Policy Analysis) (1992b), *Scanning the Future*, The Hague.

CPB (Netherlands Bureau for Economic Policy Analysis) (1993), *Wereld energie scenario's* (World Energy Scenarios), Research Memorandum no. 101, The Hague (in Dutch).

CPB (Netherlands Bureau for Economic Policy Analysis) (1996), *The Economy and the Environment: In Search of Sustainable Development (extensive summary)*, Working Paper no. 87, The Hague.

European Commission (1992), *Proposal for a Council Directive Introducing a Tax on Carbon Dioxide Emissions and Energy*, Brussels.

Pearce, D. (1991), The role of carbon taxes in adjusting to global warming, *The Economic Journal*, **101**, 938–948.

Pigou, A.C. (1932), *The Economics of Welfare*, MacMillan and Co, 4th edition.

Repetto, R., R.C. Dower, R. Jepkins and J. Geoghegan (1992), *Green Fees: How a Tax Shift Can Work for the Environment and the Economy,* World Resources Institute.

Scientific Council for Government Policy (WRR) (1992), *Environmental Policy: Strategy, Instruments and Enforcement*, The Hague.

Scientific Council for Government Policy (WRR) (1994), *Sustained Risks: A Lasting Phenomenon*, The Hague.

Steering Committee (1992), *Regulating Energy tax: Report*, Ministry of Economic Affairs, The Hague.

Wolfson, D.J. and C.C. Koopmans (1996), 'Regulatory taxation of fossil fuels: theory and policy', *Ecological Economics*, **19**(1).

PART THREE

Economic Analyses of Countries and Firms

7. Environmental regulation and competitiveness

Eirik Romstad

1 INTRODUCTION

Several proposed national environmental regulations have been shelved because they would put affected domestic industries at a competitive disadvantage. This has been a particular concern regarding trans–boundary pollutants because the national welfare gains from improved environmental quality are more likely to be offset by the welfare losses caused by the affected firms exiting the industry or moving to countries where environmental regulations are less strict.

This chapter discusses the problems of (i) potential losses in market shares if the regulations impose extra costs on the firms and (ii) the free riding element in case of trans–boundary pollutants. Pertaining to (i), this chapter will show that the relative merits of emission taxes versus tradeable emission permits depends heavily on the possibility of reimbursement under the tax scheme. This is the topic of the next section in this chapter. The effect of the regulations on firms' competitiveness enters as an important factor in reducing the free riding aspects when emissions are trans–boundary, as will be demonstrated in the third section.

In the fourth section the Porter hypothesis – that environmental regulations increase firms' competitiveness (Porter, 1990) – is investigated in more detail from a theoretical perspective and through reference to empirical studies.

2 FIRM COMPETITIVENESS AND ENVIRONMENTAL REGULATIONS

As long as the marginal damage curves are the same at various locations, both emission taxes and tradeable quotas would lead to the least abatement costs for society under perfect competition as well as the same aggregate emission level (Weitzman, 1974; Baumol and Oates, 1988). If permits are grandfathered and there are no lump sum paybacks to the firms from the tax alternative, the effects on firms' costs are, however, quite different. To see this, consider the following figure of a tradeable permit and emission tax system where the permit price becomes the same as the emission tax (initial permits are distributed at no cost to firms). The overall cost savings to society of applying an emission tax or a tradeable permit system for equal reductions for the two firms (from z^0 to z_i,

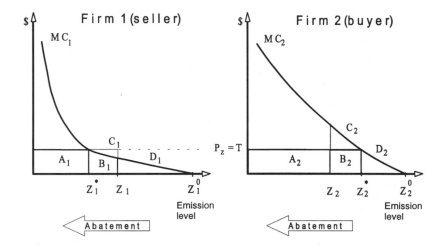

Notes: emission tax $= T = P_z =$ permit price,
$Z^0_n =$ initial emission level for firm n,
$Z^*_n =$ optimal emission level for firm n given environmental regulation,
$Z_n =$ initial emission quota for firm n.

Figure 7.1 Emission taxes and tradeable permits

where i indexes the firm) in this example equal the sum of the areas C_1 and C_2. The costs to the firms of an emission tax or a tradeable permit system depends on the additional mechanisms that are used. Assume that initial emission quotas, z_1

= z_2, are given to the firms for free under the permit system. The extra costs incurred by a uniform emission tax compared to a system of tradeable emission permits are for the seller (firm 1) the sum of the areas $A_1 + C_1$, and for the buyer (firm 2) the area A_2. If the emission permits were auctioned off, the rents associated with the tradeable permit system would be likely to vanish, making the costs to the firms of the emission tax and the tradeable emission permits the same. One way of making the costs of the two systems equal when initial quotas are given for free, is to have some lump sum paybacks in the case of the tax system.[1]

From a perspective of society one should also consider the transaction and implementation costs associated with policies. Generally the transaction costs for an emission tax without lump sum paybacks are less than the transaction costs for an equivalent tradeable emission permit system. The primary reasons for this are: (i) that the costs of setting up the (permit) exchange are likely to exceed the costs of a cost effective tax collection scheme, and (ii) that tradeable permits incur an extra decision problem/transaction for the firms, namely that of operating in the permit market.

Conversely, the costs of implementing tradeable permits are lower than is the case for taxes.[2] The primary explanation for this is found in Figure 7.1, as a tax system without lump sum paybacks to the firms reduces firm profits more than is the case for tradeable permits. Hence introducing emission taxes are likely to require more time. A recent example of this is the industrial opposition to the introduction of CO_2 taxes in Norway. Numerous other examples exist. The possibility of finding non–distorting lump sum paybacks is therefore essential in choosing between emission taxes and tradable emission permits when competitiveness issues are important.[3]

3 TRANS–BOUNDARY POLLUTION AND FREE RIDING BEHAVIOUR

Trans–boundary environmental problems fall into two categories: (i) a country's pollution affects neighbouring countries (trans–boundary emissions) or (ii) a country is affected by the neighbouring countries' pollution (trans–boundary receipts). Assume that:

- it is costly for a country to reduce its emissions,
- that reductions in emissions benefit both the country that instigates regulations as well as the neighbouring countries and
- each country's social planner (regulatory agency) seeks to maximize the country's welfare, defined by some social welfare function.

With these assumptions, the welfare function of the social planner in country i when there is only one pollutant can be expressed as:[4]

$$V_i(M_i, \mathbf{p}_i | \mathbf{Z}_i + \mathbf{Z}_{-i}) \qquad (7.1)$$

where M_i is total money income in country i,

            $\mathbf{p}_i$ is a vector of prices for private goods in country i,

            $\mathbf{Z}_i$ is a vector of public bads (pollution) originating in country i,

            $\mathbf{Z}_{-i}$ is a vector of public bads (pollution) affecting country i and originating in other countries, and

            V_i is continuous and bounded in M_i and Z $(= Z_i + Z_{-i})$.

Despite the difficulties in reaching consensus regarding the specification of the social welfare function – as demonstrated by Arrow's (1951) impossibility theorem – any valid social welfare function must exhibit the same basic properties that can be derived from individual utility maximization, that is utility increases with increasing money income, decreases (or at least does not increase) with increasing prices, and decreases with increasing supplies of public bads (like pollution). Using (7.1) this implies:

$$\frac{\partial V_i}{\partial M_i} > 0, \qquad \frac{\partial V_i}{\partial p_{ij}} \leq 0 \qquad \text{and} \qquad \frac{\partial V_i}{\partial Z} < 0 \quad \forall j \in J \qquad (7.2)$$

where j indexes the commodity and *J* denotes the index set of commodities.

The social planner is particularly concerned with the externalities (pollution), as the 'invisible hand' would correctly adjust prices and wealth if there were no externalities.

Emissions and Welfare

Using a partial equilibrium approach it can be shown that when emissions, Z_i, are reduced, money income, M_i, will fall, and prices, $\mathbf{p}_i$, will increase. From (7.2) it follows that only for emission levels above the socially optimal emission level, Z^*_i, will $\partial V_i/\partial Z_i < 0$. The magnitude of this welfare gain would be less than one would expect if only the environmental benefits were considered, that is the feedback effects on income and prices.

In an open economy these effects may differ somewhat. Krutilla (1991) shows for example that the welfare effects vary depending upon whether the commodities from the regulated production are imported or exported. Another and complicating factor is interpreting the welfare change caused by unilateral environmental regulations in country i (the country implementing such regulations) because: (i) domestic prices may not increase as much as they would without trade due to import increases[5] and (ii) domestic money income is likely to drop. It is tempting to claim that as prices do not adjust as much upward, a smaller portion of the additional costs will be accounted for, causing output to drop. This is the old argument that environmental regulations may cause firms to locate elsewhere. In discussing the environmental impacts of a single market within the European Community, Folmer and Howe (1991) play down the relocation effect, claiming that:

> Environmental Policy is only one element of a complex of factors. Other elements are the labor market, accessibility and technological development. Thus the outcome depends on the weight of environmental regulations relative to other location factors. (Folmer and Howe, 1991 p.23)

In interpreting the above statement, I believe that the essential point regarding the potential relocation of industries is not the environmental performance of proposed environmental policies, but their effects on profits and thus welfare.[6] A direct consequence of this would be that if for example one country decided to unilaterally introduce environmental taxes, the lack of response in product prices could lead to factories being closed down, thus causing a sharp drop in emissions (and a potential large welfare loss due to reduced money income). In retrospect one would conclude that the strong environmental effect of the tax would have called for a lesser tax. Thus, the use of incentive based instruments under free trade requires more 'fine tuning' than is the case in a less open economy, a conclusion also reached by Krutilla (1991) and Lothe (1996).

For trans–boundary pollutants country i's own optimal emission level and welfare depends not only on its own emissions, Z_i, but also on the emissions received from other countries, Z_{-i}. Simplifying (7.1) to embody only one pollutant yields $V_i(M_i, p_i | Z_i + Z_{-i})$. The ranking of the welfare associated with own environmental actions and those taken by other countries becomes:

$$V_i(M^0_i, p^0_i | Z^0_i + Z^r_{-i}) > V_i(M^r_i, p^r_i | Z^r_i + Z^r_{-i})$$

$$> V_i(M^0_i, p^0_i | Z^0_i + Z^0_{-i}) > V_i(M^r_i, p^r_i | Z^r_i + Z^0_{-i}) \qquad (7.3)$$

where
- Z^0_i indicates no change in emission policy in country i
- Z^r_i indicates country i regulates its emissions
- Z^r_{-i} indicates that the other countries regulate their emissions
- Z^0_{-i} indicates no change in the other countries' environmental policies.

Despite country i benefitting from environmental cooperation, it would benefit even more from everybody else regulating and not having to bear any environmental abatement costs itself (the left expression in the top line of (7.3)) as indicated in Table 7.1.

Game Theory Implications

This formulation lends itself to game theoretic analysis. It is for example easy to see that the best reply strategy of country i is always to play 'do not regulate', that is a 'Prisoner's Dilemma' situation arises. If all countries play this strategy, the Nash outcome results, yielding the welfare $V_i(M,\mathbf{p}|Z + Z_i)$. In a dynamic setting the game theory literature suggests that the 'Prisoner's dilemma' may not be the outcome. The undesirable effects on the social welfare of the countries may

Table 7.1 Payoff matrix for regulation/no regulation for country i and 'rest of the world' (bold face numbers indicate country i's ranking of the various options)

		Country i	
		Regulate	Do not regulate
Country j	Regulate	$V_i(M,\mathbf{p}|Z + Z_i)$ **(2)** ·	$V_i(M,\mathbf{p}|Z + Z_i)$ **(1)**
	Do not regulate	$V_i(M,\mathbf{p}|Z + Z_i)$ **(4)**	$V_i(M,\mathbf{p}|Z + Z_i)$ **(3)**

provide support for cooperative outcomes (c.f. the Folk theorem, Friedman, 1986). Romstad and Kriström showed that expressed from country i's perspective the Folk theorem is given by:

$$1 > \beta > \frac{\pi(o_i,r_j) - \pi(r_i,r_j)}{\pi(o_j,r_i) - \pi(o_i,o_j)} \tag{7.4}$$

where   ß is the discount factor,

$\pi(o_i,r_j)$ is the payoff to country i when it does not regulate while country j does,

$\pi(r_i,r_j)$ is the payoff to country i when both country i and j regulate,

$\pi(o_i,r_j)$ is the payoff to country i of regulating while country j does not,

$\pi(o_i, o_j)$ is the payoff to country i when neither country regulates.

The stability of this cooperative solution depends on the relative sizes of the cooperative and non–cooperative payoffs in (7.4), as is also indicated in Figure 7.2. Even though the ranking of the alternatives is unchanged, that is 'do not regulate' is still the dominant strategy for both countries in the single shot game, Figure 7.2 shows how the likelihood of cooperative behaviour from the other country increases as the horizontal difference in the payoffs between free riding, $\pi(o_i, r_j)$, and unilateral regulations, $\pi(r_i, o_j)$, decreases.[7] Also note that the overall

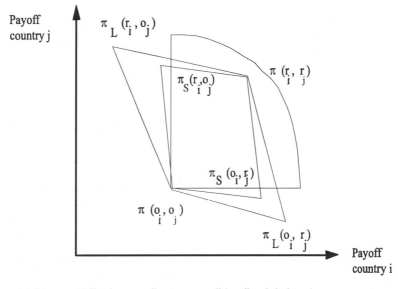

Notes: $\pi_S(\bullet)$ denotes payoffs when overall costs are small (small trade leakages),
$\pi_L(\bullet)$ denotes payoffs when overall costs are large (large trade leakages), and
$\pi(\bullet)$ denotes payoffs under Nash or cooperative behaviour in either case.
The shaded area indicates the region of possible Pareto-improvements for the two countries.

Figure 7.2   Payoff space for country i and j

stability of the cooperative solution increases as the payoffs from free riding and unilateral regulations respectively move closer to the left and bottom sides of the gray shaded area. In case the payoffs from free riding and unilateral regulations belong to the closed set formed by the gray area, the cooperative solution follows directly. Thus, Figure 7.2 underlines the argument derived from (7.4), that is choosing policy instruments with lower costs (including trade leakages), increases the likelihood of a stable cooperative solution, and makes the expected benefits from instigating regulations higher.

4 THE PORTER HYPOTHESIS

According to the Porter hypothesis (Porter, 1990), properly designed environmental policies can trigger innovation and production efficiency gains that may lead to an absolute advantage over non–regulated firms. The Porter hypothesis has recently been debated in the economics and management literature (see for example Palmer, Oates and Portney (1995); Porter and van der Linde, 1995).

At the outset empirically testing the Porter hypothesis appears one way of resolving this controversy. This is however difficult as the Porter hypothesis pre-supposes that regulations are efficient. In brief this means that if the efficiency criterion is not met, any empirical rejection of the Porter hypothesis is made on wrong premises. On this point Porter is extremely clear:

> If environmental standards are to foster the innovation offsets that arise from new technologies and approaches to production, they should also adhere to three principles. First, they must create the maximum opportunity for innovation, leaving the approach to innovation and not to the standard setting industry. Second, regulations should foster continuous improvements, rather than locking in any particular technology. Third, the regulatory process should leave as little room as possible for uncertainty at every stage. (Porter and van der Linde, 1995, p.110)

However, results from the few empirical studies that have been undertaken to test the Porter hypothesis are interesting. With current US regulations there appears to be little empirical evidence supporting Porter's claim that environmental regulations may increase the competitiveness of the regulated industries (Jaffe, et al., 1995).

Brännlund et al. (1996a) tested the Porter hypothesis on the Nordic pulp and paper industry and found even stronger evidence than in the study on the US manufacturing industry (Jaffe et al., 1995), that an increase in the stringency of environmental regulations unambiguously made the regulated firms worse off. They also tested to see if the current environmental regulations on the Nordic pulp and paper industry were efficient and found that this was not the case. Hence their empirical rejection of the Porter hypothesis could be caused by inefficient regulations. The same could also apply to Jaffe et al.'s study, as US environmental regulations generally are economically inefficient (Hahn, 1989).

Therefore, theoretical insights are still needed to resolve the Porter controversy.

Embedded in the Porter hypothesis is the notion that there exist unrealized business opportunities from voluntary firm level environmental abatement. Generally one would not expect the emission levels resulting from voluntary abatement to coincide with the optimal emission levels from the perspective of society. In the case that voluntary abatement yields insufficient reductions in emissions, this implies that firms encounter additional costs from further abatement. The existence of Porter effects on the regulated firms must therefore be viewed as a special case.

Other 'Porter effects' may however exist. One can for example envision that industries delivering abatement technologies and services in countries that first instigate environmental regulations gain a competitive advantage over firms in other countries. In brief there could be a first mover advantage for the abatement industry. The first mover advantage is limited in many cases because:

1. The conditions of the recipient and the choice of technology in the polluting firms may vary across countries, rendering abatement techniques developed for the conditions in the 'home' country less suitable for export.
2. Governments may view abatement as a potential growth industry. To fend off foreign competitors they may therefore opt to require less tested abatement technologies under development by domestic firms.

Despite being controversial, the Porter hypothesis strengthens arguments that incentive based regulations are likely to yield lower abatement costs compared to detailed command and control type regulations, in particular if argument (ii) above applies.

5 CONCLUDING REMARKS

Sections 2 and 3 present a strong theoretical case for using incentive based regulations in general and tradeable permits in particular, as this is the regulatory option that maintains incentives for firms to reduce emissions, provides cost effective allocations and solutions and leads to the least reduction in firms' profits. The latter is of particular importance when the regulated (domestic) industry faces competition from countries with less stringent environmental regulations.

The major conclusion of Section 4 is that the Porter hypothesis may be valid in special cases, but that one cannot expect it to hold in general. The reason for this is that generally there would be a discrepancy between voluntary abatement at the firm level with the associated emission levels and the emission levels that are optimal from a societal perspective. Consequently, environmental regulations will – at some level – increase the cost of production. Despite concerns that the conditions for the Porter hypothesis are not met under most current regulatory regimes, the empirical rejection of the Porter hypothesis is as expected.

In summary this chapter shows that incentive based environmental regulations generally result in lower abatement costs than command and control regulations. When regulated firms compete in an international market where the (foreign) competitors may face less stringent regulations, the additional costs associated with the choice of regulatory policy becomes important in two ways: (i) in terms of increasing the likelihood of reducing local pollution as low cost regulatory policies lead to less trade leakages with its adverse consequences for overall societal welfare; and (ii) in terms of reducing the barriers to achieving international cooperation on the control of trans–boundary pollution.

NOTES

1. Several advocates of environmental taxes have suggested lump sum repayments or two tiered tax systems due to the cost push effects of uniform environmental taxes. Reaching agreement on a repayment schedule may look like a new candidate for an 'impossibility theorem'. Regarding emission taxes that vary depending on the emission level, it is possible to construct efficient schemes of this type in the short run, but their long term dynamic effects are at best uncertain.

2. An additional disadvantage with the tradeable permit system is that there must be some minimum number of firms in the emission permit market to ensure that firms behave like price takers with respect to buying and selling permits (see Romstad and Bergland, 1996 for a more detailed treatment).

3. Grandfathering conflicts with the polluter pays principle, a cornerstone in the ethics of many environmentalists. It is reasonable to believe that if the choice is between less environmental regulation due to the instrument effect of auctioning permits and tougher environmental standards, the environmentally ethical position is to abandon the polluter pays principle.

4. This specification is consistent with the emission pattern of a trans–boundary pollutant that diffuses completely (like carbon dioxide). A more general specification is:
$V_i(M_i, p_i | Z_i + dZ_{i})$, where $d(Z_{i})$ is some diffusion function indicating how the pollutant spreads.

5. To avoid losing domestic market shares, a 'wise' government may consider taxing competing imports regardless of where they are produced to maintain the relative competitiveness of their own industries. However, even such taxes would constitute a welfare loss in the country where such taxes were introduced. The current WTO/GATT agreement opens for this under certain conditions (Lothe, 1996).

6. Romstad and Kriström (1994) write 'We do not believe Folmer and Howe would disagree on this, but from their article (Folmer and Howe, 1991), it is not clear whether they speak of profits (rents) or environmental performance, when discussing relocation effects.'

7. For country j the likelihood of cooperative behavior increases as the vertical difference in the payoffs between free riding, $\pi(r_j, o_j)$, and unilateral regulations, $\pi(o_j, r_j)$, decreases.

REFERENCES

Arrow, K.J. (1951), 'An extension of the basic theorems of classical welfare economics', in J. Neyman (ed.), *Proceedings of the Second Berkeley Symposium of Mathematical Statistics and Probability*, University of California Press, Berkeley, CA, 507–32.

Baumol, W.J. and W.E. Oates (1988), *The Theory of Environmental Policy*, Cambridge University Press, Cambridge MA.

Brännlund, R., L. Hetemäki, B. Kriström and E. Romstad (1996a), *Command and Control with a Gentle Hand: The Nordic Experience*, final report from the NERP project 'Economic Instruments in Environmental Policy: The Nordic Forest Sector', Swedish University of Agricultural Sciences, Umeå, Sweden.

Brännlund, R., L. Hetemäki, B. Kriström and E. Romstad (1996b), *Economics and the Environment – Beyond the Textbook Cases*, summary report from the NERP project 'Economic Instruments in Environmental Policy: The Nordic Forest Sector', Swedish University of Agricultural Sciences, Umeå, Sweden.

Folmer, H. and C.W. Howe (1991), 'Environmental problems and policy in the single European market', *Environmental and Resource Economics*, 1(1), 17–41.

Friedman, J.W. (1986), *Game Theory with Applications to Economics*, Oxford University Press, New York, NY.

Hahn, R.W. (1989), 'Economic prescriptions for environmental problems: how the patient followed the doctor's orders', *Journal of Economic Perspectives*, 3(2), 95–114.

Jaffe, A.B., S.R. Peterson, P.R. Portney and R.N. Stavins (1995), 'Environmental regulations and the competitiveness of U.S. manufacturing: what does the evidence tell us?', *Journal of Economic Literature*, 33(1), 132–63.

Krutilla, K. (1991), 'Environmental regulation in an open economy', *Journal of Environmental Economics and Management*, 20(2), 127–42.

Lothe, S. (1996), *Environmental Countervailing Tariffs Under the GATT Agreement in a Duopoly Model of Pollution–Intensive Industries*, Department of Economics and Social Sciences Discussion Paper #D–15/1996, The Agricultural University of Norway, Ås, Norway.

Oates, W.E., P.R. Portney and A.M. McGartland (1989), 'The net benefits of incentive based regulation: a case study of environmental standard setting', *American Economic Review*, 79(5), 1233–42.

Palmer, K., W.E. Oates and P.R. Portney (1995), 'Tightening environmental standards– the benefit– cost or the no–cost paradigm', *Journal of Economic Perspectives*, 9(4), 119–32.

Porter, M.E. (1990), *The Competitive Advantage of Nations*, Macmillan, London.

Porter, M.E. and C. van der Linde (1995), 'Toward a new conception of the environment–competitiveness relationship', *Journal of Economic Perspectives*, **6**(4), 119–32.

Romstad, E. and O. Bergland (1996), 'Manipulation of emission permit markets', in R. Nau, E. Grønn and O. Bergland (eds), *Economic and Environmental Risk and Uncertainty*, Kluwer Academic Publishing, Dordrecht.

Romstad, E. and B. Kriström (1994), *Environmental Regulations and International Competitiveness*, Department of Economics and Social Sciences Discussion Paper #D–04/1994, The Agricultural University of Norway, Ås, Norway.

Weitzman, M.L. (1974), 'Prices vs. quantities', *Review of Economic Studies*, **41**, 477–91.

8. Environmental policy and international competitiveness: the case of Germany

Rolf-Ulrich Sprenger

1 INTRODUCTION

1.1 The Context

In the last few years there has been a resurgence of interest regarding the effects of environmental policies on competitiveness. There are several reasons for this:

- Since environmental policies are becoming more stringent and more comprehensive, their potential effects on competitiveness are becoming greater.
- With the growing integration of the world economy, domestic policies, including environmental policies, may increasingly have consequences on international trade. One important consequence of import liberalization is increased competition in the domestic market, forcing firms to reduce production costs. Environmental investments could conflict with their objective of reducing costs, at least in the short run. Thus increased attention is likely to be paid to the competitive effects of environmental policies in the post–Uruguay Round period.
- Questions of competitiveness have become crucial in the debate about how best to deal with global environmental problems. Countries that take unilateral steps might be among the losers.

- The environmental credentials of products and plants are becoming more important as a factor in market access and may increasingly influence business strategies.
- Environmental policies, apart from contributing to environmental improvements, are the major driving force of the 'environmental sector', which is seen as a source of market opportunities and job creation.
- Environmental regulations are seen not only as benign in their impacts on international competitiveness of green products and green industries, but actually as a net positive force driving private firms and the economy as a whole to become more competitive in international markets. Growing attention is being given to the role of environmental standard setting as an instrument to induce technological innovation and to improve trade performance.
- Environmental and economic policies have often been viewed as in opposition and, for the most part, have been developed separately. None the less, policy makers increasingly see benefits in addressing the two together. The interactions between environmental concerns and industrial competitiveness have ramifications for many policy areas, including technology development and diffusion, export promotion and development assistance, and trade policy and negotiations.

1.2 The Scope and Organization of the Chapter

This chapter analyses the environment–competitiveness linkage from a theoretical and empirical point of view.

The remainder of this chapter is organized as follows. Section 2 outlines an analytical framework for identifying the effects of environmental policies on competitiveness. Section 3 discusses available evidence on the environment–competitiveness linkage and heavily relies on empirical data for Germany. The final section discusses some policy issues to find ways to achieve environmental goals while avoiding competitive handicaps.

2 ANALYTICAL FRAMEWORK

2.1 Typology of Competitive Impacts of Environmental Policies

Generally, environmental regulations or other environment–related pressures can have negative and positive impacts for individual firms (see Box 1). On the one hand, certain firms or industrial sectors may be

Box 1 Some competitive impacts of environmental policy

Potential *negative* impacts:	Potential *positive* impacts:
• End of pipe investments divert funds from more productive investments, thus slowing productivity growth	• Increased benefits from a cleaner environment (for example reduced health costs, increased natural resource productivity)
• Increased production costs for high compliance cost sectors, therefore reducing exports and increasing imports	• Production process changes that increase productivity
• Plants facing high compliance costs relocate to 'pollution havens' or close	• Increased innovation (for example, more efficient products)
• Reduced innovation (for example, uncertainty about regulatory acceptability of new products or processes)	• Competitive advantages for firms with less pollution intensive production processes or environmentally friendly products
• Delayed innovation (due to complex and time consuming permitting procedures)	• Increased benefits for the suppliers of environmental goods and services
• Higher than necessary compliance costs due to inflexible and inefficient command and control approach	• Possible trade surplus in the environmental goods and services sectors and increased sales from foreign demand for green products

Sources: Sprenger (1992) and US Office of Technology Assessment (1993).

affected by high compliance costs, regulatory delays, and in some cases may avoid using new technologies because of regulatory risks. A loss of competitiveness is believed to be reflected in declining exports, increasing imports, and a movement of the target industries to other countries, particularly in 'pollution intensive' industries.

On the other hand, some firms may benefit from environmental requirements if they can upgrade production processes and become more efficient. Moreover, environmental regulations can be seen as a net positive force driving private firms to become more competitive in international markets. In other cases, environmental requirements will produce commercial opportunities for those firms that develop and market environmental technologies and services.

2.2 Major Competitiveness Factors

Generally, two sets of industries are affected by environmental policies:

1. firms that must meet national environmental requirements, often while competing with firms from countries that have weaker standards or provide more assistance to their industries; and
2. firms that develop and market environmental technologies and services.

In appraising the impacts of environmental policies on competitiveness, both sets of industries have to be analysed. It is also crucial to identify the major determinants of competitiveness. Here a number of factors must be taken into account to help predict which sectors will gain or lose from environmental policies.

With respect to the regulated sectors, competitiveness effects will differ by industry according to a number of factors including significance of environmental costs, type of industry, firm size, overall competitive situation and so on (see Box 2).

The regulated industries are not only affected by new regulatory requirements, pressure on the firms to improve their environmental performance may also come from various groups within society, as Figure 8.1 shows.

– Members of the public, acting on the basis of information mostly supplied through the media. They are motivated by general, altruistic concerns, often expressed via pressure groups like Greenpeace and other environmentalist movements, or by self–interest, usually in the case of local residents in areas where new plants, are to be located – the

*Box 2 Major competitiveness effects of environmental policies
on regulated industries*

Factor 1:　　**Design of environmental policies**
– Most environmental policies – both regulations and economic instruments –
can be designed and implemented so as to minimize negative competitive
effects on industry. Potentially high compliance costs may be offset by
exemptions, rebates, subsidies or time deferrals.

Factor 2:　　**Significance of environmental costs**
– Competitiveness effects will differ by sector according to the type and scope
of environmental externalities which arise in production (for example, level of
pollution, amount of wastes, extent of resource degradation) and the share of
environmental compliance costs in overall costs.

Factor 3:　　**Offsetting effects**
– The negative effects of environmental costs on competitiveness may be offset by the positive contributions of environmental investments. Reduced input
costs, technological innovation, greater efficiency in production, reduced
clean–up costs, and marketing of environmental goods and services may
counterbalance environmental costs at the micro, meso or macroeconomic
level.

Factor 4:　　**Non–environmental factors**
– Competitiveness effects will differ by sector according to its competitive
strengths and weaknesses in non–environmental areas such as labour, capital
and technology which may heighten the effects of environmental costs.

Factor 5:　　**Type of sector**
– Competitiveness effects will differ by sector according to the location of the
sector on the flow of materials from resource extraction to consumption and
the technological advantages which can be obtained from environmental
improvements; more technically advanced sectors may reap benefits from
environmental compliance through innovations.

Factor 6:　　**Product differentiation**
– Competitiveness effects will differ by sector according to whether the sector
competes on the basis of price or product differentiation and the degree to
which it can derive advantages from marketing environment–friendly or green
products to green consumers.

Factor 7:   **International competition**
— Competitiveness effects will differ by sector according to the nature and extent of international competition and whether the sector serves primarily local or global markets; locally oriented and more monopolistic sectors will not be as affected by the relative stringency or laxity of environmental regulations.

Factor 8:   **Size of firms**
— Competitiveness effects will differ by sector according to the size of firms, the availability of scale economies in production, and the financial and technical resources available for investment in environmental enhancements; small firms will generally have more difficulties going green.

Factor 9:   **Investment cycle**
— Competitiveness effects will differ by sector according to investment cycles and the degree to which the sector is characterised by large non-recoverable expenditures on plant and equipment (high sunk costs) for some firms, shutting down capacity may be more
economical than investments in cleaner technologies.

Source: Stevens (1993) and Sprenger (1997).

so-called NIMBY (not in my backyard) syndrome;
- Customers who, for commercial, environmental or ethical reasons, wish to be assured of the environmental credentials of the intermediate or the equipment products they purchase;
- Consumers who choose products produced in ways deemed environmentally preferable ('green consumerism');
- The financial sector, including shareholders, insurance companies, providers of capital, green and ethical unit trust groups and potential or actual merger and acquisition partners, all of whom need to know the target company's current or potential environmental liabilities;
- Employees, actual or potential, as well as their shop stewards who want to be assured of the environmental credentials of the company for which they work;
- Trade unions who want to make sure that the industry for which their members work won't have to lay off their members as a consequence of non-compliance with environmental legislation;
- The environmental industry that offers solutions for environmental problems, and that offer competitive benefits to firms;
- Industrial and commercial associations that often develop voluntary agreements – for example on eco-management, eco-auditing and eco-labeling, deposit-refund systems, recycling targets – to avoid tight,

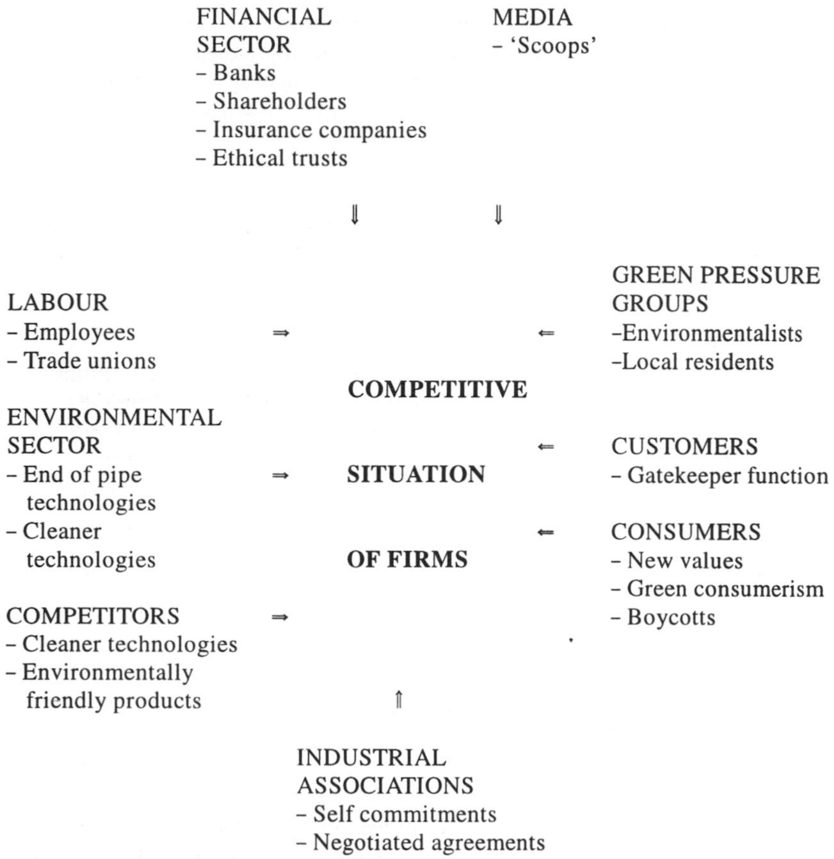

FINANCIAL   MEDIA
SECTOR   – 'Scoops'
– Banks
– Shareholders
– Insurance companies
– Ethical trusts

⇓   ⇓

                                              GREEN PRESSURE
LABOUR   GROUPS
– Employees   ⇒   ⇐   –Environmentalists
– Trade unions   –Local residents
                           COMPETITIVE
ENVIRONMENTAL
SECTOR   ⇐   CUSTOMERS
– End of pipe   ⇒   **SITUATION**   – Gatekeeper function
  technologies
– Cleaner   ⇐   CONSUMERS
  technologies   **OF FIRMS**   – New values
                                              – Green consumerism
COMPETITORS   ⇒   – Boycotts
– Cleaner technologies
– Environmentally
  friendly products   ⇑

                 INDUSTRIAL
                 ASSOCIATIONS
                 – Self commitments
                 – Negotiated agreements

Source: Sprenger, 1995 p.1650

Figure 8.1   Other environment related pressures and competitiveness

technology–forcing and less cost–effective regulations (CEST, n.d.; Sprenger, 1996).

Environmental regulations and other pressures are not the only determinants of industrial competitiveness. Other factors, such as management savvy, capital cost and availability, workforce and skills, may play more significant roles. However, environmental policies may play some role in competitiveness for some industries or firms.

While environmental regulations impose costs on the target firms, they

Box 3 Major competitiveness factors in the environmental industry

---

Factor 1: **Strength of home country environmental regulations**
– Leading international environmental firms generally come from countries
with comprehensive environmental policies and tough regulations.

Factor 2: **Design of environmental policies**
– Policies can continue to promote end of pipe solutions or can speed the use
of cleaner production processes or environmentally friendly products. The use
of economic instruments can influence innovation, which in turn can lead to
new product offerings and to export opportunities.

Factor 3: **Range of supply**
– Suppliers that design, construct or manufacture capital goods and facilities
are sometimes viewed as insufficiently concerned with service, training of
personnel, and provision of parts. More and more customers tend to require
comprehensive packages including equipment supply, after–sales service,
operation, and even assistance in financing (BOT = Build–Operate–Transfer).

Factor 4: **Company size and marketing ability.**
– Although in the past small specialized companies have operated successfully
in niche markets, the ongoing concentration of the industry will yield
conglomerate firms with more general marketing experience and the ability to
offer a wider range of products to pursue export opportunities. Domestic
environmental firms may not be attuned to export opportunities, while some
foreign competitors are more focused on international business.

Factor 5: **Financial strength**
– The small size of many suppliers in the environment industry means that
venture capital or external financing is crucial to entering the market. Access
to financial resources or support for development and demonstration activities
is important to the overall competitiveness of environmental products and
service suppliers in most countries.

Factor 6: **Export support**
– For projects in developing countries, government aid donors sometimes
offer attractive financing packages benefiting their firms. Promoting of home
country standards, practices, and testing protocols or can help create markets
for domestic technologies known to meet the standards abroad.

Factor 7: **Appropriate technologies, products, and services**
– To succeed in foreign markets, suppliers may need to adapt technologies
developed for domestic needs to the sometimes quite different conditions in
other countries. Some products used in high–standard countries may be too
expensive and sophisticated for other markets.

> *Factor 8:* **Local content regulations and tariffs**
> – In some cases, local content regulations and tariffs can limit export
> opportunities although the development of local pollution control expertise
> may create demands for more sophisticated technologies more likely to be
> supplied by imports or licensing from 'pioneer countries'.

> *Factor 9:* **Competitors in big emerging markets**
> – Several newly industrialized and advanced developing countries have
> nascent environmental industries that supply basic environmental goods for
> their own markets and also for export; as developing country environmental
> investments grow, some of these firms may well become important (regional)
> suppliers.

> *Factor 10:* **Research, development, and demonstration**.
> – The environmental market is increasingly technology–driven indicating that
> suppliers must make continuing large R&D expenditures. R&D can yield new
> and improved technologies, while demonstrations can play an important role
> in diffusing innovative technologies domestically and internationally.

Source: U.S. Office of Technology Assessment (1993).

also produce business opportunities for those firms that develop and
market products, equipment or services for environmental protection.
Generally, the most competitive environmental industries are likely to be
found in countries with stringent environmental regulations and effective
enforcement. However, many other factors are involved. Some, including
cost of capital, general export promotion policies, and overall workforce
ability are common to most or all industries. Others are more particular to
the environmental sector, as Box 3 shows.

2.3 Approaches to Assess the Environment–Competitiveness Linkage

The debate on environmental policies and international competitiveness
took off when industrialized nations began legislating and enforcing
environmental regulations with substantial compliance costs. The literature
reflecting that debate has evolved in two waves (see also Dean, 1992).

The first set of research peaked during the late 1970s and seems to have
been inspired by the growth of environmental regulations in industrialized
nations during the early to mid–1970s. The second set has come more
recently, apparently motivated by the debate over the European Single
market, and the ongoing trend of globalization.

The existing literature examines the environment–competitiveness linkage
from different angles (Jaffe et al., 1995):

1. One set of approaches has to do with the change in net exports of certain goods, the production of which is heavily regulated, and with comparisons between net exports of these goods and others produced under less regulated conditions. Thus, the magnitude and significance of an econometric parameter estimate that captures the effect of regulatory stringency in a regression explaining changes in net exports across industries could be taken as an indicator of the strength of the effects of regulation on competitiveness.
2. Another potential indicator is the extent to which the locus of production of pollution–intensive goods may shift from countries with stringent regulations toward those with less. If this is so, then there should be a general decrease in a country's share of world production of highly regulated goods and an increase in the world share of production of these goods by countries with relatively lax regulation. This normally requires statistical analyses of trade data.
3. If regulation is reducing the attractiveness of a country as a locus for investment, then there should be a relative increase in investment by domestic firms abroad in highly regulated industries. Similarly, ceteris paribus, new plants in these industries would be more likely to be located in jurisdictions with lax regulation. This 'pollution haven' hypothesis will normally involve either statistical analysis of foreign direct investment and/or surveys on investors' motives for location.
4. After having defined goods and services for environmental protection, shifts in trade flows can be examined to determine whether a growing proportion of such goods and services in worlds trade originate in countries with stricter regulations and effective enforcement. Similarly, environment–related patents can be analysed with respect to the regulation–innovation–competitiveness linkage (Lanjouw and Mody, 1996).

There are a number of reasons why the effects of environmental regulation on competitiveness may be difficult to detect:

1. The existing data are severely limited in their ability to measure the relative stringency of environmental regulation, making it difficult to use such measures in regression analyses of the effects of regulation on economic performance. First, in many studies, differences in environmental regulation are measured by environmental control costs as a percentage of value–added, or some other measure that depends critically on accurate measurement of environmental spending. Even for those OECD countries where data on environmental compliance costs are relatively good, compliance

expenditure data are notoriously unreliable. The problem is more pronounced in other OECD countries whose environmental agencies have not typically tracked environmental costs. Thus, it is likely that these analyses will find little relationship between environmental regulations and competitiveness simply because the data are of poor quality. Second, in an era of increasing reliance on incentive based and other performance based environmental regulations, accurate accounting for pollution control will become an even more pronounced problem. This is because pollution control expenditures increasingly are taking the form of process changes and product reformulations, rather than installation of end–of–pipe control equipment. It will be increasingly difficult (perhaps even impossible) to allocate accurately that part of the cost of a new plant that is attributable to environmental control. Ironically, in the future one may know less about total annual pollution control costs than at present, in spite of increased concern about these expenditures and their possible effects on competitiveness.

2. It is also difficult to estimate the impact of one (less important) factor on competitiveness, trade and location decisions. For all but the most heavily regulated industries, the cost of complying with environmental regulations appears to be a relatively small fraction of total cost of production. This being the case, environmental regulatory intensity should not be expected to be a significant determinant of competitiveness in most industries. Labour cost differentials, energy and raw materials cost differentials, infrastructure adequacy, and other factors would indeed overwhelm the regulatory effect.

3. Even 'on paper', the differences between environmental standards in the countries under review are not substantial enough to explain impacts of regulations on competitiveness, trade patterns or location decisions. Even where there are substantial differences between environmental regulations in OECD countries and developing countries, there may be some factors offsetting such arbitrations. Multinationals, for example, may be reluctant to build less–than–state–of–the–art plants in foreign countries. Thus, even significant differences in regulatory stringency may not be exploited. Moreover, it appears that even in developing countries where environmental standards (and certainly enforcement capabilities) are relatively weak, plants built by indigenous firms typically embody more pollution control – sometimes substantially more – than is required. To the extent this is true, even significant statutory differences in pollution control requirements between countries may

not result in significant effects on plant location or other manifestations of competitiveness.

4.   The contrast between the findings that some developing countries and Southern EU countries specialize in dirty industries and that environmental regulations have only modest effects on competitiveness in the developed countries could also signal measurement problems. The strong opposition and resistance of developing countries to adopting industrialized countries' environmental standards also suggests that pollution abatement cost estimates may not capture the full costs of some of the regulations. This could also explain why studies fail to find any support for the 'pollution haven' hypothesis.

5.   Another caveat is that most studies look exclusively at source discharge standards or traditional spending for pollution control equipment as measures of regulatory intensity. However if differences in 'regulatory climate' between jurisdictions, delays and litigation surrounding regulation are the greatest impediments to exporting or to new plant location, these effects will not be picked up by the conventional approaches, unless the costs of litigation and delay are highly correlated with direct compliance costs.

6.   Another factor that may temper the findings is the difficulty of measuring the effectiveness of enforcement efforts. Subtle differences in enforcement strategies are very difficult to measure, but these differences can lead to variations from country to country that could influence competitiveness.

7.   Regarding environmental industry competitiveness, empirical analysis is further complicated. Apart from data limitation to measure the relative stringency of a country's environmental policy, data on the environmental sector and trade performance are limited. One of the main obstacles is how to define, delimit and describe the environmental industry. There are a number of reasons for these measurement problems:

(a)   The industry covers a heterogeneous set of goods and services.
(b)   The boundaries of the industry are fluid.
(c)   There are difficulties in measuring many environmental goods and services, making data collection and comparisons difficult.

Trade analyses are based on several product trade codes deemed environmental. These classes are clearly not a comprehensive list of equipment related to pollution control; moreover some non–related equipment is included. Data on services are largely unavailable. Licensing, joint ventures, and multinational mergers and acquisitions further complicate the analysis. Many large environmental firms now operate on several continents. In these cases, flows of profits and royalties are difficult to compare with export earnings.

Since trade data and information are inadequate, all studies on environment–related exports and trade surpluses are based on estimates. At best, the focus is on trends and ratios rather than on absolute amounts.

8. Similar problems arise when analysing the importance of foreign patents in the field of environment–related innovations by country of origin and the regulatory intensity of these countries.

In addition to the difficulty of measuring the relative stringency of national regulations, in choosing the suitable patent classes further problems arise. If too many patent classes are selected, innovations that bear no relation to environmental protection are included and information about national activities may be swamped by movements in the mistakenly included patents. If too few are selected, relevant innovations may be left out.

2.4 Approach of this Chapter

As discussed previously, it is not easy, or at times possible, to analyse directly the competitive effects of environmental regulations. If one casts a wide enough net, defining competitiveness rather broadly and by searching for indirect as well as direct evidence, it is possible to shed some light on the environment–competitiveness linkage.

For the purpose of this chapter a set of indicators has been selected that appears to reflect the various routes through which environmental policies can conceivably affect competitiveness. The indicators that are seen to reflect the available evidence for Germany with regard to **adverse** impacts include

-   size of environmental compliance costs
-   plant closures
-   industrial relocation to 'pollution havens'
-   predominance of command and control
-   burdensome and time consuming permitting procedures.

On the other hand, indicators that may reflect **positive** impacts on competitiveness include

-   high environmental quality as a positive production and location factor
-   benefits from environmental management

–   benefits for the suppliers of environmental technologies and services
–   benefits for the suppliers of green products and clean technologies
–   benefits for the users of clean technologies.

All these indicators are not wholly satisfactory because they fail to take account of the complex adjustment mechanisms that operate when environmental regulations are imposed. Nevertheless, these indicators can be useful to sort through many of the policy debates regarding the environment–competitiveness linkage.

3   ENVIRONMENTAL POLICIES AND COMPETITIVENESS: SOME EVIDENCE FOR GERMANY

3.1   Environmental Policy Context

Germany is one of the most environmentally conscious European countries, with the most stringent environmental legislation and firmest enforcement. This is largely due to the following reasons:

–   a high–polluting, industry–intensive economy,
–   largely coal–based power generation,
–   Germany was an early victim of the effects of acid rain on the national forests, pollution of the Rhine and radioactive fallout from the Chernobyl explosion,
–   a strong economy and a secure, prosperous society allowing public attention to focus on quality of life issues, and especially
–   the urgent need to speed up the clean–up and ecological modernization of the eastern Länder (former GDR) in the process of German reunification.

3.2   Adverse Impacts of Environmental Policies on Competitiveness

3.2.1   Height of environmental compliance costs
A first indicator to support the belief that environmental regulations may have had adverse impacts on competitiveness can be seen in the regulatory stringency of German environmental legislation. Federal environmental legislation has grown significantly in Germany, particularly since 1971 (see Box 4). Regulatory programmes have given substantial rise to compliance costs (see Table 8.1).

Box 4   Major federal environmental legislation in Germany (excluding amendments)

1957	Water Management Act
1962	Detergents Act
1968	Waste Oil Act
1971	Leaded Fuel Act Protection from Aircraft Noise
1972	Waste Disposal Act; DDT Act
1974	Federal Emission Control Act Environmental Statistics Act
1975	Washing Agents and Detergents Act
1976	Nature Conservation Act Radiation Protection Ordinance Waste Water Charges Act Energy Saving Act
1980	Chemicals Act Hazardous Incidents Ordinance
1982	Sewage Sludge Ordinance
1983	Large Combustion Installations Act
1986	Hazardous Substances Ordinance Species Protection Ordinance Precautionary Radiological Protection Act Waste Avoidance and Management Act
1987	Origin of Waste Water Ordinance
1988	Small Combustion Installations Act Deposit–Refund Systems for Plastic Bottles Ordinance
1990	Environmental Impact Assessment Act Environmental Liability Act
1991	Prohibition of CFCs Ordinance Packaging Waste Ordinance
1994	Freedom of Environmental Information Act Waste Avoidance, Recycling and Disposal Act
1996	Comprehensive Waste Management Act

Source: OECD (1993b).

Table 8.1 Environmental expenditure by German industry (DM bn)

	Investment	Operating costs
1975	2.480	3.200
1976	2.390	3.610
1977	2.240	3.930
1978	2.150	4.220
1979	2.080	4.680
1980	2.660	5.160
1981	2.930	5.900
1982	3.560	6.500
1983	3.690	6.870
1984	3.500	7.330
1985	5.630	7.850
1986	7.300	8.010
1987	7.710	8.570
1988	8.030	9.370
1989	7.630	10.390
1990	7.230	11.190
1991	6.520 (1.500)[1]	12.050 –
1992	6.319 (2.500)[1]	12.790 –
1993	5.529 (3.022)[1]	13.460 –
1994	4.837 (3.806)[1]	13.960 –

Note: 1)   New eastern states.

Source: Federal Statistical Office (1996 a/b).

While comparisons are difficult, the compliance costs incurred by German manufacturers for pollution control and abatement appear to be among the highest in the world. Firms in a handful of countries such as the United States and Japan face equal costs, but they are the exception.

However, environmental compliance costs are only a relatively small share of overall costs to German industry: in most sectors they constitute less than 1 per cent of total costs or turnover (see Table 8.2). For most German manufacturing sectors, they have not been large enough, relative to other costs, to influence international competitiveness.

However, higher environmental compliance costs tend to be localized in particular sectors and firms. They are far higher than average in some pollution–intensive and natural resource sectors, such as chemicals, primary metal production, oil refining and pulp and paper. However, these sectors often represent a range of competitive positions; some of them are highly competitive internationally, with significant trade surpluses.

Environmental regulations can also have adverse impacts at the margin for sectors or firms that have competitive weaknesses because of non–environmental reasons such as higher labour costs, poor availability of capital or laggardly technology development. For these firms even small cost differences can erode relative competitive position.

A number of factors have been identified to help predict which sectors will gain or lose from stricter environmental regulations (Stevens, 1993). These include:

- design of environmental policies
- significance of environmental costs
- offsetting effects
- non–environmental factors
- type of sector
- product differentiation
- international competition
- size of firms
- investment cycle (see also Box 2).

Those which can realise competitive advantages in domestic and international markets from environmental regulations are generally industrial, can benefit from technological improvements, and market 'green products' (Stevens, 1993). The steel industry, for example, despite the relatively heavy costs it faces in complying with environmental regulations, can gain from the technical improvements which may be associated with environmental regulation, such as the development of more resource–efficient methods of production which use fewer energy inputs

Table 8.2 Cost structure in the manufacturing industry (1990; West Germany)

Sector	Gross output	Invest-ment	Environ-mental investment	Environ-mental operating costs	Personnel	Material consump-tion	Rents and leases
	DM billion	Percentage of gross output					
Electricity, gas, district heating and water supply	160.7	12.3	1.17	2.22	13.4	11.9	1.7
Mining and quarrying	29.3	7.6	1.13	1.95	44.8	29.5	0.8
Manufacturing industry		5.2	0.27	0.42	25.2	39.7	1.4
– Primary and general producer goods	489.0	5.3	0.62	–	20.4	38.2	0.9
– Capital goods	879.7	5.3	0.13	–	30.1	38.4	1.5
– Consumer goods	251.6	5.6	0.19	–	27.2	40.5	1.8
– Food, drink and tobacco	204.9	4.1	0.13	0.24	12.8	48.0	1.5
Building trade	142.2	4.2	0.06	0.05	38.0	27.2	2.1
– Construction	110.7	5.0	0.06	–	38.1	24.7	2.2
– Finishing and services	31.5	3.1	0.04	–	37.3	35.8	1.6

Note: – no figures available

Source: Federal Environment Agency (1993/1994).

and yield less waste. Automobile firms can increase market share by developing more fuel–efficient, recyclable vehicles that pollute less. The proliferation of eco–labelling, often instigated by industry itself, is an indication of how the 'greenness' of a product can be a marketing tool.

Sectors which have more difficulty gaining trade advantages from 'going green' include commodity chemicals, primary agricultural and resource based commodities such as food, minerals and wood, which compete on the basis of price rather than of product differentiation. Industrial and agricultural chemicals, for example, may realize few technological or market advantages from complying with environmental regulation, it simply raises their prices. Agricultural, mineral and wood products are in a similar position since their relative prices are all–important in the market. Primary commodities in particular have difficulty in incorporating their environmental costs into their market prices, leaving their relative competitiveness vulnerable to the degree of environmental regulations. But here, too, consumers are becoming more demanding about the environmental dimensions of production processes, as is happening with tropical timber. In the future, international labelling schemes may help even primary commodities take advantage of the growing ecological awareness of the average consumer.

3.2.2 Predominance of Command and Control

Environmental policy in Germany as in all industrialized countries is underpinned by legislation which defines the basic regulatory framework within which policy instruments are applied.

Legislation with respect to pollution in Germany since 1970 is perhaps best described by the phrase 'command and control' (see also Box 5). A pollution control agency – national, state or local – gives the 'command' – a numerical limit on the emissions of a particular pollutant from a particular point, such as a pipe or vent from an industrial process. The owner or operator of the pollution activity must then 'control' emissions from that point to comply with the command. Under the 'command and control' approach, German pollution control agencies have sought better environmental quality through rules which apply specific, uniform emission limits – generally based on a known feasible control technology – to every emission point within a regulated process.

The command and control approach produced large gains in many areas, because it dealt with sources that were easy targets, and where initial costs of control were relatively low. Despite added pollution from industrial growth, air and water quality in Germany have improved significantly since the early 1970s. But the traditional approach, despite its successes, also has serious defects:

First, rules are general statements that can't fit every case. They leave plant managers little room to adjust broad requirements to particular situations. And they treat similar processes equivalently, ignoring the chance that equivalent emission reductions might be more easily obtained from other processes in the same facility or area. Because some sources are undercontrolled under this approach, while many are controlled more than they need be, the result is excess costs – a powerful reason for industry to try to limit its obligations by resistance or delay.

Box 5 The mix of instruments for environmental management in Germany

---

Command and control
800 acts, 2,800 ordinances, and 4,700 technical instructions

Pollution charges or taxes
Wastewater: uniform scheme for all states
Hazardous waste: 3 states
Packaging waste: local schemes
Air pollution: tax differentiation on leaded
petrol and high polluting cars

User charges
Groundwater: 12 state schemes
Wastewater: local schemes
Waste disposal: local schemes

Deposit–refund schemes
Containers and packages for detergents, cleansing agents
and emulsion paints: mandatory schemes
Beverage containers

Tradeable permits
Air pollution control: offset provisions

Strict liability

Voluntary agreements
More than 90 since the early 1970s

Subsidies
Direct grants, soft loans, tax allowances:
16 programmes at federal level
95 programmes at state level

Source: Sprenger (1995).

Perhaps most important, the present system discourages innovative control approaches. A source that installs known controls can generally count on avoiding enforcement and penalties regardless of these controls' cost effectiveness. A source that develops more cost–effective or efficient measures receives no reward or credit for doing so. Worse yet, that innovative firm risks making itself the target for extra regulation, since it may have shown that it or its industry can do more. For some firms, it is simply not 'profitable' to invest in innovative efforts to do more than the minimum. Only increased innovation can guarantee improved ambient quality at reduced – rather than increasing – cost. For example, to meet national ambient air quality standards in areas with continuing pollution problems, it would be necessary to squeeze more emission reductions from sources already regulated – at steeply increasing costs per unit of reduction. It would also be necessary to seek emission reductions from small, previously unregulated sources – resulting in a more complex and expensive regulatory process which will return fewer unit reductions for each action taken.

To ease the burden that environmental regulation imposes on the target groups without jeopardizing competitiveness, more cost–effective solutions should be reached. A significant change in environmental policies would be a broader use of market–based approaches rather than legalistic and detailed regulations. Such economic instruments may achieve a more efficient allocation of abatement by relying on the knowledge and creativity that is available at the decentralized level by ensuring that pollution is abated where it is cheapest to do so. They may yield substantial cost savings by allowing polluters to determine least cost ways of meeting given standards or by equating the marginal cost of environmental protection to the level of emission charges across the whole range of activities. They can also increase flexibility for polluters by given them the freedom to choose within an overall constraint.

However, Germany continues to rely mainly on 'command and control' approaches (see Box 5). There has been no change towards replacing regulations by a purely economic approach. Indeed, economic instruments are mostly complements. Where economic instruments are used as an adjunct to other instruments, their application is far from reaching least cost solutions. In the present situation, which can be characterized by the prevalence of 'mixed systems', economic instruments cannot play their role as a cost minimizing mechanism. They can only produce suboptimal solutions because polluters have to comply with minimum requirements before they can apply economic reasoning. To conclude, there is no experience yet with economic instruments in environmental policy that permit the achievement of least cost solutions which would reduce competitive impacts on the industries concerned.

3.2.3 Burdensome and time consuming licensing procedures

Conventional forms of regulation can have effects other than just raising production cost. For example, complex, uncertain, expensive, and time consuming licensing procedures can make it difficult for manufacturers to continuously improve production processes and rapidly introduce new products.

In some cases environmental disputes over the siting of industrial facilities may have led to the cancellation of a project because the investors could not comply with the environmental requirements. In other cases lengthy legal proceedings may have delayed the construction or operation of new or modernized plants.

Systematic collection and analysis of data regarding environmental conflicts on industrial siting has been carried out only in very rare cases. A statistical analysis of data on more than 3,000 environmental disputes in the news during the 1970s revealed, for example, that 17 per cent of all the conflicts resulted in blocked projects and 8 per cent of them in relocations (UNCTC, 1985). Rates of blockage and relocation were generally higher in Germany than, for example, the United States. Oil refineries and electric utilities were the most frequently blocked types of industrial facilities, while non-ferrous metal and oil refineries were the most frequently relocated. It should be noted that a majority of the relocations were made within, rather than across, national borders. Evidence was gathered, however, that a number of chemical plants and petrochemical complexes originally destined for Denmark, West Germany and the Netherlands, were resited into Belgium, Ireland, Italy and Spain, and that a number of pollution-intensive Japanese investments were channelled to Indonesia, Malaysia, the Philippines, the Republic of Korea and Thailand. But the evidence, viewed on a world scale, did not suggest massive locational shifting.

In fact, the evidence for the loss of nonexisting jobs and layoffs in affected supplying companies is limited. Although industrial development and expansion has, in some cases, apparently been deterred or delayed by the existence of environmental regulations, the problem seems in most instances to have arisen less from the environmental standards per se, but rather from the way in which they have been implemented (for example because of uncertainty, inflexibility in the procedures adopted, or delays in certification).

Moreover, losses due to delays are of a temporary nature and even the cancellation of a proposed project does not necessarily mean that jobs are lost. The money that would have been invested in the original project might be invested in other projects. A utility company which cannot build a nuclear plant might invest in a gas- or coal-fired facility, creating new jobs in construction, operation, and maintenance. Or the utility may create jobs by investing in energy saving, energy efficiency or renewable energy. And a municipality which cannot build a waste incineration plant might invest in other public works generating similar employment effects.

Finally, merely because firms (and sometimes labour unions) blame environmental regulations for construction delays, it should not be automatically assumed that environmental requirements are the primary cause of a reported delay. Just as plant closings are often attributed to environmental regulations when there are other causes, there are many reasons why delays can and do occur. Construction delays can result from poor planning, inadequate permit applications, insufficient capital, material shortages, and strikes. Large scale industrial and construction projects are inherently complex, difficult to coordinate and time consuming. Environmental regulations often serve as an easy and politically convenient scapegoat.

3.2.4 Plant closures

Despite all complaints of layoffs and job losses due to environmental regulations, the business community and labour unions have hardly generated any data to substantiate their claims. Apart from the United States, no other country has ever carried out a systematic collection of data on plant closures and consequential employment losses due to environmental measures (Sprenger, 1997).

For the United States, the US EPA Economic Dislocation Early Warning System indicated that in the 1971–76 period only 98 plants closed because of environmental regulations. More recently, the US Bureau of Labour Statistics found that during 1988, US employers attributed only 0.1 per cent of all layoffs to environment related causes, that is 99.9 per cent of jobs lost in the US were as a result of factors other than environmental protection. Therefore, the adverse employment effects from plant closings attributable to environmental policy appear to be minuscule. Even though there have been only very rare cases where plants were allegedly closed on account of environmental regulations, these cases have been well publicized and thus have received an over-proportional attention from the public.

In the reported cases plant closures occurred in a few older, heavily polluting industries that are very capital- and energy-intensive materials producing industries and are characterized by many economically marginal plants. Plants which, allegedly, were closed for environmental reasons were, by and large, older, high cost, marginal plants that could not afford to comply with environmental requirements.

The reported plant closures and production curtailments appear to exaggerate the adverse impacts on competitiveness. Actual plant closings which, it is alleged, were caused by pollution control requirements rarely resulted from any single circumstance. Rather, the management's decision to close an industrial plant usually arose from the cumulative effect of a number of factors such as the imposition of government regulations, unfavourable market conditions, declining sales, more efficient competitors, obsolescent equipment, increased labour costs, and so on. Accordingly, reported plant closures should not be attributed solely to environmental regulations. In almost every case listed as an environment–related plant closure, other factors contributed to the decision to close. In this context, environmental regulation was generally not the overriding factor, but rather the least compelling of many reasons to suspend operations. At best, environmental regulations assumed the character of the 'straw that broke the camel's back'. Removal of the environmental restrictions would have only delayed the inevitable. Indeed, in many cases it is likely that government regulations merely acted in such circumstances to hasten the closure of plants which were already doomed.

Moreover, production in the phased–out plants tends to be shifted to other plants in multi–plant firms or to other firms in the same industry. Such factors make it difficult to assess the final impact of closings on competitiveness, although they clearly can create serious local problems, especially when they occur in areas already suffering high unemployment rates.

3.2.5 Industrial relocation[1]

National and multinational firms chose and choose to shift investment and production to other countries. Intuitively, it can be seen that stringent national environmental regulations may spur individual firms in 'dirty' industries to close existing domestic plants, deter new plant openings and/or induce relocation of production to countries with less stringent regulations.

As to the issue whether 'dirty' industries migrate in response to differences in environmentally related process standards two aspects should be considered: the 'push effect' leading to exodus of polluting industries as a result of the increased cost of more stringent environmental regulations and the 'pull effect' of lower costs due to laxer environmental policies (the 'pollution haven' hypothesis).

The industrialized countries fear that their more stringent and more comprehensive process standards may cause competitive disadvantages to affected industries and firms. Thus questions regarding 'eco–dumping', 'implicit' subsidies, and 'environmental' countervailing duties in order to 'level the competitive playing field' have come on the trade–environment agenda.

There are two important questions on the issue of eco–dumping that need to be addressed: First, how to define cost differences arising from different environmental policies as trade–distortive subsidies, as a source of 'unfair competition' or part of a 'strategic behaviour' aimed at obtaining trade benefits from deliberately setting standards at an artificially low level or from not enforcing standards. Second, are there any tangible impacts on the trade pattern, on industrial relocation to such 'pollution havens' of such strategic eco–dumping?

As to the issue of identifying the existence of strategic eco–dumping differences in standards across countries by themselves do not indicate the failure of countries with lower standards to internalize environmental costs. The Polluter Pays Principle recognizes that differences in standards can be justified by a large variety of factors such as differences in the pollution assimilative capacities, degrees of industrialization, population densities, or social objectives and priorities attached to the environment. It should further be noted that the Rio Declaration on Environment and Development states in Principle 11: 'States shall enact effective environmental legislation. Environmental standards, management objectives and priorities should reflect the environmental and development context to which they apply. Standards applied by some countries may be inappropriate and of unwarranted economic and social cost to other countries, in particular developing countries.'

Another problem comes up when a distinction is be made between those differences in environmental standards that reflect differences between assimilative capacities and social preferences across countries and those that constitute part of 'strategic policies' aimed at obtaining trade benefits form deliberately setting standards at an artificially low level (or from not enforcing standards). According to this view, a case could be made, at least in principle, for the use of countervailing duties against strategic behaviour. The theoretical literature reveals, however, that such strategical behaviour is unlikely to be practised on a rational basis. Action against this type of strategic behaviour would also be difficult to carry out, as in practice it is virtually impossible to make a distinction between 'legitimate' and 'artificial' differences of standards between countries.

In terms of plants shifting to 'pollution havens', that is countries which have less stringent pollution control regulations, evidence is scanty and anecdotal:

- In a study conducted during the late 1970s evidence was gathered that a number of chemical plants and petrochemical complexes originally destined for Denmark, the Federal Republic of Germany and the Netherlands were resited into Belgium, Ireland, Italy and Spain, and that a number of pollution–intensive Japanese investments were channelled to Indonesia, Malaysia, the Philippines, the Republic of Korea and Thailand (UNCTC, 1985).
- Another study conducted for the Conservation Foundation led to the conclusion that a few US industries have on occasion located some industrial facilities abroad for apparently pollution or workplace–health standard reasons (namely some primary–metal processing industries and those producing highly toxic chemicals such as asbestos and benzidine dyes). However, these industries are the ones that have generally also been experiencing declines in product demand, lags in technological innovation, and inadequate profits to justify substantial new capital investments for environmental or occupational safety reasons in their present locations (Duerksen and Leonhard, 1980).
- A recent survey by the US General Accounting Office suggests that a few American furniture manufacturers may have moved their operations to Mexico in response to the State of California's tightening of air pollution control standards for paint coatings and solvents (US GAO, 1991).

Yet even this evidence hardly conveys the impression that environmental standards systematically influence industrial location. Empirical research to date has failed to confirm claims that there are widespread pollution havens – countries or regions with low environmental standards which lure companies seeking to escape higher standards in their home countries. Almost all the analyses done on this issue indicate that it is a relatively minor problem with little employment impact. Three reasons are cited:

1.   differences in environmental process standards have small or negligible effects on international competitiveness or relocation of industries to countries with lower standards;
2.   even if existing environmental policies and standards are lax, the expectation often exists that eventually environmental standards will become more stringent. Investment in countries which currently have relatively lax standards may require large adjustments in the future;
3.   transnational corporations often apply the higher standards of their home country.

Empirical studies referring to industrialized countries indicate that the cost effects of environmental process standards are on average relatively small. Consequently, more stringent environmental process standards in one country do not appear to have resulted in a relocation of industries to other countries with lower standards.

Environmental costs are simply not a high enough share of overall costs in most sectors to outweigh other factors in investment decisions (see Figure 8.2). According to several surveys in West Germany during the last decade access to markets, supplies of raw materials, labour costs, political stability, the availability of infrastructure and transport costs were far more important in decisions on where to invest. Surveys of German and Japanese foreign direct investment did not even include environmental considerations as a reason to invest abroad.

The sectors where firms may be more prone to industrial flight, particularly those with high environmental costs and few market advantages from going 'green', such as minerals and commodity chemicals, are the exception rather than the rule. But that does not prevent a wide range of firms from threatening to relocate when confronted with the likelihood of higher environmental standards.

Generally, multinational firms cannot afford to base major international investment decisions on environmental considerations: regulatory requirements tend to change quickly and unpredictably. As nations experience severe pollution or waste problems first-hand, they often change their minds about being an international 'pollution haven'. Moreover, there is an increasing tendency of harmonizing product– and even process–related environmental standards in the EU member states and their European neighbour countries and an increasing convergence of standards in the triad of Europe, Japan and the USA. Finally weak environmental standards often go hand with political instability, uncertainty about future regulation, and corruption. The costs associated with the latter may cancel out any possible gains from low environmental costs.

Apart from the fact that transnational corporate investment decisions are likely to be rather insensitive to variations in environmental costs in different locations or executives expect substantial convergence to occur among national pollution standards in the medium term, the freedom to seek out low cost environmental locations may be constrained by such factors as technological interdependence (particularly in the case of integrated environmental technology) or corporate self–commitments regarding the worldwide application of the environmental standards of their home countries (as in the case of the 'Guiding Environmental Principles' of the German chemical industry).

Market related factors	Production and cost related factors	'Soft location factors'
Proximity to market	Securing stable supply of raw materials and natural resources	Political stability
Preservation and/or expansion of market share	Wages	General social conditions
Import restrictions and other trade barriers	Social security contributions	Unionization
Development of new markets	Skills of foreign labour force	Risk of strikes
Avoiding foreign exchange risk	Business–related infrastructure	Public acceptance of new technologies
	Corporate Taxes	Quality of living conditions
	Energy costs	Environmental quality
	Transport costs	Infrastructure for leisure activities
	State aid	
	Obtaining technological know–how	
	Environmental stringency	

Source: Sprenger, 1992.

Figure 8.2　Industrial location factors

As a result of more recent analyses, environmental and economic concerns that pollution havens might be exploited by individual companies have been replaced by worries about the migration of 'dirty' industries in toto to developing countries, as OECD firms shut down capacity in the industrialized world which is then taken up by developing country producers themselves. Entire sectors which are slowly disappearing from the OECD countries now account for a growing share of exports from developing countries. Environmental regulations seem to be partly responsible for promoting the exodus of basic industries, such as metal refining, oil refining, cement, pulp and paper and commodity chemicals from the developed to the developing world. The shift, however, appears to be largely attributable to the growth of local enterprises in the latter rather than to shifts in the location of transnational corporate activities (UNCTAD, 1985).

Where dirty–industry migration does take place, the advantages in terms of employment and output have to be weighed against the disadvantages. The most important disadvantages include the following: (i) industry migration will impose social costs in terms of health and safety risks for the workers as well as for these who live around the factory; (ii) products made by dirty industries may find it difficult to access the markets of countries with high environmental standards, particularly those in OECD countries; and (iii) dirty industries which migrate are typically stagnant or declining (UNCTAD, 1993).

The contrast between the findings that the south specializes in dirty industries and that environmental regulations have only modest effects on competitiveness in the north could signal measurement problems. The strong opposition and resistance of developing countries to adopting industrialized countries' environmental norms also suggests that pollution abatement cost estimates may not capture the full costs of some of the regulations. This could also explain why studies fail to find any support for the pollution haven hypothesis (Beghin et al., 1994).

3.3 Positive Impacts of Environmental Policies on Competitiveness

3.3.1 High environmental quality as a positive production and location factor

High environmental standards make it easier for companies to recruit management. After all, one of the main reasons for selecting a site is that it offers the manpower a company needs, but the availability of well–qualified personnel will be influenced considerably by the state of the local environment. Working conditions and the quality of life go hand in hand. Today, hardly anyone could deny that the image of a community or region is extremely important when recruiting top executives. This image rests to no small degree on factors such as pollution and the quality of the natural landscape.

It is important to see the close links between the debate about Germany's continued attractions for industry and the rapid ecological clean-up of the new states in the east of the country. What has happened to the area around Leipzig, Bitterfeld, Halle and Merseburg is a graphic example, illustrating that high environmental standards and a robust 'green' industry are essential to maintaining Germany as a centre of production. The most frequently cited obstacles to investment in this region are inadequate environmental infrastructure and the unresolved problems of contaminated sites. The region's ecological overhaul is also crucial to the development of the service sector, whose spatial requirements can only be met by using land once occupied by industry. This makes it essential and also economically worthwhile – not only in central urban locations – to clean up contaminated sites.

The new states could well witness similar developments to those in North Rhine–Westphalia. Of all the western states, this had the worst environment, and it was here that pollution abatement investments were highest. Nowadays, there are more companies manufacturing environmental technology in North Rhine–Westphalia than in any other German state. In other words, cleaning up and restructuring this industrial base made it an attractive proposition to draw on local labour skills and offered manufacturers of environmental technology a location close to their market.

3.3.2   Benefits from environmental management

Increasingly, the environment is playing an important part in company strategy. In the mid–eighties, high environmental standards and consumer awareness, and also keen public interest in how industry was tackling pollution issues, prompted German companies perhaps rather earlier than most to consider environmentally oriented approaches to management. In 1989 the Umweltbundesamt commissioned a questionnaire to investigate the potential for reducing costs and increasing revenue. According to the findings, only about 30 per cent of the sample believed that protecting the environment would impair their profits. Well over half took the view that a consistent application of environmental principles would improve their position in a competitive market, and that the environmental improvements they introduced would reinforce their present know-how to open up new fields of application. More than 70 per cent of those polled agreed with the statement that environment protection was vital to preserving their present industrial location. Two thirds were prepared to take environmental action in order to safeguard their business. Two out of three had actually taken concrete action of this sort in recent years, which had reduced costs or increased earnings while at the same time serving the cause of pollution abatement. One result of the survey which is particularly noteworthy was the correlation between environmental goals and company objectives for recruiting and motivating staff. 72 per cent of the companies stated that a consistent pursuit of environmental aims would exert a positive influence on the recruitment and motivation of employees. Table 8.3 shows to what extent environmental objectives matched corporate objectives in the sample.

Nowadays environmental thinking has established a foothold in very different departments of German companies: research and development, materials management, marketing, public relations. Industry has taken a number of environmental initiatives to exploit the potential more fully. The findings illustrate that an environmentally oriented marketing strategy can noticeably improve a company's commercial success (Table 8.4). Table 8.5 provides evidence that such thinking has become accepted in Germany to an exceptional degree, in comparison with other European countries.

3.3.3 Benefits for the suppliers of environmental technologies and services

Environmental technology now enjoys one of the fastest growing markets, with an annual turnover of about DM 26,000 million. In 1991, this was equivalent to 65 per cent of turnover in mining and quarrying, and just less than 13 per cent of turnover in the chemicals industry. This is due in part at least to the pioneering role which Germany has played in environmental protection. In the early 1980s, there were about 1,000 companies offering goods and services in the green technology market. Today 4,000 German companies are competing for this trade, making a considerable contribution to employment and growth.

Observers agree that the prospects for growing sales are good, as other countries will continue to attach more importance to environmental protection, generating bigger export markets for German industry and particular potential in the Single European Market. In addition, billions will be invested in domestic manufacturing facilities over the coming decade, and a big growth in sales of clean technology can be expected in the east of the country.

Germany has been especially successful with its exports of environmental technology (see Figure 8.3). In 1993, it was one of the biggest exporters of environmental goods, with a 18 per cent share of world trade. The United States accounted for 19 per cent and Japan for 13 per cent. One of the

Table 8.3   Corporate environmental activities and corporate objectives (as percentage of companies surveyed)

The effect of environmental activities on corporate aims	(very) positive	neutral	(very) negative
Company survival	60	34	6
Company independence	26	69	5
Recruiting/motivating staff	72	25	3
Solvency	16	52	32
Improved competitiveness	52	32	16
Company growth	46	53	1
Increased market share	44	55	1
Increased sales	44	55	1
Improved product quality	58	41	1
Increased profit	28	67	5
Client / market orientation	63	36	1
Improved public image	87	13	0
Improved competitive position	51	47	2

Source: Federal Environment Agency (1991).

major reasons for Germany's success with its environmental industry is that exacting national policies on environmental protection created an edge over its competitors. Germany has adopted a leading position in the widespread use of advanced technologies for reducing airborne pollution from both new and old plant. Nearly all furnaces are equipped with flue gas desulphurization and systems to cut down NO_x emissions. Emissions of organic pollutants are countered by adsorption and absorption techniques (such as solvent recovery) and thermal treatments (used, for example, in paper finishing, printing and enamelling). Biofilters to trap odour emissions have become sophisticated and are now used more widely.

Table 8.4 Environmental management and business success

Environmental management concept	Successful businesses	Unsuccessful businesses
Environment protection as a leading model		
– most important area of business	8.1	–
– own area of business	10.8	11.4
– no area of business of significance	70.3	68.2
– no comments	10.8	20.5
Environment protection in system		
– very high ranking	9.8	3.8
– high ranking	61.0	41.5
– average ranking	19.5	37.7
– low ranking	9.8	17.0
Life cycle assessment		
– applied	27.8	21.2
– planned	22.2	15.4
– irrelevant	47.2	50.0
– unknown	2.8	13.5
Environment protection in leading model		
– significant	42.0	27.6
– less significant	46.0	58.6
– not at all	12.0	13.8
Organization of environment protection in project teams		
– yes	44.0	31.0
– no	56.0	69.0
Environment protection in product development		
– much	52.9	43.5
– little	47.1	56.5

Source: Lower Saxony Ministry of the Environment (1995)

*Table 8.5　Number of sites registered in the European Eco
Management and Audit Scheme (EMAS) by member states*

Countries	as of 16 February 1996	as of 28 February 1997
Austria	6	50
Belgium	2	3
Denmark	3	16
Finland	–	4
Germany	114	509
France	3	7
Greece	–	–
Ireland	1	2
Italy	–	–
Luxembourg	–	–
Netherlands	2	11
Portugal	–	–
Spain	–	2
Sweden	1	43
United Kingdom	9	25

Sources: OJ (1996) and European Commission (1997)

The consistent employment of leading–edge pollution abatement technologies has led to major advances in this field. Now it has been shown that there is considerable technological potential for curbing pollution, environmental awareness has grown and other countries have been encouraged to tighten their policies.

Germany is set to establish a clear lead in the development and production of efficient energy systems, especially when the Residual Heat Ordinance comes into force in the near future. This applies to various types of plant, (for example heat transformers, heat exchangers, adsorbed heat pumps, absorption refrigeration, steam–powered engines, gas turbines,

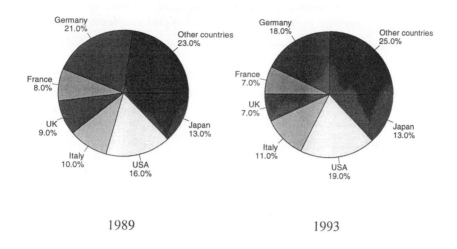

1989   1993

Source   NIW

*Figure 8.3 National shares of the world market for environmental
technologies*

cogeneration systems), energy saving production facilities, energy
supplies, and the engineering know–how behind the rational use of energy
(along with the relevant software).

  The following example illustrates the importance of a progressive
environment policy to Germany's future as a centre of trade and industry.
When selective catalytic reduction was introduced to extract the NO_x from
flue gas, German catalyst producers suffered a setback because they had
been slow to address the issue of NO_x reduction. The investment costs of
importing the first catalyst from Japan amounted to about DM 50,000 per
cubic metre. This fell to DM 20,000 per cubic metre once production
began in Germany under Japanese licence. Although German
manufacturers now have considerable experience of working with SCR
catalysts, they will not be able to increase their market share until the
licensing contracts with the Japanese producers have expired (see Table
8.6).

  Generally, the most competitive environmental industries are found in
countries with stringent environmental regulations. However, many other
factors are involved. Some, including cost of capital, general export
promotion policies, and overall workforce ability, are common to most or
all industries. Others are more particular to the environmental sector.

Table 8.6 Environmental legislation and technology licensing
         – licensing agreements in the field of flue gas denitrification –

Licensor		Licensee	
Mitsubishi	Japan	Thyssen	Germany
Mitsubishi	Japan	Siemens	Germany
Mitsubishi	Japan	Bayer	Germany
Mitsubishi	Japan	EVT	Germany
Babcock Hitachi	Japan	HI Lentjes	Germany
Babcock Hitachi	Japan	Uhde	Germany
Kawasaki HI	Japan	Deutsche Babcock	Germany
Ishikawjima Harima HI	Japan	LC Stein–Müller	Germany
Gadelius KK	Japan	Kraftanlagen Heidelberg	Germany

Source: CEST.

3.3.4 Benefits for the suppliers and users of green products and clean technologies

It is becoming increasingly obvious to both legislators and firms that control strategies are both costly to implement and inadequate as an environmental protection mechanism.

Therefore, the **preventive** strategy for environmental management is emerging as the preferred mechanism, on the basis that 'prevention is better than the cure' in both an economic and environmental sense. The preventive strategy is based on the premise that actions should be directed not to the pollutants and waste itself, but to the conditions and circumstances that have the potential to generate pollutant and waste. Elimination and/or reduction of pollutants at source, rather than treatment and disposal after the fact, is ultimately the most cost effective and efficient strategy for environmental management.

It is customary, though somewhat artificial, to distinguish between preventive strategies regarding cleaner production and cleaner products. Where cleaner production systems are more efficient in comparison with existing alternatives those companies which produce and install them earliest will also gain an advantage. Environmental policy that stimulates adoption of clean technologies could therefore lead to a competitive advantage for the suppliers and the regulated sector too. Experience in Germany appears to support this assumption (see also Table 8.7).

4 POLICY ISSUES IN THE CONTEXT OF THE ENVIRONMENT–COMPETITIVENESS LINKAGE

4.1 Innovative Approaches to Environmental Management

A number of experiments are underway as regulators and industries seek new regulatory approaches that protect the environment effectively while reducing competitive impacts on firms. These experiments include emphasis on pollution prevention; use of multimedia regulation, licensing, and inspections; development of facility–wide emission caps and performance standards; and allowing good environmental performers more choices in selecting how they will comply with regulations. The techniques explored in these experiments can complement and enhance the present regulatory tool kit, but they have yet to be widely adopted.

The basic regulatory framework for environmental policy in Germany since the 1970s can be classified as 'command and control', characterized by source and pollutant specific standards, generally based on a feasible control technology. Applied to similar sources with low initial abatement costs, this regulatory instrument was relatively efficient at reducing pollution. In recent years, however, the application of incentive based environmental policy instruments has been increasing. This shift can be explained by the following reasons:

First, government authorities perceive to a growing extent that strengthening direct emissions controls will no longer be effective once current environmental quality targets are met by pollutant specific standards.

Second, the ecological consequences of products, waste streams or standard inputs of industrial production processes defy 'end–of–pipe' mechanisms, calling for the use of policy instruments that foster environmentally friendly production and products.

Third, the number of chemicals or materials for which environmental controls are sought is steadily expanding; regulation by product becomes an increasingly unwieldy task.

The combination of these two patterns – the increasing identification of

Table 8.7 German suppliers and users of clean technologies and competitiveness

Industries	Suppliers /users as % of all respon- dents	Impacts on competitiveness					
		on domestic markets			on export markets		
		+ve	no change	-ve	+ve	no change	-ve
		in %			in %		
Suppliers:							
Primary and general producer goods	10.2	31.8	68.2	–	31.8	68.2	–
Capital goods	16.4	26.3	71.4	2.2	19.5	78.1	2.3
Consumer goods	3.3	12.8	84.6	2.6	5.9	91.2	2.9
Food, drink and tobacco	–	–	100.0	–	–	100.0	–
All industries	11.3	23.9	74.1	2.0	18.2	79.7	2.1
Users:							
Primary and general producer goods	68.1	23.3	74.4	2.3	20.3	71.6	8.1
Capital goods	45.0	20.4	76.3	3.3	15.5	79.9	4.6
Consumer goods	43.1	21.1	75.9	3.0	8.0	87.5	4.5
Food, drink and tobacco	52.2	20.0	76.0	4.0	5.3	94.7	–
All industries	48.1	21.6	75.9	3.1	13.9	81.1	5.0

Source: IFO Survey (1995).

damaging substances and the recognition of the need to switch from end–of–pipe and clean–up to products and processes – has stimulated the search for new approaches. The information/education approach relies on measures fostering transparency on firms' production and products. The measures include for example environmental impact assessments or environmental labelling. The ultimate instrument is to force polluters to accept liability.

These new regulatory patterns are reinforced by the use of economic instruments, such as user or pollution charges, deposit–refund systems, subsidy schemes and tradeable pollution permits. These instruments assign a price to the production or consumption externalities, hence encouraging polluters to curb the damaging activity.

The above mentioned approaches, and innovative instruments such as voluntary self–commitments by industries, allow businesses and households to respond flexibly to pollution reduction requirements; thus yielding savings in pollution abatement costs and fostering technical innovation.

4.2 Adjustment Assistance Measures

Where environmental regulations may generate serious hardships, the German authorities may and actually do provide a broad range of adjustment assistance measures to ease the companies' burdens. These include:

- early warning to target groups;
- step–wise implementation of regulations;
- extension of compliance dates;
- special transition provisions for existing plants;
- progressive implementation of effluent charges or eco–taxes through a step by step increase of the rates;
- exemptions from regulations, taxes or charges;
- redistribution or compensation arrangements;
- linkage of the introduction of new eco–taxes to a reduction in other taxes or social security contributions; and
- subsidy schemes including grants, soft loans, tax allowances and so on (see IFO, 1994).

Most environmental policies have been designed and implemented so as to minimise adverse competitive effects on the target groups. Potentially substantial compliance costs have been partly offset by subsidies in particular, as can be seen from a recent inventory on environment–related

Table 8.8 Overview: Subsidy programmes for environmental purposes

	Energy	Waste water	Waste	Air/ Noise	General	Total
Belgium	2	1	–	–	11	14
Denmark	9	–	3	3	6	21
France	–	18	3	2	1	24
Germany	32	14	10	13	32	101
Greece	–	–	–	4	–	4
Ireland	2	1	2	–	1	6
Italy	2	1	1	1	5	10
Luxembourg	2	2	–	4	4	12
Portugal	9	–	–	–	5	14
Spain	2	1	5	–	8	16
Netherlands	5	3	3	7	13	31
United Kingdom	3	2	3	–	5	13
TOTAL	68	43	30	34	91	266

Source: IFO Institute.

subsidies for the EC member states (Table 8.8).

4.3 Integration of Environmental and Economic Policies

Environmental and economic policies have often been viewed as in opposition and, for the most part, have been developed separately. Nonetheless, more and more, policy makers see benefits in addressing the two together. The interactions between environmental concerns and industrial competitiveness have ramifications for many policy areas, including technology development and diffusion, export promotion and development assistance, and trade policy and negotiations. Addressing these interactions could require changes in German government programmes. Among proposals now on the table are those to:

- devise a strategy to promote development and export of environmental technologies;
- create mechanisms to integrate environmental objectives into government support for manufacturing industry R&D and technology diffusion;
- work toward harmonization of EU environmental standards and bilateral and multilateral agreements on environmental standards that further environmental goals, lessen the likelihood of adverse competitiveness impacts for German firms and workers, and expand opportunities for German environmental firms at home and abroad.

NOTES

1. See, for instance, Sprenger (1979), pp. 107-114; Leonhard and Duerksen (1980), pp.51-68; Kazis and Grossmann (1982), pp. 28-30; Knödgen (1982), OECD (1993a); Jaffe et al. (1995).

DISCUSSANT: Norman Glass

Countries do not compete; companies compete. It is a mistake to confuse what is bad (or good) for a company or an industrial sector with what is bad (or good) for the economy as a whole, including consumers. Higher environmental standards may well cost money but there is not, in general, an added loss in 'competitiveness', so we do not have to have harmonized environmental standards between countries, although global and cross-boundary pollution may require concerted action if they are to be **environmentally** effective.

Higher environmental standards in an open economy may lead to economic changes including loss of jobs. However, economic changes are endemic, very large numbers of people enter and leave employment every year and avoiding transitional effects would mean never changing any policy. The key question is 'Is the environmental benefit worth the cost?'. Transitional effects may imply phasing, they do not imply accepting environmental damage permanently.

Arguments for using environmental standards to force investment and innovation or to gain a strategic trade advantage for environmental companies are not strong. It is not true that more investment or indeed more innovation is always a good thing. We cannot be sure that we do not already have too much investment and too much innovation; it depends upon their profitability. Even if strategic trade policies were feasible for Germany, they are clearly not a game everyone can play with benefit. There is nothing magical otherwise about exports; they cannot create jobs unless they do not violate the macroeconomic policy constraint and if there is macroeconomic slack, we do not have to wait for extra exports to create jobs. On the other hand, environmental policies may cost less than appears at first sight because, in the course of their implementation, innovation may reduce the costs.

Discussion

It is necessary to take account of the enforcement of regulations, as well as the regulations themselves. Environmental costs may be small, in the region of 0.5 per cent to 1.5 per cent of turnover, but if profits are of the order of 5 per cent of turnover, these costs may be significant. It is important, however, to remember that the primary objective of environmental policies is to tackle environmental problems, not to improve competitiveness or create jobs. This is why such policies are beneficial and they should not require further justification. Their benefits should be identified separately from other policies. Since labour productivity gains will be slight, eco–productivity gains should be emphasized. German companies seem to prefer regulation to tradeable permits, possibly because they often have monopolies in polluting industries. Command and control instruments are prevalent because lawyers, rather than economists, make agreements. One argument for regulation is that firms often do not operate at the production efficiency frontier, so if regulations force a change in corporate culture, efficiency may be improved. Account must be taken of distributive effects and the structural changes required and encouraged by environmental policies. Distributional effects within a country will influence the policy debate and there will also be differences in the impact of policies between different countries.

It is often the case that pollution intensive industries claim to represent all industries and although the chemical industry is supportive of environmental policies, most of industry is against these policies. However, consumer preferences are becoming greener and policies should support these policies. Small companies often identify new markets in response to new or predicted legislation, the rôle of consumers in generating new markets is often overemphasised. Given an estimated rate of time preference of 3 per cent per year in the UK, short term adjustment costs may be significant. It is also necessary to consider the interests of other stakeholders as well as shareholders in companies.

REFERENCES

Beghin, J., D. Roland–Holst and D. Van der Mensbrugghe (1994), 'A survey of the trade and environment nexus: global dimensions', in: *OECD Economic Studies No. 23*, 167-192.

CEST (n.d.), *Industry and the Environment: A Strategic Overview*, The Centre for Exploitation of Science and Technology, London.

Dean, J. (1992), 'Trade and the environment: a survey of the literature', in: Low P. (ed), *International Trade and the Environment*, World Bank Discussion Paper 159, The World Bank, Washington, D.C, 15-28.

European Commission (1997), List of sites registered in the EMAS scheme (to be published).

Federal Environment Agency (1991), 'Umweltorientierte Unternehmensführung: möglichkeiten zur kostensenkung und Erlössteigerung'. Berichte 11/91, Umweltbundesamt, Berlin.

Federal Environment Agency (1993/1994), *Environmental Protection – an Economic Asset*, Umweltbundesamt (Germany), Berlin.

Federal Statistical Office (1996a), *Umweltökonomische Gesamtrechnungen – Ausgaben und Anlagevermögen für Umweltschutz*, 1996, Statistisches Bundesamt, Wiesbaden.

Federal Statistical Office (1996b), *Investitionen für Umweltschutz im Produzierenden Gewerbe*, 1995, Statistisches Bundesamt, Wiesbaden.

IFO Institute (1994), 'Inventory on Subsidies for Environmental Purpose', IFO Institute, Munich (unpublished).

IFO Institute (1995), 'Industry Survey on Clean Technologies and Competitiveness', IFO Institute, Munich (unpublished).

Jaffe, A.B., S.R. Peterson, P.R. Portney and R.N. Stavins (1995), 'Environmental regulation and the competitiveness of US manufacturing', *Journal of Economic Literature*, **XXXIII** (March 1995), 132-63.

Kazis, R. and R.L. Grossmann (1982), *Fear at Work – Job Blackmail, Labour and the Environment*, The Pilgrim Press, New York.

Knoedgen, G. (1982), *Umweltschutz und industrielle Standortentscheidung*, Campus Verlag, Frankfurt/New York.

Lanjouw, J.O. and A. Mody (1996), 'Innovation and the international diffusion of environmentally responsive technology', *Research Policy* **25**, 549-71.

Leonhard, H.J. and C.J. Duerksen (1980), 'Environmental regulations and the location of industry. An international perspective', *Columbia Journal of World Business* **15** (1980), 52-68.

Low, P. (ed) (1992), *International Trade and the Environment*, World

Bank Discussion Papers: 159, The World Bank, Washington, DC.

OECD (1978), *Employment and Environment*, OECD, Paris.

OECD (1992), *The OECD Environment Industry: Situation, Prospects and Government Policy*, OECD, Paris.

OECD (1993a), *Environmental Policies and Industrial Competitiveness*, OECD, Paris.

OECD (1993b), *OECD Environmental Performance Reviews: Germany* OECD, Paris.

O. J. (1996), 'List of sites registered in the European eco management and audit scheme', *Official Journal of the European Communities*, No. C 223/23.

Sprenger, R.U., in collaboration with Britschkat, G. (1979), *Beschäftigungseffekte der Umweltpolitik*, Duncker & Humblot, München/Berlin.

Sprenger, R.U. (1992), *Umweltschutz als Standortfaktor*, Friedrich–Ebert Stiftung, Bonn.

Sprenger, R.U. (1995), 'Initiatives for environmental protection in Germany', in: Y. Suzuki, K. Ueta, S. Mori (eds), *Global Environmental Security*, 148–67, Springer Verlag, Berlin Heidelberg New York.

Sprenger, R.U. (1997), *Environmental Policies and Employment*, OECD, Paris.

The Lower Saxony Ministry of the Environment (1995), *Environmental Management; Perspectives for Business Success in Manufacturing in Lower Saxony*, University of Hannover, Hannover.

UNCTAD (1993), 'Trends in the field of trade and environment in the framework of international cooperation', TD/B/40(1)/6, UNCTAD, Geneva.

UNCTAD (1994), 'Sustainable Development: Trade and Environment – The Impact of Environment–related Policies in Export Competitiveness and Market Access', TD/B/41(1)/4, UNCTAD, Geneva.

United Nations Centre On Transnational Corporations (UNCTC) (1985), *Environmental Aspects of the Activities of Multinational Corporations: A Survey*, UN, New York.

US General Accounting Office (1991), 'US–Mexico Trade: Some US wood furniture firms relocated from Los Angeles area to Mexico', Report Number GAO/NSIAD-91-191, Washington, DC.

US Office Of Technology Assessment (1993), 'Industry, technology, and the environment: Competitive challanges and business opportunities', OTA-ITE-586, US GPO, Washington, DC.

9. Integrated product policy and industrial competitiveness

Frans Berkhout

1 INTEGRATION AS A THEME IN ENVIRONMENTAL POLICY

The principle of integration is by now well established in environmental policy. There has been a general recognition that environmental problems are complex and arise from deepseated patterns of production and consumption. The management of resource inputs into or waste outputs from the economy, whether by direct regulation or through market–based instruments are not sufficient by themselves in confronting this challenge. A wider perspective which sought an integrated approach to production and consumption was therefore introduced in European environmental policy in the Fifth Environmental Action Programme (5EAP) and reinforced in the White Paper on Growth, Competitiveness, Employment. A range of instruments were to be implemented within the frame of shared responsibility between producers, consumers and public administrations.

However, integration of environmental policy can take a number of forms:

1. **horizontal integration**: integrating the control of environmental impacts from industrial production sites to avoid cross–media transfers of pollution: for example, the Integrated Pollution Prevention and Control Directive (IPPC);
2. **vertical integration**: taking an integrative approach to managing environmental impacts along the product chain from cradle–to–grave: for example, life cycle approaches;

3.   **systemic integration**: taking an integrated view of alternative means of providing a good or a service: for example, a review of alternative modes of transport in achieving sustainable mobility; and
4.   **policy integration**: the integration of the environmental dimension into other areas of policy: for example, agricultural, industrial, transport and tourism policy.

This chapter is primarily concerned with policies aimed at vertical integration and their likely impacts on competitiveness. The chapter is divided into two parts. The first is concerned with describing a trend in European environmental policy towards more product–oriented policy, as opposed to process–oriented policy. 'Integration' in these policies implies a concern with the management of the environmental performance of products across their total life cycle. The second part of the paper provides an assessment of the impacts on competitiveness of the adoption of life–cycle approaches by European firms. The principal argument of the chapter is that the likely competitive impacts of product–oriented environmental policies will be determined by the technological and market context in which firms operate. Competitiveness of commodity product producers will not be greatly affected, while opportunities may exist for some firms producing final goods to seek competitive advantage as a result of these policies. On the whole European industry is better equipped to exploit these advantages than industry in North America and Japan.

2 FROM PROCESS–ORIENTED TO PRODUCT–ORIENTED ENVIRONMENTAL POLICY

While industrial and energy production remains an important source of pollution and waste in industrial economies, the relative importance of consumption–related emissions and wastes has been increasingly recognised over the past two decades. Pollution arising directly from industrial production has been falling, while pollution generated by the consumption of goods and services has been rising. Most industrial processes are relatively efficient and their emissions are contained, but growth in demand and changing patterns of use of goods have more than compensated for these gains in environmental performance. Absolute amounts of energy and materials consumed by developed economies continue to rise leading inevitably to increased environmental burdens.

The falling importance of industrial point sources is due primarily to structural change (the shift from materials– and energy–intensive industrial economies to more service–intensive economies) and technological change (improved energy efficiency and 'dematerialisation'), some of it influenced by technology standards derived from environmental regulation. These process–based controls may in some contexts be reaching their technological and economic limits. Large capital investments and regulatory effort over the past thirty years have led to greatly reduced industrial emissions. The environmental or health benefits gained through further reductions in emissions may, in some cases, not be proportionate to the costs.

At the same time, the rising importance of consumption related environmental impacts has been recognised. The great importance attached to waste management since the 1980s is a sign of this, but the same is true for many 'dissipative' emissions traditionally associated with industrial production. In setting new volatile organic compound (VOC) regulations in place in 1986, the Dutch government discovered that VOC emissions from the application of paint were three times higher than total emissions in the Netherlands from the chemicals industry. Recognition of technological limits in process control and the rising importance of consumption related emissions have led to calls, particularly in northern European countries, for policy to become more product–oriented.

These developments in policy have also responded to the emergence over the past ten years of a number of new concepts and instruments which describe approaches to product chain management. These include, among others, eco–efficiency, industrial ecology and life cycle analysis (LCA). While the focus of each is somewhat different they are related in seeking to link the social and economic 'functions' delivered through products to wider environmental consequences. Having drawn up a picture of the physical flows which make up a product chain, and classified the environmental impacts arising from this system, it is in principle possible to make a judgement about whether better environmental options are available.

In comparing environmental options a life cycle approach is used which integrates across life cycle stages and environmental impacts. The unit of analysis is not the product itself, but the function which it provides and the industrial system which supports its production, use and discard. Functions may include very specific technical definitions of performance (for example: the capacity to keep $1m^3$ of refrigerated space below 5°C with an exterior temperature of 30°C), or they may include broader 'systemic' definitions such as 'food safety' (in the case of packaging) to 'mobility' (passenger transport).

3 MANAGING PRODUCT SYSTEMS

What then is a product? In the debate about product policy, the favoured definition is usually 'final products' because they provide the clearest distinction between producers and the final consumer, especially post–consumption wastes. This definition may not always be the most appropriate. Integrated product policy explicitly recognises that product chains need to be considered, including links between producers and intermediate consumers. Products may therefore be many things: raw materials (coal, oil, wood); intermediate and final products (polyethylene, microchip, automobile); waste products (plastic recyclate, gypsum, sewage sludge); production facilities (power plant, paint shop); and infrastructure projects (packet switching device, the Channel Tunnel).

Product policy should probably be relatively neutral about what is counted 'in' and what is counted 'out', as this will vary according to the problem being tackled, and the industrial sector being considered. Policy will be directed both at broad materials flows through an economy (carbon, chlorine) as well as design and purchasing decisions relating to very specific product systems (the automobile, the battery). The ultimate objective of product policy is to encourage the innovation and consumption of 'greener' goods and services. The notion that 'services', broadly defined, may substitute for 'products' has caught the imagination of policy makers in this field.

Since products, widely defined, carry out an almost infinite number of functions and have widely differing environmental characteristics, establishing simple, universally applicable classifications of environmental performance is not tractable. Each product will have a different ecoprofile, with environmental impacts falling at different stages of the product life cycle. Nevertheless, product policy must recognise the fundamentally different resource and environmental commitments associated with different products. Three possible categories are discussed below:

1. **'dissipative' and 'non–dissipative' products**: this distinguishes between uses of materials in products so that they cannot be recovered for reuse (for example, detergents and agrochemicals) and uses in products which can be recovered for reuse (white goods and tyres). There is also an intermediate category of corrosion emissions to the environment from non–dissipative products (cadmium from tyres).
2. **'short use–life' and 'durable' products**: this distinguishes between products whose use life is short (packaging) and products which have a longer use life (buildings). The distinction between what is durable and what is not is somewhat arbitrary and will depend on the product group. A shirt with a six

year use life may be regarded as durable while durability in automobiles typically demands a use life at least twice as long.

3. **'passive' and 'active' products**: this distinguishes between products which do not themselves use energy (pans and furniture) and those which do (white goods). Energy during the use phase of an active product typically represents the largest environmental impact associated with the product. For many passive products, the key environmental impacts are associated with the production phase of the life cycle.

4 THE ROLE OF POLICY IN MANAGING PRODUCT SYSTEMS

In seeking to manage product systems policy makers are faced with new problems: Which products should be the focus of policy? How can 'green' products be distinguished from the rest? What policy levers exist to influence product systems? How can these policies be coordinated? How effective can product policy be in making patterns of production and consumption more sustainable?

Governments do not have the competences or the powers to devise and implement an interventionist product policy. For instance, governments do not have the skills to analyse the inputs and outputs of product systems; they are not in a position to evaluate independently the environmental and economic benefits and costs of products; and their capacity to influence the materials or energy profile of products is indirect. Lastly, in many cases, governments do not have the authority to define on environmental grounds whether or not a product may be produced or consumed. Governments therefore need to share responsibility for product policies with other stakeholders. In many cases this may be through market–based instruments, but there will remain a need for regulatory 'steering'. Preferences of consumers by themselves cannot be expected to guide the development of more sustainable product systems.

Apart from requiring the creation of new competences and frameworks for environmental policy, a transition towards product–oriented policies faces political and legal obstacles. The key problem is over consumer sovereignty, but there are other concerns: the sheer diversity of products on the market; the number of actors engaged in producing and consuming products; and potential barriers to free trade of product policies.

1. **Consumer sovereignty**: The right of consumers to consume can be limited only where wide consensus exists that a given product or use is illegitimate, as with regulations and procedures which secure health and safety. Indeed,

consumers have been extremely sensitive to hazards to health, and strong penalties exist for firms who are seen not to protect their customers from unacceptable risks. Introducing environmental aspects into the management of products is possible when those impacts are widely accepted as being significant, as with ozone depleting substances, but far more difficult when scientific or political consensus does not exist. For most product groups, governments find it difficult to intervene directly in the right to consume, even in cases where environmental harms may be widely believed to result.

2. **Product system diversity**: There are too many products for public authorities to monitor and manage directly through policy. The total number of products available in European markets numbers in the millions. Most firms do not understand the life cycle impacts of the products they are involved in producing. Governments are even less able to do this.

3. **Value chain complexity**: Many actors are involved in the production and consumption of products. Direct regulation of consumers in respect of the environmental performance is difficult, and would frequently face legal challenge. The case of cigarettes demonstrates the limits of direct governmental restriction of the rights of consumers even where harm has been effectively proven. Much more important in the long run have been changing social attitudes to smoking, a development in which governments have played an significant role.

Direct regulation of producers will also not be straightforward. There has been a tendency in the 1990s, first in waste management policy but also in product policy for greater responsibility for product system management to be placed with producers. However, establishing how to distribute this responsibility is a thorny problem. Supply chains in industry are typically long and complex, and for many complex products the greater proportion of production is not done by the final producer. One approach is to seek to distribute responsibility for product system management across the supply chain evenly. This approach has been pioneered in the VALPAK organisation created in the UK to implement the EU Packaging and Packaging Waste Directive. The opposite approach is to place full responsibility for product management on one member of the supply chain, usually the final producer who is the largest and most technologically capable member of the product chain. This is the approach favoured in the German end–of–life vehicle voluntary agreement which sets out recovery and recycling targets for automobile manufacturers.

4. **Global scope of product systems**: The resource requirements and environmental impacts of product systems cross national and regional boundaries. There are inherent tensions between trade rules which prohibit differential treatment of imported goods if they are identical in function, and product policies which discriminate between similar products on the basis of

the methods used to produce them, the materials they contain, or the way they are powered.

To summarise, for public authorities the transition from process–oriented to product–oriented policy means a transition from intervening directly in the environmental impacts of single sites with well–known technological and resource characteristics operated by single industrial firms, to modifying indirectly the imprecisely known environmental impacts of product systems involving many stakeholders. This transition has major implications for the whole structure of environmental policy which are only now beginning to be understood.

5 POLICY RESPONSES

Product policy represents a new area of policy with new objectives, instruments, problems and possibilities. A wider network of partnerships between national and international actors needs to be created, with rights and responsibilities reallocated among public authorities, producers and consumers. The policy process must become more open, interactive and cooperative, placing greater stress on voluntary actions and market instruments, with public authorities taking the role of facilitators and arbitrators, rather than as enforcers of rules laid down in legislation. This is not to underestimate the continuing great importance of environmental legislation.

Three types of policy response have developed in the EU, none of them as yet strong or well developed. At the macro level, countries like the Netherlands, Germany and Sweden have set in train broad frameworks for managing key substance flows through national economies and rates of emissions of pollutants to the environment. Policies will emerge which attempt to influence the dynamics of aggregate demand in the economy and link this with environmental impact in key sectors including energy, agriculture and industry. The new Kreislaufwirtschafts- und Abfallgesetz (Closed–loop Economy and Waste Law, 1996) in Germany, and the Swedish Ecocycle Law (1993) are forerunners of this approach.

At the meso level, voluntary agreements have been negotiated between governments and industry which implements extended producer responsibility (EPR), shared responsibility and Product Stewardship for specific product groups. The Swedish Ecocycle Commission has recommended that the concept of producer responsibility should be applied generically to all product groups in future. It is assumed that the costs of product system management will be passed on to the consumer, and that competition will ensure an efficient reconstruction of product systems. To date, policies which extend producer responsibility have been concerned primarily with waste management.

At the micro level, more environmental information is becoming available in the market. This may be directed at consumers, at private and public sector procurement, and at producers aiming to develop 'green' products. Environmental declaration and labelling schemes are increasingly based on the cradle-to-grave concept. There are many unanswered questions about the effectiveness of information instruments. Ecolabels have proven problematic to negotiate, and their impact on the behaviour of consumers, and on innovation of 'greener' products by industry, is likely to be marginal.

Surveying this picture, we can suggest a simple model for the development of product–oriented policies which might be termed the **reverse chain management model**. This suggests that product policies develop backwards along the product system in a series of stages, gradually becoming more comprehensive in scope and impact. In an initial phase, environmental policy is process–oriented and concerned primarily with control of emissions, both static and mobile. In the first phase of product policy development, responsibility for waste management is shifted from government and the consumer and is imposed on producers, so extending producer responsibility. In the next phase, information policies that aim to improve and open access to environmental information about products are introduced. In the final phase legal responsibility and information policies are supported by research and technology development (RTD) policies, charges and taxes, and voluntary agreements aimed at stimulating innovation and market take–up of green products. The scope of product policy therefore moves from waste management, to information up and down the product chain, to innovation policies aimed at producers.

Given that product policy encompasses a portfolio of instruments which act at different points along the product chain, the definition of what is meant by product policy has not yet stabilised. A recent European Commission study suggested that integrated product policy was 'public policy which aims explicitly to modify the environmental performance of product systems'. Included in this definition are five types of policies:

1. to provide information on the life cycle environmental performance along the supply chain to customers and consumers (that is eco–labels);
2. to encourage the development of 'green' products and services (that is eco–design programmes);
3. to create markets for 'green' products and services (that is green public purchasing initiatives);

4. to promote the recovery, reuse and recycling of materials (that is take–back obligations); and
5. to redistribute responsibility for managing product systems away from customers and government, towards producers (producer responsibility).

A key issue is over the place of policies to encourage energy efficiency and 'detoxification' through the removal or management of toxic materials contained in product systems. In each case what is being sought is policy which considers energy, chemicals and wastes in the context of the product systems which consume and generate them, rather than as separate problems in their own right. The great challenge for a product–oriented policy is to reconsider rather traditional problems in environmental policy in the light of the economic activities which give rise to them.

6 THE ROLE OF INDUSTRY

European industry has played a leading role in defining the scope of product oriented environmental policies. The Dutch chemical industries trade association (VNCI) produced an influential Product Policy document in 1992, the World Business Council for Sustainable Development has been active in defining eco–efficiency, and firms have been active participants in debates about Industrial Ecology (AT&T), Extended Producer Responsibility (Electrolux and others), Life Cycle Assessment (LCA) (Volvo, Procter and Gamble, Dow–Europe), and promoters of information instruments (in sectors such a retailing and cosmetics).

Through concepts such as 'functional sales' firms situated both upstream and downstream along the product chain have begun thinking about a transition away from core businesses based on the sale of products alone, to a business delivering 'functions' or services to consumers. The extension of market relationships based on leasing and service agreements to new markets is one element of industry thinking. Final producers or their proxies would just retain ownership of the product itself, and instead market the service. Maintenance, reconditioning and recovery of the product would become one of the normal roles of producers. The producer would retain a continuing relationship with the consumer. Leasing relationships are being enabled by technology, in particular the capacity to collect and manage data about consumers, their preferences and their behaviour. They are also being encouraged by the commodification of services like the supply of electricity. Energy costs are no longer separated from product costs, but can be provided as part of a service by a single service provider, whether a final producer or a retailer. These changes are set to transform the structure of industry in ways which are difficult to foresee. They also present a problem for an analysis of competitiveness impacts. The notion of competitiveness assumes that the rules of the game remain the same.

In taking this leading role, industry has responded to market pressures from consumers and competitors, while also seeking to bring greater balance to environmental debates. Industry is also responding to the extension of producer responsibility to manage and reduce environmental impacts across product life cycles. These developments have potentially major implications for competition and competitiveness. For instance, setting formal or informal eco criteria for a product group inevitably discriminates against those products which do not meet the criteria. On a broader scale, endowed national energy infrastructures have a profound impact on the ecoprofile of many of the products produced in that economy. German aluminium looks 'dirty' when compared with Norwegian aluminium (coal–fired versus hydro electricity generation). As environmental criteria rise in importance in private and public sector purchasing, such differences may become an important component of comparative and competitive advantage.

Product policies therefore arise out of two converging trends: the need to integrate vertically environmental policy; and market and technological opportunities that are encouraging firms to manage the life cycles of the products they produce. These tendencies are not yet pervasive across all sectors, nor are they yet fully aligned. The implications for competitiveness of industry are also not yet evident. A good proxy however is an analysis of the competitive impacts of the adoption of life cycle approaches by firms. We have shown above that a life cycle approach lies at the core of product–oriented environmental policy, and also that industry is playing a leading role in shaping and implementing these policies. The analysis reported here is based on a two surveys of 60 European firms in six industrial sectors carried out during 1995 and 1996. The sectors included: aluminium; chemicals; building materials; electronic goods; automobiles; and consumer products (see Berkhout and Howes, 1997).

7 LIFE CYCLE ASSESSMENT

Life cycle assessment is a framework for learning about the environmental impacts of products from the 'cradle to the grave'. The approach has two roots: traditional engineering and process analysis; and energy analysis which developed during the 1970s after the first oil shock. Up to the 1980s, most analysis concentrated on materials and energy efficiency in process technologies. For many bulk commodities energy analysis will provide a large proportion of the picture. In the late 1980s there was a desire, especially in industries increasingly affected by heavier and less predictable environmental pressures, for non–energy related impacts to be included.

The objective of a life cycle study is to assess the total environmental impact of a product. A full LCA would include the whole life cycle of a product system, stretching from raw material extraction through materials processing, component production, final assembly, distribution, use, recycling and waste management. A classical study would include a description of the product system and its mass and energy balances (inventory stage), an accounting of the environmental and resource impacts of the system (classification and characterisation) and finally some valuation of the impacts (normalisation and valuation).

Most life cycle studies cover only a limited set of life cycle components and many do not include a formal assessment step. More limited 'cradle–to–grave' life cycle inventory (LCI) studies typically provide mass and energy balances and environmental emissions inventories for the production of intermediate products, such as commodity plastics (Boustead, 1994/95). Downstream production, use and waste management activities are not considered, and no attempt at classifying or valuing impacts is made. Analysis will normally be limited to physical features of the system and impacts on ecological systems, to the exclusion of safety and ethical concerns.

Life cycle studies have been used to understand three types of problem:
(i) assessments of single products to provide data about their ecoprofiles (an example is the recent European surfactant life cycle inventory study, Stalmans et al., 1995); (ii) comparisons of process routes in the production of substitutable products or processes (the studies on paper and polystyrene foam hot drink cups, Hocking, 1991); and (iii) comparisons of alternative routes for delivering a service or function (mobility, warmth, painting). Most life cycle studies have been comparative assessments of similar products, whether final or intermediate products. Within industry the application of life cycle–based knowledge is to inform a firm or a sector group about the competitive position of its products and processes.

8 ADOPTION OF LIFE CYCLE APPROACHES BY INDUSTRY

European industrial firms have taken highly differentiated strategies in learning and adopting life cycle approaches (LCA). They are differentiated across sectors, between firms within the same sector, and between business units within the same firm. Even in sectors where there is greater commitment to more integrated approaches to design and product system management, firms display a diversity of attitudes to the instrument.

One explanation of this diversity is that firms are still in an early phase of a new business activity, and that with learning and experience convergence will occur in the behaviour of firms. For instance, in sectors where collaborative life cycle studies have played an important role, such as plastics, there is greater similarity between firms. Another explanation is that firms have very different interests and capabilities in the adoption of a new 'life cycle' perspective on product innovation and management. A highly differentiated picture is therefore to be expected. However, although life cycle approaches are still at an early stage of development, it is possible to define a number of strategies in learning and adoption taken by firms. In particular, position along the product life cycle (whether upstream or downstream), and the nature of the product (whether simple or complex), have an important bearing on adoption strategies. The technological and market context in which the firm operates therefore determines its adoption of life cycle approaches.

Like all innovations, life cycle approaches require adopting firms to develop new competences (to analyse life cycle resource and environmental impacts of their products), and to make changes to their organisational routines (to act profitably on this knowledge in managing product life cycles). Applications may be in decision making or opinion forming, both inside and outside the firm. The process of learning and adoption is usually not unproblematic, and takes time. LCA is a rather unconventional innovation. It is not a piece of technology that can be applied to a defined task, nor is it a formal management or accounting approach for which a process of adoption has already been elaborated. Although LCA is primarily an analytical technique, it may also be used as a framework to communicate a wide range of messages to diverse audiences. There is frequently a problem in finding a 'fit' for LCA within firms, partly explained by uncertainty about what role it may play in meeting the firm's objectives, financial, technological or environmental.

Firms initiate learning and adoption of LCA in three ways: they subcontract life cycle studies to outside consultants; they develop in-house competences; and they participate in collaborative life cycle studies. This activity is now pervasive across European industry. Significant life cycle activities are now underway in all industrial sectors, except tobacco products. Many large firms have invested in life cycle studies and many have established in-house competences and capabilities (databases, LCA software). Relationships with external consultants are sustained either independently, or through collaborative industry studies.

As in-house competences mature, and as decisive applications begin to be made, a higher premium is placed on autonomy and confidentiality. However, the process whereby life cycle approaches become embedded in business processes follows distinct pathways in different sectors. The main factors influencing adoption by European firms are: whether the key driver is regulatory or market pressure; the control exerted by a firm over the product chain; whether the decision to adopt is 'top–down' or 'bottom–up'; the balance of internal and external applications of LCA; and the appropriability to business of life cycle approaches.

Regulatory or Market Drivers

Direct technology–based regulation is still the main driver of environmental initiatives in industry. It has also played an important role in encouraging firms to adopt life cycle approaches. Where regulation is the main driver of the adoption of life cycle approaches (plastics waste management legislation, or end–of–life vehicle voluntary agreements) the response among firms has typically been defensive, in collaborating in seeking to influence public policy. Large studies reviewing how waste management options are funded are usually carried out by third parties (academics or consulting firms). For instance, in the negotiations over the European plastics waste directive LCA studies were influential in shifting, on environmental grounds, legislation away from an emphasis on mechanical recycling, to promote hybrid approaches with lower recovery targets which include incineration.

The market may influence adoption if LCA–based claims are employed in competition between products or processes. This may take the form of cross–sectoral competion between substitutable materials types (steel versus aluminium in the automotive sector, plastic versus paper in packaging), or intra–sectoral competition between substitute products (disposable versus reusable diapers). In cases of cross–sectoral competition, firms tend to collaborate in defending their environmental credentials, and thereby securing their competitive positions. The result has been a catalogue of industry life cycle inventory studies for commodity products (for instance, Association of Plastics Manufacturers of Europe, APME, European LCI Surfactant Study Group, CEFIC/ECOSOL). These data are used in marketing, but they also feed into life cycle studies for intermediate and final products conducted by industrial producers further up the production chain. Intra–sectoral competition in final goods markets has become less common because it lays firms open to counter claims, and because it requires them to reveal a significant amount of environmental data about their production processes.

Control over the Product Chain

A generic product chain includes raw materials extraction, materials processing, assembly of final product, use, waste management (and recycling) stages. Firms situated along this product chain will exercise control over different stages of the chain, and will have varying capacity to extend this control to other stages. On the whole, the larger, more vertically integrated, and more centrally placed in the product chain a firm is, the greater will be the degree of control it can exercise over that product system. Assemblers of final products are the orchestrators of product life cycles and have the greatest knowledge about the composition and performance of the product. Through their purchasing and design decisions they have the potential to exert greatest influence in shaping ecoprofiles of goods and services. They are frequently also under the most direct regulatory and market pressure to improve the life cycle environmental performance of products. Final goods producers therefore appear to have a greater capacity to capture benefits of improvements to life cycle performance of products.

The reality is less clear cut. Commodity producers have invested more heavily in LCA and appear today to extract more clear cut competitive advantages from their investment. This is partly because the adoption process began relatively early. Moreover, their needs in adopting the approach tend to be relatively simple, and require few organisational or technological innovations. Participation in collaborative LCI studies involves the collation of mass and energy balance, and emissions data which is often already collected by the firm. The initial objective is usually to avoid having to make costly changes to manufacturing processes or management responsibilities by being able to argue that current ecoprofiles of products are no worse than those of alternatives. For final goods producers the predicament is quite different. They face substantial investments in the development of new data gathering and analytical capabilities, which may lead to technological innovations and organisational changes. While final goods producers may benefit from life cycle approaches in the longer run, they also face large obstacles in doing so.

Top–down or Bottom–up

Adoption of LCA by firms has been stimulated either by top management and marketing functions, or has emerged internally within research and development functions. Management and marketing functions have tended to respond to definite external stimuli, whether regulation or market driven, which represent competitive threats to the firm. These include life cycle–based claims by competitors and new regulatory initiatives with an impact on the life cycle costs of products. Under these conditions firms quickly established in–house LCA competences, usually as well funded centralised functions with links to similar functions in other companies in the sector. This pattern is typical in commodity producing sectors like chemicals, forest products and aluminium. It also occurs in final goods producing sectors where there may be a clear market advantage in making life cycle–based claims (as in sectors in which an ecolabel is being negotiated).

Research and technical departments have been the principal route for LCA adoption in sectors where there is a need to respond to longer term, less direct threats to competitiveness. In these sectors, engineers facing new demands for environmentally friendly products have seen LCA as a problem solving framework which could be applied in design and development. In–house competences have been established more slowly in these circumstances in small decentralised teams with research and development functions, sometimes distributed across several divisions within the firm. External links tend to be weaker in these cases, and the approach adopted is more internally–oriented. This pattern is more typical of intermediate and final goods producing sectors like building materials, automobiles and electronic goods.

Internal or External

Life cycle studies can be used by firms externally in marketing or lobbying opinion, or they may be used internally to support business decisions within firms. These two orientations encourage different approaches to LCA adoption. Externally–oriented applications involve the defensive or offensive use of LCA–based claims to external stakeholders (customers, policy makers, LCA practitioners and others). Publication of life cycle studies will usually be required to support such claims. It has been estimated that less than 20 per cent of LCA studies are available in the open literature (OECD, 1995). To be credible these studies need to meet minimum standards of transparency and peer review. This excludes the use of commercially confidential data and requires formal external evaluation. Production of formal studies may also require specialist LCA competences. Consultants therefore play an important role in these applications.

Internally–oriented applications involve the production of knowledge which can be used in benchmarking existing processes and products, and in the development of new technologies and products. At a more general level they may inform business strategy through the encouragement of 'life cycle thinking'. Activities to support this wide range of needs are diverse, ranging from large formal studies to simpler assessment integrated into computer based decision tools for product designers. Internal studies are generally not published and do not need to meet formal criteria for thoroughness and transparency. Such studies are almost exclusively conducted by in-house LCA practitioners.

Appropriability

The adoption of life cycle approaches by firms will depend on the benefits which can be captured by firms from knowledge about the relative ecoprofile of products. In most sectors direct economic or other benefits cannot be appropriated by firms because: life cycles are fragmented between producers, consumers and waste managers; the environmental benefits arising from a life cycle-based product change are spread across these actors as well as others who would have borne the burden of environmental externalities; there has rarely been direct regulatory pressure to take account of life cycle environmental externalities; and because consumer preferences for product ecoprofile improvements are variable across markets and through time. Early marketing uses of life cycle-based claims have demonstrated that such information can easily be manipulated and refuted, leaving confusion and resentment among some consumers.

The competitive benefits available to firms are usually indirect, and may be defensive (protecting market share or countering new regulations), or developmental (supporting product development and product strategy). With defensive uses the goal is to influence the regulatory or market environment, while with more developmental uses there may be technological or organisational benefits for firms which are nevertheless difficult to communicate in the market. LCA-based claims are difficult for firms to sustain individually in the marketplace because consumers cannot evaluate them and because such claims elicit LCA-based counter-claims. LCA-based claims have a greater chance of being accepted if they are supported by a wider and more authoritative community of experts.

Impacts of life cycle approaches on indicators such as costs, quality and sales are difficult to measure. Firms in several sectors (automobiles, electronic goods, building materials) are still struggling to understand how LCA and life cycle approaches benefit them.

Conclusions

Broadly speaking, where the competitive benefits are at the sectoral level, firms engage in externally oriented, large scale, collaborative life cycle inventory studies. This approach is typical of upstream, commodity producing sectors. Where competitive benefits can be appropriated by individual firms life cycle approaches tend to be internally oriented, confidential, small scale,

Table 9.1 Pattern of LCA activities in European industrial firms

	Commodity products	Intermediate and simple products	Complex products
Orientation of life cycle activities	External • marketing • policy process	External and internal	Internal • decision-support
Study structure	Collaborative	Collaborative and independent	Independent
Study practitioner	Third party and in–house studies	In–house and third party studies	In–house studies
Study scope	Cradle–to–grave life cycle inventory (LCI) studies	Scoping total product cycle LCI studies	Total product cycle LCI/LCA studies
Data origin	Internally–generated	Internally– and externally–generated (upstream)	Externally–generated (upstream and down stream)
Evaluation of impacts	No evaluation	Limited evaluation	Some evaluation
Adoption process	Top–down	Variable	Bottom–up
Collaboration	On data	On data	On methodology

integrated into product development and less standardised. Studies tend to consider the total life cycle. This approach is more typical of downstream assemblers of final goods. Intermediate and simple products occupy an intermediate position between these two extremes, sharing characteristics with both. Table 9.1 presents this synthesis.

9   IMPACTS OF LIFE CYCLE APPROACHES ON COMPETITIVENESS

There is no single definition of what makes a firm competitive. Broadly, competitive advantage grows out of the way firms organise and perform activities (human resource management, technology development, procurement, marketing, environmental management). Porter (1985) and others argue that firms create value for their customers by performing these activities, and that this, in turn, generates value for the firm when customers pay for the good or service. A firm is profitable when the costs of providing 'buyer value' are less than income. Competitive advantage over rivals is achieved in two ways: by providing buyer value more efficiently (lower cost), or by performing activities in a unique way to provide buyer value which commands a premium price (differentiation).

Impacts on firm competitiveness of life cycle approaches are as yet hard to measure directly. Instead, they need to be inferred building on observations about learning and adoption strategies. The main impacts are likely to be over the longer term, as innovative firms capture competitive opportunities which are presented by the reconstruction of product systems according to life cycle–based heuristics. Firm based life cycle approaches may have an influence on price competitiveness. For instance, they may uncover new opportunities to improve efficiency through energy and materials savings. The transmission of life cycle inventory information from supplier to customer may provide the customer with proxy data on the costs of the supplier, providing new opportunities for price bargaining. Such data may also be used to exclude certain suppliers on environmental grounds. However, examples of these sorts of direct effects on the price competitiveness of firms are currently rare. Life cycle approaches are not usually invoked where significant additional costs would be borne by the firm.

Life cycle approaches will have a more significant impact on competitiveness through improving resource productivity and environmental efficiency (what might be termed 'environmental productivity'). These impacts will occur over the longer term through innovation and the redefinition of a firm's or an industry's production frontier. In the discussion below we consider likely impacts of life cycle approaches on environmental productivity of firms. Given that learning and adoption strategies of firms are determined by their technological, market and regulatory context, impacts on competitiveness will follow a similar pattern.

Commodity Producers

Competition in commodity production is based primarily on price. The main determinants of competitiveness in these sectors are the cost of energy and materials inputs, the 'yield' from well established, mature processes, and the costs of environmental management. In general, there is a strong correlation between materials– and energy–efficiency and competitiveness. The search for new technological opportunities is already oriented towards improving resource efficiency, whereas tightening emissions controls and market preferences for greener commodities are already forcing many commodity producing firms to consider environmental performance as part of their technology strategy. Life cycle approaches add little to the capabilities and direction of technical change in upstream producers, although 'benchmark' ecoprofiles may help less competitive producers to set targets for process improvement.

The main competitive impact of industry–led life cycle initiatives has been to assist in maintaining 'static' competitiveness by giving producers a tool for defending a product in the market against environmental claims made by competitors, or in defence against new regulations on environmental grounds. In this defensive mode firms have sought to stymie environmental threats to their competitiveness.

Final Goods Producers

Competition between final goods producers is based on function and quality, as well as price. The main determinants of competitiveness are a capability to respond quickly to consumer demand to provide innovative products, an ability to coordinate rapid product innovation, and to manage and control costs in the supply chain. Product innovation is a key component of commercial success, while there is generally a weak link between materials and energy efficiency of products and the competitiveness of firms.

Producers of final products, are also in the best position to improve the ecoprofiles of products. Life cycle approaches are most likely to stimulate innovation, and thereby to encourage 'dynamic competitiveness', amongst final goods producing sectors. Internally–oriented, developmental applications of LCA are beginning to be made in those sectors where market demands or regulatory pressures for life cycle improvements are greatest (consumer goods, automobiles). However, integration may carry high financial and organisational costs, while the ability of the firm to appropriate the benefits of life cycle–oriented improvements of product systems may be limited. One of the roles of product policy is to create the legal and market framework for innovative firms to capture competitive advantage through managing product life cycles.

10 CONCLUSIONS

This chapter has dealt with two discussions: the first concerned with the emergence of product–oriented environmental policy in Europe; the second concerned with the adoption by European industry of life cycle approaches in the management of product systems. The two discussions are linked since product policy aims to develop regulatory, market based and informational instruments which improve the environmental performance of product systems. Industry is likely to play a key role in formulating and implementing this policy.

It has been argued that the main impacts on competitiveness of firms of product policies will be felt amongst producers of final goods and services. This is primarily because of the central product life cycle positions that producers occupy. In this position they are impacted both by signals from upstream about the rising price and changing composition of resources, as well as signals from downstream about tighter restrictions on waste management and new consumer preferences. Materials and design choices made by final goods also determine to a large extent the ecoprofile of the product system, and it is here that policy must intervene. Price signals alone, such as those transmitted by ecotaxes, are unlikely to be sufficient to steer product system changes. Lastly, final goods producers appear to have the greatest competitive interest in searching for life cycle environmental improvements, and for seeking to reconsider product systems by innovating more efficient ways of providing the service embodied in the products they sell. Product policies will be most effective if they are targeted at final goods producers, and their main impact on competitiveness will be in injecting new knowledge into markets, so encouraging competition along a new dimension. This knowledge will in various ways encourage innovations while establishing new parameters for market competitiveness.

There are two main obstacles to the dynamic articulation of policy and industrial objectives. First, the regulatory and policy framework within which industry operates sends conflicting signals. Current environmental, industrial and economic policy was not created against the background of an integrated assessment of the environmental impacts of these measures. Environmental policy today is a patchwork, accreted through a long history of crisis management and conflict resolution. There are few core principles or common priorities. Firms seeking to establish selection mechanisms for product or process innovation which take account of the total life cycle are likely to be confounded by this lack of integration in policy.

Second, if industry is to play a positive role in product policy, the conditions whereby it can appropriate competitive benefits from life cycle environmental improvements need to be more clearly defined. Firms will respond innovatively only when there are clear commercial interests in doing so. In the short term this will be achieved through extended producer responsibility imposed far more pervasively than it is today, and in the longer term through the creation of new markets for services which aim to replace many current patterns of product ownership. One solution to the environmental problems of consumption is to remove from the consumer the responsibility for managing the product.

DISCUSSANT: Sue Scott

Rather like input–output analysis, life–cycle analysis has considerable appeal which is often enhanced by the unanticipated or counter–intuitive nature of the findings. For example, a recent study (cited in *The Economist*, 17.12.1995) shows that re–using bottles was more harmful to the environment than recycling them, when one took into account all stages in the life cycle, from cradle to grave.

Apart from having this appeal, what in fact does life–cycle analysis (LCA) actually do? The answer is that, in addition to providing information thereby enabling efficient decisions to be taken, it

- helps with marketing, if the product has good LCA characteristics,
- helps producers to counter claims of competitors,
- bridges the information gap if measures other than market–based measures need to be adopted to protect the environment.

On this latter point it would be interesting to know to what extent LCA has been used to help with environmental policy. One's supposition is that it could be used, for background information, in such tasks as the formulation of the conditions for Integrated Pollution Control licensing, which some countries operate. These non–market based measures have to be applied in certain circumstances, such as when the 'pollutant' is deadly, lumpy or hard to meter, or has irreversible effects. These circumstances apart, however, if society could get on with taxing and/or charging for the major pollutants, that is for the social as well as for the private costs, this would ensure that the less damaging products were produced and LCA would tend to be superfluous –

except, importantly perhaps, as a check or indeed in helping to determine the actual levels of pollution tax or charge. It is not clear where LCA has a niche advantage.

We should try to think this through with an example to see to what extent LCA can contribute to environmental policy. We can instance some situation where any product, it might be strawberry jam, is under- or over-provided (or it might be pollution abatement which is under-provided, or assimilative capacity which is over-demanded). Suppose that strawberry jam is, for historical reasons, supplied free by society: would we then want to calculate the costs for each stage of strawberry jam production, and sum them to see if strawberry jam production was justified? Or would we just remove the price restriction? Similarly, for the generality of environmental resources, we need to ask when does or does not the market based measure seem appropriate? As mentioned, it may largely be only where the market based measure is not appropriate that LCA has its major role, though LCA may also have a supportive role in other cases, where it can help with valuation. It would be useful to have these roles spelt out.

I will round off by straying from this final session's brief to the theme of the project of which this workshop is a part: the application of market-based instruments for sustainable development. It is often stated that economists can make their best impact by addressing the big micro distortions. A big micro distortion is the non-charging of external costs imposed by polluters. Consequently, we should not be unduly exercised by, for example, whether or not there is a double dividend. One dividend is enough; it is the getting rid of a big micro distortion. The Inter-governmental Conference is underway at present to review the EU Treaty. There will be additional clauses inserted in the Treaty relating to the environment, with statements about 'integrating' the environment in policies and about 'ensuring sustainability' and the like. Getting these clauses adopted is likely to require some effort, and may actually amount to rather little. But if any of us has any influence, we should recommend a short cut. Specifically, the IGC should simply seek to give more prominence and force to what is currently an obscure clause buried in article 130r subsection 2, namely the Polluter Pays Principle.

Discussion

An argument for the adoption of life cycle approaches is that they help firms to compete more effectively; if more information were available to stakeholders, better choices would be made. It is necessary to consider more than just price signals. It is now an accepted management tool – for example life cycle analyses are now used by the UK Department of the Environment to evaluate policies. Life cycle analysis could be used when it is difficult to use other instruments, since it requires more information. One example would be nutrient balance in agriculture – it is difficult to intervene, but life cycle analyses could be undertaken.

It is possible to standardise approaches to environmental problems using market based instruments. This can be achieved through codes of practice and international standards (for example the ISO standards) although these are very general.

Considering the role of regulation in encouraging innovation, external changes may force firms to become more up to date. They may not know their production frontier, but they may well know that they could do better. There is considerable differentiation between firms; adoption of the current best practice would enable improvements to be made. Managers spend a lot of time on environmental issues, which may have opportunity costs of failure to innovate in other areas.

REFERENCES

Berkhout, F. and R. Howes (1997), The adoption of life cycle approached by industry: patterns and impacts, in *Resources, Conservation and Recycling*, **16** (forthcoming).

Boustead, I. (1994/5), *Eco-profiles of the European plastics industry: Report 2: Olefin Feedstock Sources; Report 3: Polyethylene and Polypropylene; Report 4: Polystyrene; Report 5: Co-product allocation in chlorine plants; Report 6: Polyvinyl chloride; Report 7: PVDC (Polyvinylidene chloride)*, APME, Brussels.

Hocking, M.B. (1991), 'Relative merits of polystyrene foam and paper in hot drink cups: implications for packaging', *Environmental Management*, **15**(6), 731–47.

OECD (1995), *An overview of the Life Cycle Approach to product and process environmental analysis and management*, Paris.

Porter, M.E. (1985), *Competitive Advantage: Creating and Sustaining Superior Performance*, The Free Press, New York, 1985.

Stalmans, M. et al. (1995), 'European Life-Cycle Inventory for Detergent Surfactants Production', *Tenside Surfactant Detergents* **32**, 84–109.

10. 'Green' product development: factors in competition

Robin Roy, Mark Smith and Stephen Potter

1 INTRODUCTION

Most studies of business and the environment have focused on company environmental policies and responses to regulation and other environmental pressures, typically focusing on pollution from production processes and on waste management (for example Vaughan and Mickle, 1993). Few studies exist of firms designing, or redesigning, products with reduced environment impacts, and those which do tend to focus on projects in large companies with established environmental policies (for example Oakley, 1993). This chapter draws from one of the few studies to examine green product development projects in small as well as in medium-sized and large firms (Smith, Roy and Potter, 1996).

It is useful to define what is meant by 'green design'. The US Office of Technology Assessment defines green design as: 'a design process in which environmental attributes are treated as **design objectives**, rather than as **constraints**.....green design incorporates environmental objectives with minimum loss to product performance, useful life or functionality' (OTA, 1992). Thus, green design is simply the **development of products taking account of their impact on the natural environment – as well as the more usual factors such as performance, aesthetics, cost, safety, and so on**.

This chapter concerns products which include both what have been described as **incremental 'green designs'** and **systematic 'ecodesigns'** (Ryan et al., 1992). 'Green' designs are developed to tackle one or two specific, often high profile, environmental problems (for example eliminating CFCs, reducing landfill waste) without systematic consideration of their total environmental impact. Green products comprise the majority of projects in this study. 'Ecodesign' represents a significant advance in that it involves designing a product to **consider and balance all the areas of adverse environmental impact throughout its life cycle** from raw materials acquisition through manufacture and use to final disposal (that is from 'cradle to grave'). There are very few examples of attempts at an ecodesign approach in our survey.

None of the projects, however, involved any attempt to move towards what has been described as **sustainable product development,** in which the function of the product is considered and alternative environmentally sustainable means for providing it are examined – including replacing the product with a service, or even questioning whether the product is really needed (Dewberry and Goggin, 1996; Manzini, 1996).

2 THE FIRMS AND PRODUCTS

The material in this chapter is based on a series of structured interviews with senior management, marketing and technical design staff in sixteen firms, carried out between 1991 and 1995, using a method similar to that developed for an earlier study on the 'Commercial Impacts of Design' (CID) (Potter et al., 1991; Roy and Potter, 1993). As in the CID project, the objectives were to identify design inputs and commercial outcomes at the product level and to understand the business and other aims underlying product development. Thus it was intended to study the planning and development of a sample of 'green' products within their commercial context.

The project sought to include a mixture of sizes and types of company. Small firms were mainly selected from those that had won, or been commended in, the 'Green Product' category of the Royal Society for Arts (RSA) 'Better Environment Awards for Industry'. Larger companies were selected from those participating in the lighting and domestic appliance product groups of the EU Ecolabelling programme, plus firms which made 'green' products commended by environmental organisations. The sample comprised mainly British-based firms, although six of these were overseas owned. The study also included overseas interviews in an Australian-based subsidiary of a UK company and in an American firm.

Half (8) of the firms were small with less than 100 employees. This group included some very small start-up businesses, such as a four-person business operating from a shop basement. The other eight businesses were medium-sized, defined for this study as having 100-499 employees, or large with 1000 or more UK staff, including some very large international company groups with one division based in Britain. The firms, products and size/ownership of the businesses where the interviews took place are summarised in Table 10.1.

Table 10.1 Companies and 'green' products in the study

Company[1]	Size/Ownership	'Green' Product	Product Area
Nitech	Small/UK	Rechargeable battery/lamps	Lighting
Starlowe Lighting	Small/UK	Low energy floodlight	Lighting
GE Lighting	Large/Overseas	Compact fluorescent lamps (CFLs)/ fittings	Lighting
Osram	Large/Overseas	Compact fluorescent lamps	Lighting
GTE/Silvania	Medium/Overseas	Compact fluorescent lamps	Lighting
Frigidaire	Large/Overseas	Low CFC and energy saving refrigerators	Appliances
Hoover Major Appliances	Large/Overseas	'New Wave' energy, water and detergent saving washing machines	Appliances
Stelrad Ideal	Large/UK	Condensing gas central heating boiler	Appliances
Atmosol	Small/UK	Compressed gas propelled aerosol	Packaging
SC Johnson Wax	Medium/Overseas	Recycled packaging for Shake n'Vac, etc.	Cleaning
Environmental Paints	Small/UK	Organic solvent-free paints (ECOS)	Paint
Grace Dearborn	Medium/Overseas	Cooling water treatment system	Pollution abatement
Trannon Furniture	Small/UK	Furniture from forest thinnings/coppicing	Furniture
Gestetner Australasia	Small/UK	'Boomerang' remanufactured laser toner cartridge	Office supplies
Pax Guns	Small/UK	'Prometheus' lead-free air gun pellets	Miscellaneous
Fibrescreed	Small/UK	Road/runway repair material from recycled tyres	Miscellaneous

Note: 1. Some of the companies have changed name and/or ownership since the study was carried out.

The small firms were typically created to manufacture a particular new design or invention, while the large firms were usually extending or complementing their product range, or exploiting a particular technology to gain a commercial advantage. Some of the small enterprises, such as Environmental Paints, were in direct competition with much larger, well-established firms. Others, including Nitech, had in effect created an entirely new market; in this case for high-performance rechargeable batteries and portable lighting. At the other end of the spectrum were the large, international firms, including the compact fluorescent lamp (CFL) manufacturers, who already produce other types of lighting, including traditional incandescent lamps. CFLs represent a diversification into new, energy-efficient lighting, originally designed for commercial purposes, and recently adapted for domestic applications.

3   ENVIRONMENTAL FACTORS IN COMPETITION

A significant feature of the products in this study is that most were not originally designed to be 'green', although their production, use or disposal involved reduced environmental impacts. Instead the firms concerned aimed to develop a product that would perform better, create a new market, increase or maintain their market share, or satisfy market demands or regulatory pressures. Environmental factors were thus deliberately or incidentally taken into account in pursuit of commercial and market aims.

Given the commercial focus of the projects it was not surprising that, with one exception, the firms in this sample did not attempt to sell their 'green' products primarily on their 'environmental friendliness'. This was because some firms initially did not recognise the environmental advantages of their product. Other firms understood that the environmental performance of a product is not usually the highest priority in terms of competitive advantage and other attributes are more crucial to commercial success. In common with other studies of green products (for example Wong et al., 1995; NCC, 1996), this sample indicated that to be commercially successful, the products had to be competitive in terms of performance, quality and value for money. Products need to work well, be of high quality and offer economic value before environmental factors enter the list of customer requirements. These are the elements which generally give products a competitive advantage.

Specific information was gathered in the survey in order to establish a more precise picture of competition factors in the 'green' products market. Each respondent was asked to select three key attributes from a list of eleven which in their opinion conferred a competitive edge when the product was launched on the market. The results are presented in Table 10.2, which shows the factors ranked in order of significance derived from the total number of responses.

In this study, it is clear that features pertaining to performance, quality and reliability are the most highly rated attributes of a competitive product. Quality and reliability characteristics included longevity and low maintenance. These aspects may also bestow environmental advantages due to a reduction in material resources needed to replace and maintain products, but may not be marketed as an environmental benefit or even perceived as such. For many products, value for money and reduced operating costs were also important factors in customer choice.

Table 10.2 Competitive edge factors in rank order

Rank	Feature
1	Specification/Performance
2	Quality/Reliability
3	Value for money
4	Environmental friendliness
5	Price
6	Marketing/Promotion
7	Styling/Visual appearance
8	Customisation
9	Ergonomics/Safety
10	Response/Delivery time
11	After-sales support

'Environmental friendliness' ranked fourth and, although it is not the most crucial factor in competition, it is significant that it is rated more highly than price alone. As an illustration, furniture made by Trannon gains its competitive advantage not from its price, but because it is of high quality and well-designed, as well as being made from forestry thinnings or coppiced wood, a renewable and under-utilised resource.

Other examples drawn from the firms in this survey also indicate that the priority in product development is designing for performance. Nitech's rechargeable batteries, lead-free air-gun pellets from Pax Guns and Starlowe's low-energy flood lighting system technically outperform rival products. Performance and quality of the product are typically the primary competitive features rather than environmental attributes. As one interviewee commented; **'we did not actually design it to be "green", but to be a good product.'**

The survey also sought to determine how much of each product's commercial performance could be attributed to the environmental issues it addressed, and how much was dependent on other characteristics. In the great majority of cases (11 or 69%) environmental issues alone were considered insignificant. Trannon noted that it had only sold very few chairs on the basis of their 'green' attributes. SC Johnson Wax deliberately did not communicate to consumers any environmental premium associated with product packaging made from recycled plastics. GE, Osram, GTE, Starlowe and Nitech all considered product longevity, reliability, low maintenance and cost savings of their lighting products as more valuable attributes than any environmental benefits. Gestetner and Stelrad emphasised the importance of cost saving to the user as the primary incentive to purchase their 'green' products – our interviewee at Stelrad observed **'Environment is a "comfort factor", a reinforcement to the basic motivation of buying because running costs are low'**.

In fact at the time of the interviews, only Environmental Paints attributed the sales of its VOC-free paint predominantly to its environmental features, although emphasising that the green paint's technical performance must be as good as conventional paints. Subsequently, the firm came to recognise the need for competitive pricing following the entry of the major manufacturers into the 'green' paint market. But this was too late to save the firm, which ceased production after three years.

The low priority given to environmental factors in many markets does not mean that there are not circumstances in which 'green' products can provide a competitive advantage. Nitech and Fibrescreed both observed that environmental factors were mostly insignificant in customer choice, but that attitudes towards environmental issues were changing. Fibrescreed, for example, reported growing environmental interest, expressed by the British Airports Authority and some local authorities, in their recycled runway/road repair material. Regulation could also shift the balance in favour of environmental factors. GE, for example, estimated that about 50 per cent of sales may be attributable to environmental concerns, but only if the European Union (EU) Eco-labelling scheme for lighting materialised.

Pax Guns also observed that environmental performance is of significance only in certain export markets, notably Sweden, otherwise it is the superior performance of the product which determines purchasing decisions. But the firm did carry out a survey of their air gun pellet users to ascertain the degree of environmental concern among customers. This involved a competition to write a 'jingle', of which the winning entry was: **'They're fast and consistent, non-toxic and clean, so me and my gun are environmentally "green"'**. This indicates again, in a different context, the importance attached to product quality (Pax plastic and zinc pellets are more accurate than lead ones), which may be augmented by environmental performance. Environmental performance in isolation is clearly regarded as insufficient incentive for the successful marketing of a 'green' product, even to environmentally-aware consumers.

The broad conclusion that can be drawn from these observations is that the environmental performance of a product is not usually the highest priority in terms of competitive advantage and other attributes are more crucial to market success. In order to compete effectively, the products had to be up among the leaders in terms of performance and quality, as well as offering value for money. Improvements in environmental performance only become a significant competitive factor once such levels of product performance quality and value are attained. This conclusion is similar to that reached in other studies of products such as 'green' detergents and recycled paper (Wong et al., 1995). It helps to explain the frequent company strategy regarding 'greening' existing product lines rather than establishing separate 'green' product ranges, and confirms that the firms in this survey focused on designing for performance and quality.

4 COMMERCIAL OUTCOMES

A series of questions in the interviews was designed to ascertain the commercial impacts of these projects, including: annual sales, gross profit margin, market share and exports of the products. Information was also gathered on the costs of developing the products from concept to market launch, including all design, development, plant, tooling and initial marketing costs. The costs, sales and profit data permitted the payback period of the projects to be calculated. This was measured in terms of the amount of time from product launch it took for the total investment in the project to be recouped. If detailed financial data were not available, respondents were asked to provide a qualitative indication of the commercial success of the project.

The financial data in this study needs to be treated with caution, given that detailed information was only obtained from six of the small companies, together with sales and export data from three of the large companies. Nevertheless some tentative conclusions can be drawn.

Profit margins for the 'green' products are broadly similar to comparable 'non-green' products. The average gross profit margin of the green products developed by the small enterprises in this survey (at 44 per cent) is similar to the average for similar types of products from the previous Commercial Impacts of Design (CID) survey (37 per cent before the subsidised design project and 46 per cent after it – Potter et al., 1991) and is within the margin of error for such a small sample. This suggests that environmental features do not add much value to a product and hence there is limited scope for firms to 'price up' green products (especially given that in some cases production costs of these products were reduced through energy and material conservation). This is consistent with the earlier conclusion that environmental factors only start to convey a competitive advantage to a product after performance, quality and value for money are equal or superior to other products.

One difference was that the cost of developing the 'green' products was higher than for typical non-green products in the earlier CID study. Since both types of product had similar profit margins, the green products therefore experienced a longer payback period. Repayment on total investment was on average a little more than 2 years for the green products developed by the small enterprises in this survey, compared to 15.5 months for similar projects in the CID non-green sample of product and engineering/industrial design projects (Potter et al., 1991).

This longer payback time for 'green' products is supported by a recent survey of Dutch companies which took part in two government sponsored 'Ecodesign' programmes designed to assist firms incorporate environmental factors in product design. The products generated during these programmes (which ranged from an office chair and a gas hob to a plant tray) exhibited similar payback times to the products in this study (Brezet et al., 1996).

From the perspective of the national economy the international trade impacts of the 'green' products deserves consideration. This study suggests that green products do not necessarily lead to higher exports, although particular products can perform well in certain environmentally-aware export markets. The benchmark CID study showed average exports were 19 per cent of sales, with engineering/industrial design projects exporting over 40 per cent of sales, the most appropriate category for comparison with the majority of the 'green' products in this survey. For the 'green' products made by small firms, exports averaged less than 15 per cent of sales, but there was a large range, from no exports through to a proportion in excess of 65 per cent. Exports for the large firms also covered a large range from zero to 90 per cent. This result is partly because small firms tend not to be major exporters, while for the large firms exports depended on the acceptability of their product in overseas markets. For example, small wall-mounted gas central heating boilers, such as made by Stelrad Ideal, are designed for the UK market, whereas larger, floor-mounted boilers are preferred elsewhere.

Nevertheless for those firms, large or small, that were operating in certain environmentally-sensitive export markets, the environmental performance of the product was often crucial and enabled them to succeed in exporting a significant proportion of their output. Hoover, for example, believed that the environmental performance of its New Wave washing machine range, supported by the award of an EU Ecolabel, was an important factor in the company's penetration of the environmentally-aware German market, in which the company doubled its market share in 1994, and they viewed similar opportunities for export to Scandinavia. Even so Hoover found it necessary to produce lower–priced, but less environmentally efficient, models for the volume UK and Southern European markets.

5 CONCLUSIONS

With a few exceptions, the firms in this study did not set out to produce a 'greener' product. Most firms aimed to develop a product that would perform better, create a new market, enable them to increase or maintain their market share, or respond to market demands or regulatory pressures. Environmental factors were thus· incidentally or deliberately taken into account in pursuit of commercial and market aims. This is in agreement with other studies (for example Green ct al., 1994) which point to the importance of commercial pressures and existing or anticipated regulation as the two main stimuli for the development of greener products.

In the light of the commercial aims of these projects, it is not surprising that most of the companies adopted an incremental 'green design' approach to the incorporation of environmental factors in product development. This focused on one or two environmental issues of particular concern to the firm – most often materials choice and the environmental impacts of production, followed by concern for reducing the energy and pollution impacts of the product in use and with recycling materials at the end of product life.

In this study, none of the firms routinely adopted a systematic 'ecodesign' approach to product development in an attempt to reduce environmental impacts over the life cycle of the product from 'cradle to grave'. However, some of the firms had broadened from exclusively considering environmental impacts of the product during either the production or the use phase to considering the environmental impacts of its materials, distribution and disposal, indicating a learning process involving a shift from 'green design' towards 'ecodesign'.

This and other studies indicate that the development of 'green' products that have a reduced environmental impact arising from their materials, manufacture, distribution, use or disposal is still relatively rare, especially in the UK and among small companies. Nevertheless, this study has shown that the development of green products can be a very worthwhile activity. The majority of green product development projects were commercially profitable, with small firms creating new industrial/commercial niche markets with innovative 'green' products and larger firms developing their consumer or commercial markets with environmentally improved products. However, the study also emphasises that the environmental performance of a green product is not usually the primary factor in its commercial success. To succeed in the market the products had first to be competitive in terms of performance, quality and value.

For well–designed products, good environmental performance can provide an additional attraction to customers, especially in certain export markets. This provides a commercial incentive for companies to develop green products. But for more widespread development and market acceptance of green products, and for the application of more comprehensive 'ecodesign' approaches, various forms of new environmental regulation are likely to be needed.

REFERENCES

Dewberry, E and P. Goggin (1996), 'Spaceship ecodesign', *Co-design*, No. 5/6, 12-17.

Brezet, J.C., A. Zweers, P. van Duyse and R.E. de Wijn (1996), *Economic benefits of Ecodesign*, Faculty of Industrial Design Engineering, Delft University of Technology, Delft, The Netherlands, June.

Green, K., A. McMeekin and A. Irwin (1994), 'Technological trajectories and R&D for environmental innovation in UK firms', *Futures*, **26**(10), 1047–59.

Manzini, E. (1996), 'Design in transition', *Eco Design*, **IV**(1), 15–16.

National Consumer Council (1996), *Green Claims: A consumer investigation into marketing claims about the environment*, NCC, London.

Oakley, B.T. (1993), 'Total quality product design – how to integrate environmental criteria into the product realization process', *Total Quality Environmental Management*, Spring, 309-21.

Office of Technology Assessment (1992), *Green Products by Design. Choices for a cleaner environment*, Congress of the United States, Office of Technology Assessment, Washington DC, October.

Potter, S., R. Roy, C. Capon, M. Bruce, V. Walsh and J. Lewis (1991), *The Benefits and Costs of Investment in Design: Using professional design expertise in product, engineering and graphics projects*, Report DIG-03, Design Innovation Group, The Open University and UMIST.

Roy, R. and S. Potter (1993), 'The commercial impacts of investment in design', *Design Studies*, **14**(2), April, 171–93.

Smith, M.T., R. Roy and S. Potter (1996), *The Commercial Impacts of Green Product Development*, Report DIG–05, Design Innovation Group, The Open University, Milton Keynes (ISBN 07492 883310).

Ryan, C., M. Hosken and D. Greene (1992), 'EcoDesign: design and the response to the greening of the international market', *Design Studies*, **13**(1), January, 5–22.

Vaughan, D. and C. Mickle (1993), *Environmental Profiles of European Business*, Earthscan/Royal Institute of International Affairs, London.

Wong, V., W. Turner and P. Stoneman (1995), 'Market strategies and market prospects for environmentally friendly consumer products', Warwick Business School Research Bureau, Paper No. 165, University of Warwick, Coventry, March (ISSN 0265-5976).

Index